THE
FALL AND RISE
OF WOMEN

HOW WOMEN CAN CHANGE THE WORLD

WINFRIED SEDHOFF

Copyright © 2016 Winfried Sedhoff

Version 2.0. All rights reserved. No part of this publication may be reproduced, stored in a retrieval system or transmitted in any form or by any means, electronic, mechanical, photocopying, recording or otherwise, without the prior written permission of the copyright holder.

Disclaimer

Some of the examples in this book represent experiences of real people. Names have been changed and identifying details omitted to help protect their anonymity. The original work of this book and its suggestions are in no way affiliated with other courses and books regarding how to be an 'authentic woman' or to improve the 'essence of woman'. Any similarity or resemblance is purely coincidental.

To women,

the rock and foundation upon which to build a better world

Contents

Acknowledgements xiii
Introduction xiv
How woman was cast from paradise xxii
Chapter 1: Introduction to the Balance of Self Model 1
Chapter 2: The inevitable downfall 7
Chapter 3: The influence of chronic threat 10
Chapter 4: Settling as farmers 16
Introduction to seven steps 23
Step 1: Respect 25
Chapter 5: Respect yourself 26
Chapter 6: Respect other women 33
Chapter 7: Respect authentic men 46
Step 2: Grow friendship 51
Chapter 8: Types of friendships 52
Chapter 9: Friendships with women 58
Chapter 10: Friendships with men 66
Chapter 11: Friendships with family and community 85
Step 3: Listen to you 93
Chapter 12: Communicate with the Inner Self 94
Chapter 13: Questions to resolve emotional pains 112
Chapter 14: Questions to resolve fears 118
Chapter 15: Questions to help with future choices 129
Chapter 16: Questions to understand Essence of Woman .. 136
Step 4: Be attractive 141
Chapter 17: Enhance your Personal Self 144
Chapter 18: Make self time 150
Chapter 19: Increase contact with Land 152
Chapter 20: Take back choices 156
Chapter 21: Increase self-worth and self-respect 159
Chapter 22: Treat yourself as a best friend 165
Chapter 23: Increase Personal Self in children 169

Step 5: Be sex-wise 173
Chapter 24: Sex and basic human needs 175
Chapter 25: Sexual desire mismatch 180
Chapter 26: Overcome sexual desire mismatch 188
Chapter 27: Mismatch solutions 194
Chapter 28: Sex to raise the Essence of Woman 199

Step 6: Get actively involved 205
Chapter 29: Types of education 207
Chapter 30: Socially recognized education 210
Chapter 31: Personal education 217
Chapter 32: Active involvement 225

Step 7: Enhance your spirituality 237
Chapter 33: Stories 239
Chapter 34: The great danger of the spiritual 246
Chapter 35: Connect with the spirit 254
Chapter 36: Create stories of spirits true to your heart 260

Create a more secure world 267
Chapter 37: How the seven steps reduce chronic threat 268
Chapter 38: Realistic hope 274

Appendices
Appendix 1
A balance for parents 277
Appendix 2
Further reading 278
Notes 279
About the Author 281

Comprehensive contents

Acknowledgements xiii
Introduction xiv
How woman was cast from paradise xxii
Chapter 1: Introduction to the Balance of Self Model 1
   Personal Self 3
   Community Self 4
   Family Self 5
   Land 5
Chapter 2: The inevitable downfall 7
Chapter 3: The influence of chronic threat 10
Chapter 4: Settling as farmers 16
Introduction to seven steps 23
Step 1: Respect 25
Chapter 5: Respect yourself 26
   Take pride in yourself 26
Chapter 6: Respect other women 33
   Praise and encourage 33
   Speak well of women 38
   When women disrespect you 38
   Be proud of other women 45
Chapter 7: Respect authentic men 46
Step 2: Grow friendship 51
Chapter 8: Types of friendships 52
   Casual vs close friendship 55
Chapter 9: Friendships with women 58
   Enhance and create friendships 60
   Warning 65
Chapter 10: Friendships with men 66
   Friendship with your partner 69
      Close friendship keeps him real 69
      Close friendships with partner 72
   Friendships with other men 77

Friendship with another man with relationship..........................78
Friendship with a man without relationship............................82
Three NEVERS of friendship with a man......................................84
Chapter 11: Friendships with family and community.....................85
Family friendships...86
Warning..89
Community friendships..90

Step 3: Listen to you...94
Chapter 12: Communicate with the Inner Self...............................94
Make time: The most important activity...............................97
Practice activity 1: Right place..98
Find a safe place...99
Clear all distractions..99
Practice activity 2: Right mind..101
Breathing..101
Mindfulness..102
Technique 1: Zen meditation..103
Technique 2: Toy boats on a stream...................................105
Technique 3: Feeling the breath...106
Mindfulness to Inner Self...107
Practice activity 3: Right question......................................110
Chapter 13: Questions to resolve emotional pains.....................112
A word of caution...116
Chapter 14: Questions to resolve fears..118
What are you afraid of?..122
Warning...124
Resolve the fears...125
Chapter 15: Questions to help with future choices....................129
Create realistic hope...132
Create a future of purpose...134
Chapter 16: Questions to understand Essence of Woman........136
Your Essence of Woman...137

Step 4: Be attractive..141
Chapter 17: Enhance your Personal Self.....................................144
Six steps to increase Personal Self......................................146
Chapter 18: Make self time...150

Quiet time..150
Personal enjoyment time..150
Chapter 19: Increase contact with Land 152
Use culture..154
Chapter 20: Take back choices..156
Suggestions to increase choice....................................157
Chapter 21: Increase self-worth and self-respect..............159
Increase self-worth..159
    Be deserving 159
    Don't put yourself last 161
    Learn to say no 162
Increase self-respect..162
Chapter 22: Treat yourself as a best friend 165
Chapter 23: Increase Personal Self in children..................169

Step 5: Be sex-wise..173
Chapter 24: Sex and basic human needs............................175
Self Sex..176
Social Sex..176
Family-Positive Sex..177
Chapter 25: Sexual desire mismatch 180
Mismatch of dreams and intentions............................181
Mismatch of dreams and actions 183
Mismatch of strength of desire....................................184
Why sexual desire mismatch?......................................186
Chapter 26: Overcome sexual desire mismatch..................188
Honestly, what type of sex is that?..............................189
    Points to clarify..190
Four simple sex rules 193
Chapter 27: Mismatch solutions..194
Overcome and prevent dreams and intentions mismatches..............194
Overcome and prevent dreams and actions mismatches 195
Overcome and prevent strength of desire mismatch 196
Chapter 28: Sex to raise the Essence of Woman 199
What about romantic love?..202

Step 6: Get actively involved..205

Chapter 29: Types of education 207
Chapter 30: Socially recognized education 210
    Can a woman have too much formal education? 212
    Recommendations for formal education 215
Chapter 31: Personal education 217
    What is personal education? 218
    How to increase personal education 218
Chapter 32: Active involvement 225
    Self 225
    Family 228
    Local community 232
    Matters of state 233
    Active involvement in governments 234

Step 7: Enhance your spirituality 237
Chapter 33: Stories 239
Chapter 34: The great danger of the spiritual 246
Chapter 35: Connect with the spirit 254
    See the world as spirits 256
    Keep it practical 258
Chapter 36: Create stories of spirits true to your heart 260
    Create stories with spirits 262
    Stories through actions 263
    Warning 265

Create a more secure world 267
Chapter 37: How the seven steps reduce chronic threat 268
    Step 1: Respect 268
    Step 2: Friendship 269
    Step 3: Listen to you 270
    Step 4: Be attractive 271
    Step 5: Be sex-wise 271
    Step 6: Be actively involved 272
    Step 7: Enhance your spirituality 272
Chapter 38: Realistic hope 274

Appendices

Appendix 1
A balance for parents 277
Appendix 2
Further reading 278
Notes 279
About the Author 281

Acknowledgements

Every woman I have had the privilege to meet, or know, has made this book possible. Each one has left an impression, at times, profound. From my mother to my sister, to intelligent and accomplished women I met from childhood onwards, the world has molded me, and determined the nature of this work, through their great influence. To the female patients who have trusted me with their hearts, I offer a special thanks; without you this book most definitely would not have been possible. In particular, I'd like to thank my editor, Jessica Perini.

Jessica has helped keep this book grounded and real. She has ensured I have kept the work both relevant and accurate; her research and suggestions have been invaluable. As part of the target audience it has been wonderful to get her feedback.

Other thanks must go to those who have also read the work, and made comments or suggestions along the way, including Celeste Rossetto, Diana Deane, and Dr Rick Sapsford, an insightful, and experienced, GP counseling colleague. A special mention also goes to Joanne Walters, who has not only read the work but found it inspirational enough to use it to begin to create women's support groups. Her vision holds great promise. I hope to continue to assist her as best I can so women can find solace and validation with each other, as they once did. I too wish no woman to never feel unsupported, unsafe, uncared for, or alone.

To all of you who see the value in helping women become the most authentic, and best women they can be, may I acknowledge your efforts now and into the future. We share a similar dream.

Introduction

The Keres Indians of Laguna Pueblo in North America tell a tale of Thought Woman and the origin of the world.

In her book *The Sacred Hoop: Recovering the feminine in American Indian traditions*, Paula Gunn Allen describes, 'In the beginning *Tse che nako*, Thought Woman finished everything, thoughts and the names of all things. She finished also the languages.'[1]

Thought Woman is considered the spirit of creation that 'informs right balance, right harmony, and these in turn order all relationships in conformity with her law'. She is considered 'the supreme Spirit, she is both Mother and Father to all people and to all creatures'. They say she brought building, agriculture, memory, intuition, social systems, religion, creativity, dance, among many other things, and 'blessed the people with the ability to provide for themselves and their progeny'. She was not a male ruler who punished those who defied her; she is the spirit of a woman who brought life, balance, and an ability to make our own decisions to humanity.

The Keres Indians believe Thought Woman will return and help restore balance in the world. That is the vision of this book – to help modern women elevate themselves to the revered ancient woman of the past – respected, acknowledged, empowered, so she, in turn, can transform society.

◎

This book is dedicated to you women out there. Because I have seen your power, value, and your role in society denigrated. You're not paid the same as men, you hit the glass ceiling protected by men, and are unappreciated at home and as a mother. You are objectified in the media to the point of contempt. Women like you all over the world are being oppressed, abused, and disrespected simply for being the person nature intended. You're often regarded as inferior, subservient, or lowly compared to men who are commonly valued more highly. There has been a fall of woman – a downfall – and it has seen, and continues to see, our relationships suffer, our families become dysfunctional, and our communities fragment and fall apart racked by violence and disunity leading to unnecessary wars, extremes of wealth and poverty, mass starvation, and destruction of the natural world on an unprecedented scale. The fall of woman – as we shall soon see – was inevitable. What is not inevitable is that it stays this way.

Nature unwittingly made it like this. As will soon become apparent, at first nature made the power and influence of women much higher. The power of desires that define a woman – the Essence of Woman – were strong. They were at least the equal of the power of the desires at the heart of men – the Essence of Man – if not greater. The Essence of Woman was in balance with the Essence of Man and for millennia women were respected, highly valued, and greatly appreciated by their families and community; they held great sway. In some cultures – such as the Cherokee and Iroquois Nations of the United States before the colonization of white man – to be a woman was to be revered. But nature created some potential weaknesses, and the right conditions to turn all that on its head. We have been living the traumatic legacy of these weaknesses and circumstances ever since.

Nature also provided us with a solution.

We live in a time when gender roles have blurred and we are no longer true to our authentic selves. Many women have lost what it means to be true to being a woman, and behave more like men, or immature girls. Many men have also lost touch with the authentic man in them, and no longer know how to be the 'Real Men' women need them to be. This is leaving many men and women confused, not knowing who they are, or who they are supposed to be. Many of us find ourselves in unsatisfying relationships because we are no longer able to fulfill each other's most basic relationship needs. The shortage of authentic men is leaving many women deeply unsatisfied.

In the quest to restore balance between the Essence of Woman and the Essence of Man we could try to lower the Essence of Man, bring the power of his desires down so the desires of woman can rise in comparison, but this will only make matters worse. Lower the Essence of Man and there will be fewer authentic men to satisfy women. In the end nature only left us with one realistic option:

Raise the power of the natural womanly qualities within you: become the most authentic woman possible.

Nature refined in you the qualities of the woman it needs you to be. You can see these qualities reflected in your deepest womanly desires and feel them in the depths of your heart. No man can raise the power and influence of these desires for you. No man can make you an authentic woman with great inner power, confidence, and wisdom. Only you can truly raise the Essence of Woman in your being, and around the world. Only you – and women like you – have access to the true heart of an authentic woman that can restore balance and harmony.

Deep inside you resides the spirit of an ancient woman suppressed. She knows your heart. She knows your womanly needs, as she has known the needs of the hearts of women over the ages. She can have great power and influence among us once more. She can offer us friendship, caring and nurturing, improved health, insight, tolerance and compassion. Her wisdom can help us find a path for a society that is lost and struggling to find its way. She does not want you to be someone you are not. She simply asks that you listen to your Inner Self and hear her. She wishes you to once again feel her warm embrace, and realize her natural power.

The aim of this book is two-fold. Firstly to help correct the imbalance between the Essence of Woman and the Essence of Man by assisting you to better understand why the Essence of Woman fell, and to help you to raise it and keep it raised so that you, your daughter, and your daughter's daughter, and indeed all women, can live more satisfying and fulfilling lives. The second is to help you feel true to yourself as a woman and take pride in the woman you naturally are. As you blossom then you will finally be treated with the respect and appreciation you deserve, and you can live the deeply satisfying life that nature intended.

In the process you will also help create a more equitable, peaceful, and balanced world.

How can I – a man – teach a woman to be authentic?

Ultimately I can't.

I can't tell you what you should do, or what your place is in society. But, after years of counseling women I can ask many questions that may help you unearth insights and understandings, and I can offer tools and guidance, so you can explore and increase your own Essence of Woman.

In the following chapters we look at why the Essence of Woman fell, and why its fall was inevitable. We explore what powerful yet simple forces can lower it, suppress it, and keep it suppressed. Once we understand what you're up against we can develop practical steps to help you counter such forces. We begin by introducing a practical and simple model that can help us better understand our basic human desires. The model is called the Balance of Self (BOS) Model.

In the first chapter we'll introduce the BOS Model then refer back to it throughout the book. As you shall soon see it's a powerful yet simple model offering personal and social insights. For example it can give you a much better understanding of friendship and how to improve your relationships. It can also help you better understand how you choose to have sex can either increase the Essence of Woman or lower it. Are troubles with relationships getting in the way of you feeling complete as a woman? We can use the insights of the BOS Model to improve them.

With a better practical understanding of the desires that drive many of our thoughts and behaviors it's easier to understand the inevitable fall of the Essence of Woman. In Chapter 3 you will discover how women and our society in general, respond poorly to chronic threat. We will see what chronic threat is and why it is so bad for us, and why it's especially bad for women and the Essence of Woman. Chronic threat is the first of two reasons behind the inevitable downfall of women. Going from nomadic tribes to farmers and settlers was a part of our human evolution. Farming had the potential to provide enough for all and give us common social equitable goals that could unite us; instead society fared badly due to resulting extremes of wealth and poverty, and wars, famine, and suffering. We are yet to understand the full impact that this evolution has on our societies; but one thing is certain, women did not, and still do not fare well. Becoming farmers and settlers was the second reason behind women's demise.

In this book we look at seven practical steps to help you improve your relationships, your family life, and your power and satisfaction as a woman in our society – steps to raise the power and influence of women so that it never falls again. They are:

- Step 1: Respect yourself, her, and him
- Step 2: Grow friendship
- Step 3: Listen to the real you
- Step 4: Be attractive
- Step 5: Be sex-wise
- Step 6: Be actively involved in decisions
- Step 7: Enhance your spirituality.

In Step 1 we acknowledge the Essence of Woman cannot be raised without respect. With simple practical suggestions you will learn to increase respect for yourself, but also for the men and women around you. This can go a long way to restoring balance with the Essence of Man. This step alone can transform your relationship and how others treat you. It is a critical first step in your journey towards realizing your greatest potential.

In Step 2 we will increase your fulfillment as a woman in friendships with:

- other women
- family and greater community and
- your partner.

As we shall soon see these friendships are critical to you being and remaining true to yourself. So is the right type of friendship with your partner. Get the friendship wrong and you risk your relationship and drive your partner away. Know how to get it right and you can have years of fulfillment in each other's company. In this section you will learn how to build a deeper bond to each other. This will go a long way towards helping you realize your authentic self.

Step 3 will arguably be the most important step of the seven, not just for you but for us all. Here you will learn to communicate with your Inner Self. Up till now you may have learnt to listen to your gut. Some call it instinct. You will learn to communicate with it directly and honestly and this incorruptible part of you will let you know what you need, and help you see the best path for your life, and how to get there. Your every desire is written inside your Inner Self, which sees far more than you are consciously aware of. Learn to communicate with it directly and you will have a truly amazing resource at your disposal. For example, communicating with your Inner Self can help you make relationship decisions. Should you stay or go? It can help give you direction in life, decide on a career, or a path that will work best for you. It can also help you feel truly confident as a woman of inner power and insight. Learning to communicate with your Inner Self can help you connect with your authentic woman in its purest form.

In Step 4 you will learn to enhance your attractiveness and keep it. Attraction is about promising, and being able, to satisfy important relationship needs. Don't get me wrong, there's far more to it than just appearance. Looks might get attention, but they don't keep it. Being attractive gets both attention and helps keep it. In this step you will learn what authentic men find attractive and learn to develop one quality we all find attractive: a strong personal self. A strong personal self helps you stay true to the genuine you. Maintaining a strong personal self will help you not lose yourself in your relationship. In this section we outline ten practical and simple ways to develop and keep a strong personal self.

Sex is powerful. It can either enhance us or leave us empty and miserable. It can improve our relationships or destroy them, increase the Essence of Woman or lower it. In Step 5 we will learn the many different desires sex tries to fulfill; not all will leave you truly satisfied, or enhance you. You will learn about sex in a way you may never have considered. Whatever sex you decide to have you can become what I call 'sex-wise': that is, know how to use it to build and maintain close relationships. Your sexual choices can affect the levels of respect and value of women everywhere.

In Step 6 we learn the value of being educated and involved and we also look at important ways you can make a difference and still be true to the person you naturally are. We need women to be more actively involved in decision making so the Essence of Woman not only rises in you, but also spreads through families and communities. Being actively involved in decision making means getting educated and involved, but there's more to being well educated than just schooling. You may also need to increase your personal education, so you can become more understanding, tolerant, compassionate, and wise.

Enhancing your spirituality is a positive and deeply personal way to raise your Essence of Woman. It enhances an emotional connection with the world, each other, and yourself. It also offers a sense of meaning and purpose and helps nourish you inside. In Step 7 you will learn to reconnect with the world on a spiritual level. The key, as we shall soon see, lies in understanding stories. Stories you tell yourself can change not only you, but they can restore balance to the world. As balance is restored so is the value and power of women.

Remember, our aim is to help you live a life that feels honest, true, and is deeply and lastingly satisfying. It is not to try to make you into what I, or anyone else, wants or needs you to be.

Imagine a time when women are revered once more - where to be a woman is to be respected, never denigrated, and never used or abused or treated like property. A time when a woman can walk the streets proud and empowered, and without harassment, and be given equal pay and recognition for an equal or similar job. Imagine a time when women are more satisfied in stable fulfilling relationships with men who once again know how to be real – authentic – men. Consider a time where women are being heard in every aspect of life, valued for their wisdom, and respected for their compassion and tolerance, where poverty is reduced, the sick are cared for, and the world is once again treated with care and respect – a time of greater balance and harmony. This time may be closer than you think.

As a woman you have more power and influence than you may know. Only you can give human life to the world; you are of a chosen life-giving people. Your natural innate closeness to your precious children makes you perfectly placed to mold the hearts and minds of generations to come and transform the world. Your naturally endowed caring and nurturing desires make you prioritize people – you are more likely to want to share than many men. You, as an authentic woman, evoking the power of the spirit of the ancient woman within, are perfectly placed to restore balance and harmony to the world. You can be our beacon of hope.

By the end of these seven steps – like the Thought Woman – you can transform society and finally restore the 'right balance' and 'right harmony' with each other, the world, and yourself.

How woman was cast from paradise

All change is not growth, as all movement is not forward.
Ellen Glasgow

In the early fifteenth century, in the region of the St Lawrence River, the Jesuits, under the leadership of Father Paul Le Jeune, were determined to 'civilize' the Montagnais-Naskapi Indians. A peaceful easy living people, where physical abuse was considered a terrible crime, children were never given more than a simple reprimand, and the chief led not by force of power but the eloquence of his words, women held great influence – this was a largely matrilineal society; property and power was passed down the female line. To the French this way of living was unacceptable; they needed to transform them into peasant-serfs, to show them that a woman's proper place is under the authority of her husband, and the people should obey their leaders – they needed to change them as they had their Indian's counterparts in France centuries earlier. To this end they coerced or captured the children, placed them into school and taught them to obey by battering, neglecting, torturing, imprisoning, and psychologically tormenting them to 'educate' them. They informed the men that French women do not rule their husbands – they instigated male rule and dominance. Men who did not conform – and there were many – would not be given the backing of the church or political institutions – power was transferred only to the men who agreed to the French system. For Le Jeune understood – as Paula Gunn Allen points out in her book *The Sacred Hoop: Recovering the feminine in American Indian traditions* – to assault the peaceful system founded on giving power to women requires child terrorization, male dominance, and the submission of women to male authority.

The Montagnais provide a clear example of the fall of women in society at the hands of male-dominant oppressors. This wasn't just limited to the Americas. Women all over the world were to suffer a similar unjust and unwarranted fate. Many are still suffering today.

The downfall of women was inevitable. Women as a group were always going to be treated as inferior to men, undervalued, underappreciated, and disrespected. By understanding human desires we can come to terms with why it was always going to be this way, why it should never have been allowed to happen, and what you can do to help change it.

How do we understand our human desires? There are so many. We have desires for food, water, warmth, intimacy, and friendship … the list goes on.

We begin by recognizing we are just a personal mix of the same basic ingredients.

Chapter 1: Introduction to the Balance of Self Model

Search inside your heart and you will find a basic mix of fears and desires: the same mix from which all humans are composed. In many ways we are much like a cake: with the same basic ingredients of flour, sugar, eggs, butter, milk, and soda we can make many different cakes. A sponge or a pudding, a slice, or a wedding cake. Add extra flavors for a chocolate, orange, or lemon cake. At the heart we have the same basic ingredients mixed in different amounts. Just as at our core we are made up of the same basic human desires. We are different thanks to the changing strength of our desires and are never exactly the same from this day to the next – the balance of ingredients keeps changing inside us.

The Balance of Self (BOS) Model is a summary of our basic human desires; those we must have if we are to survive – the basic ingredients. This simple dynamic model can help us make sense of what desires we have and how they become stronger and weaker under different conditions, such as those that can lead to the oppression, abuse, and disrespect of women. The model can help us better understand ourselves.

The BOS Model can be best expressed in a diagram.

The Balance of Self Model

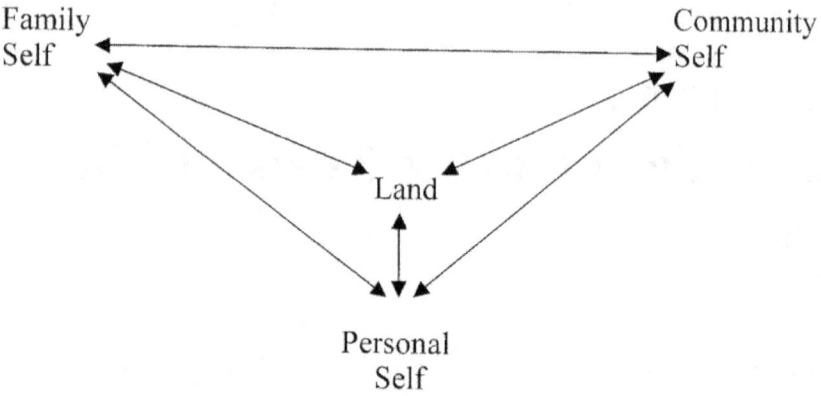

The main components in the BOS Model are termed the Three Human Essences: Personal Self, Family Self, and Community Self. They summarize the essence of what drives us to be human, to act and behave as a human being, as opposed to acting like a bird or a cat. If you had the desires of a bird for example you would want to fly from tree to tree, or hover high in the sky searching for something to eat. Thankfully we don't have such desires or more than a few of us would have some very painful bruises or broken limbs.

The Human Essences are a summary of our human motivations and desires grouped into three parts.

In the center of the model is the supplementary component Land.
Let us consider each of the components in turn and begin to see how they make us whom we are so we can clarify their part in the fall of the Essence of Woman and what part they play in an authentic woman's life.

Personal Self

Personal Self desires help keep us alive and healthy in our own right. Not surprisingly some of its desires include those of hunger, thirst, and the desire for warmth and shelter, for without these we wouldn't be able to survive. But Personal Self can represent much more than that.

Personal Self has five components that change how we see and treat ourselves:

1. Self-worth
2. Self-respect
3. A sense of knowing what we think and feel in our own right
4. Sense of choice
5. Being our best friend

We are unlikely to meet our own personal needs if we don't think we are worthwhile, don't respect ourselves, don't know ourselves well enough to recognize our needs, don't think we have a choice in having our needs met, or if we treat our self as an enemy rather than a close and trusted best friend.

Personal Self is about stripping away the influences of others and then uncovering who we are.

Would you know whom you are when no one is around and you don't have to answer to anybody? When you strip away the role of mother, friend, worker, and companion, who are you? Personal Self is about having a strong sense of your individuality, an identity that isn't determined by the influences of others. It is the closest we can find to an honest and true sense of genuine and unique self.

Personal Self is considered the foundation of the BOS Model as without a strong Personal Self we will never truly be ourselves, and never find true and honest fulfillment in any part of our life. When we try to be someone we're not we don't satisfy our needs, just the needs of the person we think we should be.

Community Self

You and I find security in numbers; among others we can call friends who can be trusted to be there to help us survive. We are social. We are made to find comfort in each other. Nature made us this way because we survive better in numbers, working together as groups, whether it is to fight off the savage tiger attacking our children, or hunting together to bring down the wild beast. The Ten Basic Desires of Community Self that ensure we fulfill our social needs, are the need to be:

1. valued
2. noticed
3. appreciated
4. heard
5. considered the same (sameness)
6. validated/approved
7. respected
8. cared for
9. supported
10. protected.

In simple terms, we are driven to have these needs met by others, and other people are driven to have these needs met by us. We all want to be noticed and valued, heard, appreciated, respected, cared for and supported by others. We also want to be approved of, and to not seem too different – to have a sense of sameness or similarity.

We can summarize these desires as the needs at the core of friendship; if these needs are unmet there is no friendship.

Soon we will learn how to use our understanding of these basic social needs to create friendship in our lives and our relationships that can be close and profound.

When we begin to understand the sheer power of Community Self desires we start to see why the fall of woman was inevitable. We also better understand some important differences between women and men, especially in terms of how we communicate and can use sex. Want to understand how to avoid being hurt and disappointed in your sexual relationships with men? It can become clearer once we better understand the desires at the heart of Community Self.

Family Self

A family is ultimately a small community. What distinguishes it from a community in this model is that the bonds are so strong that it shouldn't forsake you in your hour of need, whereas a community may abandon you. A family is a very special small community with its own specific desires.

> **There are many Family Self desires but it is enough to know for now that the desires that ultimately make us an authentic woman or an authentic man are Family Self desires.**

Family Self desires include all the desires that drive us to be part of a family and have a family of our own. It includes the desires that drive us to build a mutually satisfying sexual relationship and bond so we stay together as a couple and care for our children so they can thrive later as adults.

Desires for an authentic man and to have a happy family are Family Self desires women are naturally born with. We can have amazing mutually fulfilling relationships and create more stable families once we both learn to be true to the Family Self desires at the heart of our authentic self.

Land

Land represents everything that is not human; it includes the sky, the stars, the air, the trees, the animals, and the earth itself.

How is this relevant?

Land becomes a tool we will use later, much as the Aboriginal Australians once did.

Years ago, before Europeans invaded Australia, many of the Aboriginal Australians had an interesting way of connecting with their world and themselves. They would go on what Europeans called 'walkabout'. Some would roam the land and survive for many months or more at a time without any company. In essence developing an identity that was their own, a personal sense of who they were in the natural world and the universe in their own right. They used the land to increase their Personal Self.

When we are on our own, when we are left for long enough with only the world for company, we can get to know what we, as individuals, think and feel.

Land can help us reconnect with the world and ourselves.

Land can help us clearly see we are more than just a man or a woman in a community and family; we are an important part of so much more that extends beyond us. When we are away from nature, and spend most of our time with others, it can be easy to lose sight of this.

Land can be a powerful tool to help us become more realistic and find a more satisfying and sustainable balance in our lives. It is in the center of the BOS Model because its impact defines much of who and what we can become.

We will use the Land in one of the seven steps to help raise your Essence of Woman and help you connect with your true Inner Self.

With a practical model to help us understand our basic human desires we can now move on to why the fall of the Essence of Woman was inevitable.

Chapter 2:
The inevitable downfall

'He would have killed me …' Ms Barbara Sheehan, a regular church going 50-year-old mother of two grown children tried to explain outside the State Supreme Court in Queens. She was accused of murdering her police officer husband in a hail of bullets after years of his abuse.

Ms Sheehan described, in a *New York Times* article published 18 September 2011, that she had suffered abuse – and her children would back her up – that included 'smashing her head against a cinder-block wall during a vacation in Jamaica in 2007, throwing boiling hot pasta sauce at her', and being punched in the face the evening before the killing took place.

'Ms Sheehan's family said she often appeared anxious and would show up at family events made up to cover bruises and black eyes.'

As she quite reasonably pointed out outside the court where she was being tried for murder, 'I am being made the victim twice.'

In October 2013 Ms Sheehan was admitted to a correctional facility where she is expected to serve out a sentence of at least three years. Community and family members continue to petition for her release.

Ms Sheehan in enduring years of abuse is not alone. According to the Center for Disease Control and Prevention, Atlanta, Georgia, nearly one in four women (24.3 percent) in the United States have experienced rape, physical violence, and/or stalking by an intimate partner,[2] almost a quarter of all women in the United States. That is one woman in every woman's doubles tennis match. But that is probably a gross under estimate of the level of abuse women suffer in the US. The numbers don't include all the women who regularly suffer the psychological abuse of being shouted at, ignored, or put down, told they are worthless or useless and who, for whatever reason, fear, intimidation, or low self-esteem, never report the abuse.

Unacceptably high levels of violence against women are not restricted to the USA. In an Australian survey[3] conducted in 1996 twenty-three percent of women who had been married or in a de facto relationship experienced violence at some time in their relationship. Of women who had been in a previous relationship forty-two percent reported violence by their previous partner. Some twelve percent of women who reported violence by their current partner at some time during their relationship said they currently lived in fear. A 2005 World Health Organization survey found that among women aged fifteen to forty-nine years between fifteen percent of women in Japan and seventy-one percent of women in Ethiopia reported physical and/or sexual violence by an intimate partner in their lifetime.[4]

The Essence of Woman has truly fallen. This abuse would almost never happen – certainly not to this extent – if the Essence of Woman was raised and women were truly respected. We wouldn't abuse, disrespect, or oppress qualities we held in high regard.

The fact that so much abuse, oppression, and disrespect of women remains indicates we as a society do not truly value women.

However this wasn't always the case.

As some stories of North American tribes living before European settlement suggest[5] women were not treated as inferior. In fact – as mentioned earlier – in many tribes such as the Cherokee and tribes of the Iroquois Nation women were revered and held great power. In tribal cultures often everyone has a say in community affairs. Women are highly respected for their vital role in many tribal communities. It is reasonable to assume this was true for thousands of years; that women were truly valued as women by many of their people and the Essence of Woman among them was high. Then something changed, and what a woman represented – the Essence of Woman – fell into decline.

What changed? Why did the Essence of Woman fall? And how can knowing this help us raise the Essence of Woman now and in the future?

The downfall of the Essence of Women is due to two main factors:
1. The influence of chronic threat
2. Settling as farmers.

These two reasons combined made the downfall of the Essence of Women inevitable, and continues to contribute to its low levels today.

Nature made us with potential flaws that just happen to show themselves under certain all too common conditions.

The first of these circumstances is chronic, or long lasting, threat.

Chapter 3:
The influence of chronic threat

Threaten a dog, back it onto a corner, and it will show its teeth. It is reacting in a predictable way to the threat; defending itself. Threaten us for long enough and our reaction is just as predictable, but with devastating consequences for women, the Essence of Woman, our families, communities, and the world.

What do we mean by threat?

In a nutshell, a threat is something that could harm or kill those who are dear to us, or us. For example, back when we lived in tribes typical threats would include fierce predators, such as lions and tigers, starvation, thirst, and of course, other people such as other tribes, villages, nations, or individuals. If they looked like they might harm us, take the life of a relative or friend, or they took what we needed to survive, they were a threat.

Nature made us behave in specific ways when under threat. But today we react as if we are still in a tribe.

When something threatened us when we lived in our tribe – before we lived in towns and villages – we would race to each other for help; we found safety and security among close friends and relatives, and often our close friends were our relatives. When something threatened one of us it threatened all of us. We came together for each other. Nature also made us look towards and support those who could protect us best.

Who can protect us best in times of threat?

The providers and protectors.

When we were under attack from a neighboring tribe – perhaps they wanted to steal food, or seek payback for the last time we fought and one of them died – the hunters and strong fighters would protect us. Nature made men stronger and faster than most women; hence better suited to that role. If the tribe lived in a land with available game and other food was scarce men were also more valued under threat of starvation (otherwise everyone who could bring in food would be more valuable, including women).

Put simply, place us under threat and the desires of the Essence of Man – to provide and protect – become dominant in the tribe.

Threat raises the value and influence of the Essence of Man and lowers the value and influence of the Essence of Woman. It creates an imbalance between them. When the threat has passed men can go back to being no more important than the rest of the tribe, and the Essence of Man can expect to return to its previous standing.

It is a reasonable natural strategy. Support and value those most able to keep us alive when we need them most and we all have a better chance of surviving. But what if the threat lasts much longer? What happens if the threat lasts for months, years, or decades, and it becomes a chronic threat? Then a terrible trend develops, the Essence of Man dominates for much longer and women begin to suffer. The chronic threat creates a prolonged imbalance between the Essence of Woman and the Essence of Man.

What is the result of such a lasting imbalance?

Since women's roles and desires are not as valued, women become undervalued. They are not as respected or appreciated as much as men, and are considered less important and can even be made to feel inferior to men.

These effects might not happen in days or weeks, but the longer the threat the longer a woman's role becomes less important to the community. Eventually the vital primary roles of caring and nurturing give way to desires of providing and protecting. What naturally satisfies a woman's heart becomes less critical than what naturally satisfies a man's. The flow-on effects of this can make matters worse. Soon women will be driven to act and behave like men.

Why?

Two main reasons.

Firstly, so they have their basic human needs met; so they can be heard, noticed, valued, respected, and appreciated as human beings – needs we can now recognize as vital basic social needs listed in the Balance of Self (BOS) Model. No human being wants to be taken for granted and suffer abuse.

Secondly, so there will be more people to provide for and protect our tribe in such stressful and dangerous times. With more women becoming fighters and hunters the tribe has a better chance of surviving the threat. The survival of the tribe is paramount. If it doesn't survive we don't survive. The children can wait.

As the chronic threat continues soon the natural roles of men and women in society begin to blur. Then the stability and satisfaction of everyone in the society is at risk.

As threat persists for longer and longer more and more women begin to act like men and take on provider and protector roles, such as being soldiers and hunters.

If they live in cities or villages under chronic threat this can manifest itself as women working in jobs men would traditionally do. If men aren't available for long periods of time because they are fighting or protecting us then women will have to do many of the provider and protector roles. A good example of this was during World War 2 where, as the men left to fight, women began to work in factories to keep the war-machine running. Everyone was called up to do their part to counter the threat of the enemy.

The longer women work as providers and protectors the more their role in society blurs. If women are taking on many male roles what does that leave men to do? If a woman is better at providing and protecting than the man, and the children still need to be cared for, many men can be left to fill this role. Then they too no longer fill their traditional or natural male role, and their role as a man in society also becomes blurred. The more the roles are swapped the more men and women can struggle to know what it means to be a man or a woman as they no longer live true to the roles that nature defined for us. As a result men and women across society feel less satisfied. This influence can spread itself across generations.

Keep a state of chronic threat in a society for long enough and generation after generation the Essence of Woman will fall lower and lower.

If the threat remains where is the incentive to be an authentic woman? Especially if being this means women are oppressed and abused by men, and undervalued by society. Fewer authentic women in society, leads to fewer authentic men, and as a result more unfulfilled relationships, relationships failing, and families torn apart as the basic needs in their relationships aren't met. How can we expect to be truly satisfied in our relationships if our partner isn't able to meet the most basic of needs, those that nature programmed inside us? Unstable families threaten the cornerstone of a stable society.

I recall a young woman once sharing that one of her deepest fears was to become a mother. Not because she worried about having children, but because of the effect it would have on her career. She was deeply angry that men didn't have the same pressure placed on them to care for children as women do. For her a career was far more important than being a mother.

When the Essence of Man dominates women will not want to care for the children as much as they otherwise would. As a result we can expect many children will grow up feeling neglected and unsatisfied. Neglected and unsatisfied children make for disturbed and troubled adults unsure how to meet their basic human needs. Troubled adults are more likely to fight a system that they feel is unable to satisfy their basic human desires. Generation after generation this can get worse and worse until the very fabric of our societies are put at risk by more and more troubled people committing crimes, fighting the system that is failing them.

Do you live in an environment or society that is under a state of chronic threat?

Perhaps the better question is do you value the role of provider and protector more than that of carer and nurturer? Do you value and respect the desires of the Essence of Man over the desires of the Essence of Woman? If you do then perhaps you live in a country or environment that is under a state of chronic threat?

Chronic threat is very common.

Today countries all over the world are in a state of chronic threat. In some countries the threat is more obvious, such as mass starvation, war, or the threat of war or attack. In all these countries we can expect the oppression and abuse of women. Good examples can be found in countries like Afghanistan where war seems to have never left the country, where the terrain is harsh, food is scarce, and neighboring tribes still fight each other. Here all too many women are abused, oppressed, violated, and have little say in the running of their communities, let alone their country. In other countries the chronic threat is less obvious, but it's still powerful none the less.

In every modern city in the world – especially in the USA and many other western nations – some degree of a state of chronic threat exists. The media plays a critical role. For instance, the introduction of television in the USA in the 1950s saw the number of murders double within ten to fifteen years – the time necessary for the children who watched the television to reflect what they had been influenced by into actions and behaviors as adults. Television alone has been considered a causal factor in perhaps half of rapes, assaults, and other interpersonal violence in the US.[6] Increase the levels of rapes, assaults, and interpersonal violence and the level of threat in a community is raised. When the media focuses on violence, crime, and the terrorist threat it increases fear among the people. This fear directly contributes to the level of chronic threat – to live under constant fear is a state of threat. The longer the media focus on fear – using fear to gain attention and market audience – the longer the state of chronic threat exists among those who are influenced by them. Fear of violence can also lead many people to own guns to protect themselves, further adding to the level of threat.

A 2007 survey of international gun ownership in one hundred and seventy-eight countries found the US averaged over eighty-eight guns per one hundred people. The next highest was Yemen (fifty-four guns per one hundred), then Sweden with forty-five. The lowest was Tunisia with 0.1. Owning guns makes people a threat to everyone else – do you feel safe when you see a person you don't know carrying a gun they can use at any time? The armed person could have a really bad day, year, or month, and decide to take it out on those around them without warning – using their powerful weapon – with tragic consequences. How many people can walk their street at night and feel completely safe in the USA? How many feel they can count on each other, or the government, to provide for them if they have no shelter and nothing to eat? How many can be sure others will care for them if they are sick?

When we can't be sure of our safety, having enough to eat, or know that others will care for us, then no matter how advanced our cities or societies, or how well armed we are, we are living under a state of threat. If this continues for months or years it becomes chronic. A state of chronic threat now envelops the world. We don't feel safe. We don't feel we can count on those around us to care for and protect us as we feel we need. Not surprisingly the Essence of Woman remains low in most parts of the world and women are abused, disrespected, oppressed, and unvalued as a result.

Was a state of chronic threat inevitable? Was it always going to happen that so many of us would always feel unsafe and insecure and let the desires of man dominate us?

It was inevitable, once we stopped being nomadic tribes and started to become farmers.

Chapter 4:
Settling as farmers

Think of a farm and you might imagine cows, or sheep, or fields of corn or wheat. Maybe a few ducks and chickens. Perhaps even fields of rice. We are so used to the meat in our supermarkets and our bread, milk, eggs, and cereal in the morning we forget that the farming that fills our pantries and refrigerators is all very new. For over a million years – earliest archeological evidence of human-like creatures dates back at least 1.5 million years – we hardly farmed at all, and over this time the Essence of Woman was probably doing ok. We can't be certain of course. But if the stories of many tribes in North America before white man suggest, and the evidence of equality between genders found in unthreatened remote tribes in places like the Amazon show us today, it is more than a reasonable assumption. Then we did what no other humans had done before; we learnt to cultivate, and we learnt to farm animals. Nature kindly created just the right conditions which meant we could settle and stop being nomadic tribes. From the moment we settled to farm the Essence of Woman didn't stand a chance.

It doesn't sound like a big deal. A group of people around 12 400 BC in the Eastern Mediterranean – in an area known today as the Fertile Crescent – herded goats and grew early grasses with seeds we would later call crops. So what's the big deal? Where is the fuss? The fuss is that this simple change in our way of life altered how men would behave to fulfill their male desires. It would ensure most people in the world would live under the fear of chronic threat. 'How could something as simple as farming do this?' you ask.

**Farming spreads a state of chronic threat.
It begins with the creation of wealth.**

When we were nomadic tribes we had no need for wealth; the accumulation of stuff we wanted to hoard or keep. We might carry a bit of extra dried food, or extra water to see us to our next camp, but taking lots of pots, jewelry, or extra clothes would mean more to carry. Besides we could find most of what we needed and take it from the land as we went. If we needed fish or to hunt we would do so. We would follow the food according the seasons. If there wasn't enough we'd move. Then we decided to settle.

Once you no longer move to find what you need to survive you have to start accumulating – food in particular – to survive. You accumulate just in case of bad seasons such as times of drought. Stay in one place and the more food you can gather such as goats, cattle, pigs or sheep, grain, or fruits, the more secure you will feel knowing your family will make it through the tough times. We call this accumulation of excess wealth.

We had no need of wealth when we were nomadic. We needed it to help us survive once we became settlers.

With wealth comes surplus, more than we need. That allows for greater trade; we can trade the surplus for things we want or need. When we were nomadic we might have traded some stones or shells with other tribes we met, now we can trade much more and get much more in return such as garments and tools we could never make ourselves, or trinkets and goods that come from places we never visit. With wealth we also create villages and towns that eventually become cities – we can now supply them with the surplus food we grow on our farms. Soon, thanks to the desires of men, we also create the need for power and status.

Nature created men to protect us and help keep us safe and secure from threats. Once we settle new threats arise. Chief among these threats is the threat of other men. Other men can take our wealth and threaten the survival of our families. It isn't enough that we can accumulate wealth when we are farmers; we also need to influence others so they will not take our wealth and – better still – protect it so it remains safe and secure. How do we influence others to keep our wealth safe? With what we recognize as status and power.

Become a person of some status – such as becoming an important leader – and more people listen to us and are prepared to do what we say. The more important we seem to be to the community the more status we can have and the more we can expect others to help us in our hour of need. A society is going to protect those it values most. It can expect to allow those with status to accumulate and keep their wealth so that the society knows they are secure. We can also create influence with power.

Through use of force, intimidation, threats, and offering 'incentives' or 'gifts' others can't refuse – bribes – we can increase our influence with other people so that more people will do our bidding. We know this as power. The more influence we have the more power we appear to have. Have enough influence and control of other people and you can have an army of followers to help increase and protect your wealth. Wealth itself also becomes a source of power. We can buy influence; we can purchase help and ensure our accumulated wealth is secure. For example, we can buy the support of leaders, security forces, or armies. Wealth can buy enormous power and influence, just look at the influence of wealthy companies and people. How much influence and power do they have in our society and our governments? The more influence and power we have the safer and more secure we feel.

The bottom line is that once we became farmers men were always going to express their male desires in a very specific way.

Men were always going to be driven to try to create safety and security for our group and themselves through power, wealth, and status.

Unfortunately with powerful drives for wealth, power and status we create high levels of chronic threat in our societies and across the globe.

How does that happen?

We can never have enough to ever feel truly secure and safe. That means we were always going to take the search for wealth, power, and status to the extreme.

Create a struggle for wealth, power, and status and you create ruthless competition. Everyone is grappling for the same wealth; competing to be the most safe and secure. As a result everyone becomes a potential – or real – threat. The more others become a threat the more we are driven to accumulate even greater wealth, power, and status. The cycle is never ending. We can never have enough to ever feel completely safe and secure. That makes us insatiable.

We initially tried to feel safe and secure by accumulating enough to protect us from the bad seasons. Now we try to protect what we accumulate for any crisis we can think of. But we can never be sure the seasons or conditions won't be so terrible we all die. We can never feel completely safe, as there's always someone with more wealth, power, and status that can threaten our own.

Worse still by us simply competing with others to have ever-more wealth and power we leave the majority of people in extremes of starvation and poverty, and then these people too become a threat.

We can never have so much that the majority of people won't take it from us if they choose to. We can see a good example of this in the Russian Revolution of 1917.

In Tsarist Russia towards the end of World War 1, the masses of poor and starving people overthrew the autocracy. Tsar Nicholas II and his family were executed. One of the most powerful and wealthy families of the world had everything taken from them in a matter of months. Before long the whole government had fallen and was replaced by a new set of people seeking power, wealth, and status under the guise of communism. Even the wealthiest and most powerful can fall when the majority of people decide it's time.

The great irony is that the more wealth, power and status we amass in our quest for safety and security, the more vulnerable and insecure we feel.

The more we strive to satisfy our desires for wealth, power, and status the more we make enemies and potential enemies. Those who do not have our level of wealth and power feel threatened by us. And the more wealthy and powerful we become the more we threaten those with more wealth and power than ourselves. Soon we have a few with almost all the wealth feeling threatened by the majority who have almost none of it. The very nature of striving to find safety and security in wealth, power, and status is taken to extremes.

By excessively striving to accumulate wealth, power, and status we create increased levels of chronic threat both in our societies and across the globe.

In a society primarily driven by male dominant desires for wealth, power, and status we are all competitors. It's us versus them. We don't work together or as friends, we are driven to use other people to get want we want. This self-serving behavior makes others a real or potential threat; they are our competitors. If our government works on the same principles it will leave us to fight it out among ourselves, it will not try to even-out the wealth through taxation and offer social supports to the needy. This can leave people starving, homeless, without medical care, and struggling to survive; making them a threat to everyone else, as they will want everyone else's money, power and possessions. Live in a society driven by the desires for wealth, power and status and we can expect to have huge extremes in the differences in wealth and a large number of people forgotten or trodden on, collateral damage in the fight to get to the top. The more people who are simply competing rather than helping each other, and the more people who go without, in comparison; the greater the level of chronic threat in our society. But the threat doesn't stop there.

Why stop trying to accumulate wealth, power, and status in one country when you can accumulate it in countries around you, or all over the world? As we have seen the male dominant desires for wealth and power are insatiable. Once they drive us, other countries and peoples also become competition and a potential threat, and a potential source of even more wealth and power. Eventually those motivated enough for wealth, power, and status can be expected to invade or fight other countries to spread their power and influence so that they can become so great and powerful no one dares touch them – so they can feel as secure as they possibly can. We know it as building empires. As empires are made they spread chronic threat across the globe.

Over two thousand years ago Rome built its empire by spreading the fight for greater wealth, status, and power across Europe and some of Asia and North Africa. With their decline other empires arose to take their place, each trying to increase its power and wealth by taking over or fighting other countries. Eventually this fighting between empires led to the 'war to end all wars', World War 1, but the fighting didn't stop there. Soon we had World War 2 as Germany fought to build its own empire. Empire building continues today as countries send powerful companies overseas to fight for more wealth, status, and power, as a means to increase their influence across the world. They spread the idea of competition in societies and teach more and more people to be threats rather than friends. They spread wars as governments fight to compete for wealth and power on their companies' and their wealthy individuals' behalf. This leaves whole countries in a state of chronic threat, as they no longer feel safe next to each other. It leaves millions feeling threatened by the wealthy who they know don't care for them.

It was inevitable we would settle and become farmers; nature kindly gave us animals and plants that made this possible. It was inevitable, thanks to the desires at the heart of men, this would lead to the desires for wealth, status, and power. This led to extremes of wealth and poverty and spread conflict around the world. It also created a chronic threat worldwide that would lower the Essence of Woman and see women undervalued, disrespected, unappreciated, abused, and oppressed globally.

Your fate as a woman was sealed millions of years ago.

The downfall of the Essence of Woman was inevitable. It isn't inevitable that it stays that way.

Ⓘ

The following parts outline seven simple steps to help you uncover the authentic woman within. Each step significantly reduces the level of chronic threat in our society. This ongoing destructive cycle can stop; your natural caring and nurturing nature can counter it. You can help eliminate extremes of wealth and poverty, and make our societies finally feel safe. You don't need to do anything exceptional to achieve this; all you need to do, should you choose to, is listen more to your heart and your Inner Self, and be true to what nature has written inside you; the spirit of the ancient woman within.

Introduction to seven steps

> *Awelye means women's ceremony and stems from the Anmatyrre language that is now shared by many language groups of the Central Desert [Central Australia]. Awelye also refers to the designs that women paint on each others' bodies using ocher and other natural pigments at the beginning of the ceremonies. During these ceremonies Aboriginal women call on their ancestors, show respect for their country and demonstrate their responsibility for the wellbeing of their community. The ceremonies reflect women's roles as the nurturer, healer and caretaker of their families and community. These ceremonies celebrate the fertility of the land and the food the land provides. Awelye is women's business and is never done in the presence of men.*
>
> Gisela Wendling[7]

It is not for a man to tell – or show – a woman how to be a woman; that is for women to show and teach each other.

After all who can know the desires of women better than a woman?

I am respecting an old and wise tradition.

The Aboriginal tribes of the Central Deserts of Australia maintain and recognize the importance of separating what's called men's business and women's business. Each gender holds sacred ceremonies that the other gender cannot watch. Each has their own mythological characters to enact; the men have male characters in the sacred men's ceremony, and the women have female characters in their sacred ceremony. Through each ceremony the men and women learn their roles in society. Men learning from men, and the women from women.

This wise tradition is worthy of recognition and respect. I cannot know as much about being a woman as a woman can. And neither can I know what it is to realize being one. What I can do is offer a framework for you to consider so you as a woman can learn for yourself and share with other women what it is to be a woman true to herself in today's society.

Consider the next seven steps a guide and set of recommendations.

The aim is to help you learn to listen to your heart, the heart that still resonates of ancient mothers inside you, and to learn what you can do to embrace the authentic woman within. At the same time we aim to raise the Essence of Woman so that it continues to rise and never falls again.

As we apply the following steps try to imagine the powerful spirit of the ancient woman within – wanting to know you, yearning to speak with you through your heart. Listen to her wisdom.

Step 1: Respect

If you want to be respected by others the great thing is to respect yourself. Only by that, only by self-respect will you compel others to respect you.
                                        Fyodor Dostoevsky[8]

As I stood before a small group of women and men at the seminar I asked them a question:

'Do you respect yourself?' I saw many nod their heads. 'Please raise your hand if you respect yourself, and treat yourself with respect.'

Almost everyone raised a hand, many not very much, just enough to be noticed.

'Great,' I said. 'That's most of you. Now let me ask you another way.'

The room was the size of a small lecture hall. Everyone sat in a semi-circle facing me as I stood in front of a small stage. There was a mixture of ages from late teens to mid-seventies.

'Would you harm someone you really respected?' I asked.

Many shook their heads.

'Would you recommend they harm themselves?'

Again they shook their heads.

'Would you recommend they did anything unhealthy?'

Everyone seemed in agreement they wouldn't.

'So how do you treat yourself? Do you do everything you know you should do to keep fit and healthy? Do you eat well, exercise as much as you should, take care of yourself as you know you should?'

Some people smiled.

'Raise your hand again if you do all you should do to be as fit and healthy as you can be.'

Not one of them raised their hand.

'Now what does that say about our actual level of self-respect?'

Chapter 5:
Respect yourself

Now I'm going to ask you: Do you respect yourself as a woman? Do you care for the woman you are, as you know you should?

If women don't respect themselves as women then why should men respect them as women? Why should their children, why should anyone?

Respect begins by respecting ourselves. And we all want respect; see the Ten Desires of Community Self in the Balance of Self (BOS) Model.

When you see people abusing themselves with drugs and neglecting themselves do they inspire your respect? Not really, it is hard to respect them when they don't respect themselves isn't it? When we respect ourselves others respect us. We can begin to respect ourselves by taking pride in ourselves.

Take pride in yourself

She holds herself with genuine confidence; knows in her heart she is being true. In her every task she exudes a self-assurance. She has no time for frivolities like trends or girlish fashions. She focuses on what matters to a woman's heart the most. Every child benefits from her ability, and every adult offers her thanks for her caring interest, and the world benefits from her benevolence. She is a woman filled with the power of glowing pride. The honest pride of being an authentic woman that radiates and shines and is clearly visible for everyone to see.

When you are proud you show it in your actions, how you hold yourself, and in every other aspect obvious to others. When you are proud you will act like you are worthy of respect and it will shine from you like a warm glowing light.

Pride should come from the heart; it must feel true for others to notice.

Pride that is faked – false pride – is irritating. It is as if the person is lying to us. How many times has someone else's false pride irritated you? The person acts proud, but you know it is fake. Genuine pride on the other hand rings true, and never seems artificial or contrived. Pride from the heart is a great way to enhance the authentic woman qualities inside you in a way that false pride can never do. Genuine pride can be a most useful tool.

Pride is akin to a personal life filter. Just as a water filter filters away harmful sediment to refine the quality of water so too pride can help us refine ourselves and remove harmful impurities. One of the ways pride does this is by promoting repetition.

Suppose you take pride in keeping a clean house or room – it makes you feel good inside to know it is as clean as you would like it, and that you made it this way. Then every time you clean the house or room you feel genuinely good inside, like giving yourself a positive reward. Take pride in it and you will do it well, and feel genuinely good and want to do it again. We are more likely to repeat what we take pride in. By repeating it – and always wanting to do it well – we can get faster and more efficient, refining what we do.

Of course this process of using pride as a means of refinement can work against us.

For example, if we take pride in creating misery for others – perhaps because we want the attention – then we refine and reinforce creating torment. This will make others want to avoid us – or even punish us – making our lives more miserable. What we take pride in matters; it will reinforce and refine parts of who we are; what we do, how we act and behave, and how others will treat us.

The reason false pride doesn't help us is that it doesn't inspire us to do the task well, or do it again – it doesn't feel genuinely good. It doesn't help us refine positive qualities in ourselves. So not only does false-pride irritate others it works against bettering ourselves.

Take genuine pride in your authentic womanly qualities and you refine them, you do them well, repeat them, and filter out what doesn't work – you refine and filter yourself to become a purer authentic woman. The more you find to be proud of inside you the more you will find to respect and value. Genuine pride and respect inside women can then spread.

The qualities in which you take pride will be reflected in other women. When you are proud of them they are more likely to be proud of themselves – you have shown them something of themselves to be proud of. Having honest pride in the authentic woman inside you then becomes a source of respect and pride for the authentic woman qualities in all women. Respect and pride for all women begins within.

If you are struggling to know what to be proud of as a woman consider the following examples:

1. you naturally care for people and children more than wealth, power, or status
2. you value your ancient heritage and the women of ages past that still speak to your heart
3. you are one of a chosen people able to create and give life to the world
4. nature has given you the sacred task of molding the hearts and minds of our young that determines the happiness of generations to come
5. you are inherently a sharer rather than a user of the world and its people as men tend to be
6. you have a natural sensuality and the amazing experiences that come with it, when you let yourself be true to it
7. you personally have great power as a woman to change the world simply by being yourself
8. you can restore balance to the world, something men currently cannot do.

Women have innate power. In the age of the domination of man it can be easy to forget this and begin to believe your innate womanly qualities have little or no influence or value. Yet inside you is the very essence that can change the world. You are the life-giver, the determiner of the quality, satisfaction, and balance of all future life. Inside you resides qualities no man can ever truly know or completely comprehend. You can give and offer what he cannot. This will often scare him.

A man may take pride in competition and conquest. The resulting levels of destruction can threaten us all. He is largely driven by desires to provide and protect. Women on the other hand can take pride in building the foundations of lasting peace, life satisfaction, and creating a sustainable balance with the natural world, all grown from the transformational innate desires inside every woman – caring and nurturing. Women can make mans' need for conquest and destruction obsolete by making the giving and caring for life the priority. This will scare many men, especially those relying on conquest and destruction to give their life direction and meaning. Create a more peaceful and caring world and what will men have to provide and protect us from?

What more can you be proud of as a woman than qualities that can improve not only your life but the lives of your children, and generations to come? Qualities nature endowed in you that promote peace, caring, and a greater sustainable balance with the natural world?

When you are true to yourself, there is no reason for false pride.

As you develop your pride in being a woman you increase your confidence. You won't have to answer to anyone about whether you're authentic; you'll know it clearly in your heart. You will know your actions are coming from a part of you that you deeply respect, your Essence of Woman, the spirit of the ancient wise woman inside. How will you know if you have lost this pride? By how you let yourself be treated, and how you treat yourself.

Some examples of indications you have lost pride include:
1. doubting yourself as a woman
2. letting others abuse or disrespect you
3. having many short-term relationships

4. letting men control you or order you around
5. giving sex to men you do not know
6. using your looks to gain status and influence
7. no longer caring for your health and appearance
8. putting status and wealth ahead of time with your children
9. no longer caring for the people, the plants, the animals, and the world around you.
10. being a user of others and the world rather than nurturing and supporting them.

When you do not take pride in your authentic womanhood you stop acting like a woman.

Lack of pride means you no longer consider the future of your children – including possible future children, and children everywhere – as your priority, instead you act as though other things are more important. When you have lost pride you will, predictably, let yourself go. No longer will you care for your health, your appearance, or your fitness. If you have an addiction for instance, then you're surely not proud of the woman you have become.

Ideally, our society should help us feel proud of our natural womanly and manly qualities. The unique qualities of an authentic woman should be recognized and revered so that genuine pride in being authentic can be nurtured in every woman. Unfortunately, civilization will not increase the levels of pride in authentic women, not while chronic threat exists, and wealth, power, and status remain our primary drives. But you can increase it right now, in spite of our dysfunctional society and the male dominant imbalance. You can be the much-needed example simply by taking pride in the truth you feel within.

When you are proud of the woman within then you will radiate it like a beacon.

Not only will you promote pride and respect by recognizing it in others you will automatically promote it without saying a word, and women everywhere will wonder what you have that they lack and know in their hearts they need.

Imagine being the confident and self-assured woman described at the beginning of the chapter, filled with glowing pride. What would it feel like to be such a woman? How would it change your life, and the lives of the women, families, and world around you?

When you let yourself feel the great pride you should feel in being a woman you show the spirit of the ancient woman inside you the respect she truly deserves. It is so much easier to respect her if you are also proud of her. It is so much easier to respect yourself if you are proud of yourself.

If you are struggling to be proud then write what you are proud of; your own version of the examples above. Look at the list every night. In a world that no longer values women's true qualities, remind yourself to take pride in the woman you naturally are. Remember what you are proud of and what you should always respect.

Respect can be a powerful way to increase the number of authentic women in our society. Respect the desires and qualities at the heart of a woman – the Essence of Woman – and we encourage it. The more women are encouraged the more authentic women we will have in our society, the higher the Essence of Woman will rise. It is similar with men.

Respect the desires at the heart of a man and you encourage him to be the man you need him to be. Interestingly by respecting him you also increase the Essence of Woman in our society. How does this happen?

The more you respect the Essence of Man, the more likely it is men will respect the Essence of Woman in return. You will recall in the BOS Model one of our Community Self desires is to be like others – the desire for sameness. When we set the example, others are likely to follow. Respect a man as a man and he is more likely to respect you as a woman. Respect works both ways. We get what we give.

Raising the Essence of Woman inside you begins by respecting yourself, then other authentic women *and* authentic men.

What does this mean? How do we do it? The next chapter looks at respecting women.

Chapter 6:
Respect other women

As we shall see it isn't enough that you learn to respect yourself as a woman to raise your Essence of Woman, you also need to respect the Essence of Woman in all women. Women have much to be proud of; yet it's easy to lose sight of this in a male-dominated world. Learn to show respect to the Essence of Women and you will finally begin to know in your heart how valuable and important you are to all of society. We can respect other women in three practical ways:
1. using praise and encouragement
2. speaking well of them
3. being proud of them.

Let's look at each point in more detail.

Praise and encourage

Praise and encouragement go a long way to changing how we act and behave. Praise a child, for instance, and they are more likely to do what you praised them for – such as cleaning their room. Together praise and encouragement change behavior to help mold a child into who we want them to become. It's no different with adults. We increase the Essence of Woman by praising and encouraging her, so she can be guided and nurtured to be the natural woman she is.

What qualities should we regularly praise and encourage? Those that we recognize in the heart and inner being of every woman; caring and nurturing, and especially mothering.

Caring and nurturing in all its forms should always be encouraged and praised.

Don't you feel better about yourself if others validate you? The same is true for other women. The more you validate the womanly qualities of caring and nurturing the more you give women the confidence to continue to express and show these qualities, qualities true to a woman's heart that help her feel fulfilled and satisfied. Women everywhere could do with more praise and encouragement for being women. So could you.

The way to get other women to show praise and encouragement to you is to show it to others. You can't force women to praise and encourage your womanly qualities since that disrespects them by not giving them a choice. But you can praise and encourage every woman you meet when you see them caring and nurturing in any part of their life. Be the example. As we noted before, thanks to our desire of sameness – to be like others – they will be more likely to give praise and encouragement back to you once you show them by example first.

And I'm not just talking about caring for children. Caring and nurturing activities that should be regularly praised and encouraged can include caring for:

- friends and relatives, especially those who are sick or in need
- strangers, such as the homeless or the poor
- parents and the elderly
- our community's youth
- those who are sick, especially as a health professional such as a nurse, doctor, or healthcare worker
- and nurturing children, not only ours but all children we may encounter (in the end they are all our children)
- sick animals
- plants, trees, and the natural world, and nurturing them to grow strong and in balance
- the planet.

If you see women doing any of these activities praise them for it. If it's your daughter encourage her to follow her heart and praise any caring and nurturing activities she wishes to try. Help her feel satisfied as a woman and show her how important caring and nurturing is for us all. Caring and nurturing in a family and society is a critical part of human life, without it we can feel alone, neglected, and suffer the unnecessary pains of illness and injury. Women who live true to their heart are wonderful carers and nurturers. I'm sure you will agree all of our societies could do with more caring and nurturing.

Encourage the caring and nurturing of any woman, no matter her age, and you empower the Essence of Woman within her and help it spread among the people.

A caring and nurturing role that especially needs praise and encouragement is that of being a mother. No duty can validate and satisfy a woman's natural caring and nurturing desires more than this one. One of the most powerful ways to show respect for the Essence of Woman and help raise it is to praise, encourage, and support mothering.

Unfortunately in this modern world the task of mothers is completely undervalued and underappreciated. But it wasn't always like this. For example, many North American Indian women prior to European settlement recognized that women determined the morals, ethics, and character of the future men and women of the tribe and as a result they had strong family and community support. Many tribes had medicine women to care for their health. Everyone helped raise the children and the mother's important role was highly valued and respected.

We no longer consider the role of mother of as much importance. Evidence is found in the lack of support we show modern mothers today.

We can see evidence of the undervaluing of a mother's role in the plight and struggle of mothers everyday. The life of Sarah is an all too common example.

Sarah – not her real name – a young woman in her early thirties and mother of two active lovely children under five years old came to see me. Within moments of sitting down she started crying telling me that she wondered why she couldn't cope. She was working part-time, and otherwise spent most of her day with her children, cleaning the house, and cooking; she was exhausted by the time her husband arrived late in the evenings. Where were her supports? Her husband worked long hours and was always home late. Her parents and extended family lived hundreds of miles away. She had no family immediately available to help her. She could barely find time to meet her few friends and she told me she would often cry uncontrollably at night. She felt terribly lonely.

Sarah was no isolated example. I have met many mothers struggling to raise a family alone, trying to cope without family support. I remember one young mother without support once claiming her mother refused to look after the grandchildren. Not because she was too old – I have met many elderly grandmothers who do a fine job – but because she said it was now her daughter's turn. You see she had to do it alone; there was no one to help her, now her daughter had to do the same. Besides, now she was retired, she had lots of travel plans, lots to do, and no time to babysit.

The value of a mother and mothering in a society can be measured by the supports of the family and society that are offered to them. What value is the role of mother given in our modern society? How little are we actually supporting the mothers struggling to be authentic women in our modern world?

Where once the role of mother was revered and everyone gathered around mothers to support them in their most vital role, now being a mother has become an afterthought, and secondary to other apparently more important things.

It is not uncommon to hear women being criticized by female colleagues for putting family and being a mother ahead of the once-in-a-lifetime lucrative career. Usually the criticism comes from women who aren't mothers, or who sacrificed being a full-time mother to have a career.

Today we see a growing number of children in daycare as their mothers work. If mothering were the most important job in our society would we really be giving our children to complete strangers to look after them as a substitute? Would our society really abandon single mothers and force them to work rather than support them to focus on being a mother and building the social supports their children, and they need? If mothering were the most valued job in our communities would so many women be choosing other jobs instead? Would we insist they work to maintain what we perceive as a higher standard of living; higher status and wealth? Many women are taking on the provider and protector role over being a mother and woman, some by necessity or their family would starve, others by choice. If we regarded being a mother the most important job would we let this happen? Is that really what we want?

Unless we support motherhood and its vital role in our society by encouragement, praise, and giving lots of physical support, the role of being a mother will continue to not be valued by our society. If women decide to be a mother ahead of making more money and having a career we need to offer all the praise and encouragement we can. And if women need help being mothers we need to be there for them. Women, and especially mothers, need the close support and encouragement of all the women that they can find.

If you want to raise your Essence of Woman show respect to the Essence of Woman in other women, especially the Essence of Woman in mothers. Praise it, nurture it, encourage it, and support it, and the Essence of Woman will naturally rise in you as well.

So next time you see a woman, any woman, it could be your mother, your sister, your niece, your daughter, your boss, your neighbor, your friend, or a complete stranger, give them praise and encouragement every time you see them show qualities of an authentic woman. Offer support to the mothers around you. Don't abandon them; that will just lessen the Essence of Woman among all women. Increase the Essence of Woman everywhere through simple praise and encouragement and the respect for women will be raised once more. Some simple words and acts of support can help change a society, improve life in our families, and help create a more satisfying life.

Speak well of women

Imagine deep in the center of every woman is the spirit of a wise tribal woman. The spirit of ancient woman shared among the hearts of all women. You may not notice the wise ancient woman inside you. You may not even see her in other women, especially those who no longer live true to the desires of the spirit inside them. We all struggle to remain true to our inner nature in our inherently dysfunctional modern world. Yet even in the most troubled, angry, misguided woman the spirit of the wise ancient woman resides. What you do to any woman – including yourself – you do to the spirit of ancient woman and the Essence of Women everywhere.

If the Essence of Woman is to be raised and the spirit of ancient women is to be respected everywhere, every woman should never speak ill of any other woman.

That sounds easier than it really is. How hard is it not to speak ill of a woman who has abused or disrespected you; someone who has spat at you, ignored you, told lies about you, or cursed you and humiliated you in front of others? How hard is it to not speak poorly to yourself if you don't meet your own high expectations? It is easy to be critical and want to punish others around us. If others are critical and punish us we are likely to treat ourselves the same way. What we need are some strategies to help stop the spread of ill spoken of women. There are two strategies you can apply. Firstly, by learning when another woman disrespects you, don't speak ill of them back. And secondly, by preventing the ill will and abusive words being spoken in the first place – prevention.

When women disrespect you

When a woman, or women, speak badly of you – spreading horrible lies or rumors, abusing you to your face – how should you react? Our natural instinct is often to fight back, perhaps curse them, or some other form of retaliation, but is that wise? To reflect on your options, let's think of ourselves as behaving much like a pack of wolves.

Imagine a pack of wolves, like those roaming Yellowstone National Park. Suppose one of these wild wolves bites another in the pack. What options does the bitten wolf have? They can cower and submit, in which case they will likely be bitten again and others will follow suit to work out the order of dominance in the pack; who gets what priority to the food when the prey is killed. They can run away, in which case they will lose their place in the pack and have to make it alone – not a good outcome for a wolf, they hunt better together. Or they can bite back. Biting back sends a message, you hurt me you get hurt too, so don't do it again. This helps them keep their position in the pack and prevents other challenges. We might think we are so much more advanced than a wolf, but we often respond in a similar way.

When someone hurts us, physically or emotionally, our natural instinct is to bite back.

Remember your last argument, perhaps it was with your partner, perhaps someone at work or someone you just met. When they started to abuse you how did you react? Did you let them continue to abuse you – submit? Did you run away? Or did you shout, argue, or abuse them back? Did you say or do something to hurt them? Then you bit them back.

We know others will abuse and disrespect us at some time, it can be hard to avoid when we live with other people. The question is what is the best approach when someone abuses us so we don't lower the Essence of Woman through our actions or response? Should we submit, run away, or bite back?

Consider the alternatives.

Suppose someone swears at you, tells lies about you, or abuses you in some other unacceptable way. You respond by backing off and running away, will the abuse and disrespect just stop? It might for a moment; until you meet the abuser again, or until there is another opportunity for them to abuse you, then we can expect it to start again. Why? You didn't give them any reason not to do it again.

Remember in the schoolyard, when one person was weaker than everyone else? Did everyone come around them and protect them or did the majority abuse, bully, or disrespect them too? Yes, the weakest were often treated worst of all. Even our schoolyards are like a wolf pack. The weakest can run away but can expect to be abused again and again until they give those abusing them reason not to continue.

What about cowering and submitting?

The next time the abuser gets a chance, or has a reason to abuse you, then you will be the victim of their abuse and disrespect again, for the same reasons we just mentioned, you haven't given them a reason not to. They can also continue to abuse you to feel more secure.

When a wolf attacks a lower member of the order in its pack it can help it feel secure in its current position; a reassurance, and a sign to others about how strong it is and not to mess with it. So if any of the wolves below in the pecking order show weakness they better watch out, any sign of weakness can lead to an attack! Similarly, when we live in competitive societies seeking to feel secure in our position in our pack – the people around us, such as in a schoolyard or work – we too can be driven to attack those below us to feel more secure as a way of feeling more secure ourselves. When we start to feel less secure we can begin to feel more secure by attacking those we consider to be below us.

This is one reason why women are often more abused in relationships. The more they submit to their partner's abuse the more their partner will abuse them. The sign of weakness does not foster care and compassion, instead if fosters a desire to hurt and abuse them more for being so weak. And if a man feels insecure in either the relationship or among his peers – perhaps he was made to feel worthless because he suffered or suffers abuse himself – then he will be more likely to abuse a weaker woman to help him feel more secure. Every time he feels insecure he will abuse her. Every time she cowers she makes herself lower and lower in the pack – in this case the family, or relationship – and open to ever-more abuse.

The same situation can happen at work. Those who are most insecure can be driven to bully and attack you. The more you submit the more likely it is that the bullying will continue, and anyone else who is feeling insecure will likely join in.

What about if you just bite back?

Hurt them when they hurt you and they are less likely to do it again; this protects your self-respect. This is often what we will do when someone hurts us; almost by reflex. If we have any worthwhile self-respect we will bite back, often say nasty things, or get into a fight until the other person submits. It is a great way to stop others continuing to abuse us, but the down-side is that it can all too quickly get out of hand.

Going tit for tat we just keep hurting each other. They hurt us we hurt them. We seek revenge. Revenge is simply our way of ensuring the other person won't abuse or disrespect us again. But it can get out of hand and what starts as a small disagreement can end up as a family feud, battle, or physical violence. Like the famous Hatfield-McCoy feud between two families in West Virginia-Kentucky that lasted from 1863 to 1891, where nearly a dozen people died as a result. Even in our relationships it's easy to get in a tit for tat exchange. They hurt us, they may not even know they did it, but we hurt them back in return, then they hurt us and we hurt them and so on. When we are together long enough we know where the emotional tender spots are, we can know how to hurt each other really well. Biting back can have its advantages but it can all too quickly escalate.

How do these options affect the levels of the Essence of Woman?

Cower or run away when another woman abuses or disrespects you and you let her disrespect not only you, but also your spirit, and your Essence of Woman will fall as a result. Every time you cower or run away the Essence of Woman continues to fall.

Bite back on the other hand, defend your self-respect and defend the Spirit of Woman – the spirit of ancient woman inside every woman – from assault, and you can keep your Essence of Woman raised. But keep fighting, getting involved in revenge and payback means you both lose; the Essence of Woman continues to be lowered in both of you, and in society and women everywhere.

Fight each other and you fight the other's Essence of Woman and abuse and disrespect her too.

As we mentioned earlier what you do to the spirit of any woman you do to the spirit of women everywhere. So if another woman abuses or disrespects you, they hurt you intentionally, what should you do?

The ideal scenario is to be friends, and we will work on communication in Step 2. However some women will not want to be your friend no matter what. In that case what's the best option?

Defend the Essence of Woman inside you!

The key is to do it in a way that doesn't lower the Essence of Woman in both of you. How do we do this? Below is a set of strategies that might help.

Don't just bite back

Biting back is a natural instinct, but it can easily spiral. Stop, take a breath, take control and hold your ground.

Don't walk away or submit

Unless you know you'll do or say something you'll regret, hold your ground, appear strong and firm. If you leave you make them feel stronger, and you'll look weaker in their eyes.

Get angry

Get very angry. They are not only abusing you but the Essence of Woman in you and all women. The Essence deserves to be defended, so do you. Channel your anger and make it tell them very clearly 'this is unacceptable, and don't you ever say that or do that to me ever again'.

Don't make threats just say your piece confidently, using your anger to make you strong, make sure you are heard then move on so an ongoing exchange doesn't develop.

Unite as women

Explain that enough women suffer abuse and disrespect at the hands of men, you live by the code of never disrespecting other women; you want to help make them united and strong. This will make you appear friendly. We don't tend to disrespect or abuse our friends. It can also help gain an ally in the fight to increase the Essence of Women everywhere.

Don't keep ignoring it

Abuse and disrespect are like a slow acting cumulative poison; they can make you really sick, or kill you. It doesn't go away by ignoring it. If you need help to develop your strategy, or the approaches you have tried haven't worked, then seek professional help. Many skilled counselors and therapists are trained in such matters.

Stand your ground, don't back away, get angry and focus that anger to defend your Essence of Woman and Spirit of Woman; she deserves to be defended. Don't go tit for tat; don't let the abuse continue. Let the woman who abused you know when just one woman brings another woman down she brings down the spirit of all women and ensures that men will continue to dominate. Women need to stick together and unite so the Spirit of Woman can be strong. Abusing or disrespecting other women is not the answer.

Let us be clear here. We are not talking about strategies for when we disagree. We can still disagree with someone without abusing or disrespecting them. Keep a discussion on topic and never attack the person personally and we can learn greatly from each other.

We should all feel able to disagree with others; it helps us maintain a vital sense of self. Abuse and disrespect on the other hand are a personal attack, not a challenging of ideas or opinions, and should be dealt with before they are allowed to spread and damage the Essence of Woman everywhere.

In the end it's your choice how you respond to the abuse and disrespect of other women. You could try to unite as women first. You might recognize this won't make a difference. It's your choice. You determine whether you raise the Essence of Woman inside you and other women or lower it.

Prevention

Preferably we should all work to prevent ill will and abuse among women. The key to doing this is self-control, self-awareness, and living by a personal code.

Don't ever speak ill of women and they're less likely to speak ill of you.

Below you'll find some simple strategies to help you only speak well of other women. Speaking includes any other form of communication, including texting.

- **Think before you speak.** If you think what you are about to say about a woman will be offensive, don't say it.
- **Don't agree with others who speak ill of women.** Never validate a woman's attacks on another woman. That attack is an attack on the spirit of all women.
- **Explain your code.** When other women speak ill of you or others let them know your code of conduct, and why. See 'Unite as women', above.
- **Choose kind and encouraging words.** Everyone has a 'good' side. Focus on the positives of other women, never the negatives, no matter how horrible the other woman may appear to be.
- **Promote the positives.** Encourage and praise the authentic women qualities you see. Validate them as women and they will be more likely to do the same.

I remember a friend telling me that not everyone likes bananas. He was told by a wise counselor that you couldn't make a person like bananas who doesn't, no matter how hard you try. He was right. We aren't going to like everyone we meet, and not everyone is going to like us. We won't be able to be close friends with everyone.

Whether you like another woman or not treat her as though you are speaking to the wise ancient woman inside her. The qualities of this ancient woman will blossom and help us all.

The more you treat women as wise ancient tribal women, worthy of respect and honor, the more women will act and behave as wise women worthy of respect and honor, and the more the Essence of Woman will rise among you.

Teach your daughters by being the example. Show them by always speaking well of other women every day.

Be proud of other women

We have just seen the great value in being proud of the natural woman you are. The more you are proud of your authentic womanly qualities the more you have to respect and value about yourself. Enhance and grow this sense of genuine pride in you as a woman and you are perfectly placed to be proud of other women and be their example. Your growing womanly pride can also offer you strength to be able to share it. With this greater inner strength you can then confidently remind other women – if they don't already know – of the great and powerful womanly qualities they carry within themselves.

For example, discuss the list of proud womanly qualities – mentioned earlier – with other women. Share with them your own list; what you find makes you proud to be an authentic woman. Show them – if they are interested – how genuine pride can help raise their Essence of Woman, and help them to see how much there is about them worthy of respect and value. Let your daughters and nieces know how proud you are of their authentic womanly qualities so they too increase pride in themselves and can pass it on to the women of the next generation. Share the pride among women and you increase the respect among women.

Women deserve enormous respect. When societies no longer realize how important they are then it's up to you to take pride in yourself and show it. Help raise the Essence of Woman and increase the spirit of the wise ancient woman in women everywhere, by always praising and encouraging women's true qualities, always speaking well of women, and always being proud of the authentic woman within. When you respect these qualities eventually so will everyone else. Don't expect respect if you don't have and show it first.

You can also raise the Essence of Woman, and increase the number of authentic men, by always respecting the man who is true to himself.

Chapter 7:
Respect authentic men

Rob would come home exhausted from a long day at the office. Tina cooked a basic meal of meat and vegies, she hated cooking; she felt she had better things to do with her time. Her four-year-old son from another relationship, Max, played quietly by himself in his room, as he did most days, when he wasn't in childcare – Tina almost never played with him herself, not if she could avoid it. Rob dreaded coming home; it would almost always lead to a fight. From the moment he walked in the door Tina was at him. 'Don't sit down, you need a shower. Hurry up, dinner's getting cold, you're late!' Then he'd be in even more trouble for not noticing she had her hair styled and cut.

'What do you think?' she asked.

Rob was too tired to notice.

'You never pay attention. You don't love me.' She threw the plate down onto the table.

'Now hold on,' Rob began to protest, 'I work all day …'

'And for what?' Tina interrupted, 'for this …?' she said dismissively.

'This house I have to clean, and I have to pay the bills for …'

Rob had learnt to argue with Tina; he never had to in his previous relationships. He found if he didn't argue the abuse would get worse. By the end of the evening he just wanted to sleep.

Suddenly Tina demanded attention and affection in bed. Rob felt so emotionally detached from Tina and so demoralized following her attack he barely moved. Tina threw back the sheets as she jumped out of bed.

'What kind of man are you? I'm sleeping next door with my son, at least he loves me.'

It was just another day for Rob, nothing he did was good enough, and everything was always his fault. He was so exhausted he just fell asleep.

If we look at Rob's example we can see it's easy to blame men, they get so much wrong and don't have a clue about many things, especially when it comes to women, but is disrespecting them the answer?

Just as disrespecting a woman lowers the Essence of Woman, disrespecting a man also lowers his Essence of Man. As women keep telling me there is a shortage of 'Real Men', but will lowering the Essence of Man really help?

When you respect him as a man you increase the authentic man inside him, just as respecting yourself as a woman increases the authentic woman in you.

But what about all the men who disrespect and abuse you, or don't meet your needs? How should you treat them? The same way you'd respect a woman:

- use praise and encouragement
- speak well of him
- be proud of him.

Praise and encourage the qualities of a man and he will act more like a 'Real Man'. Every man has an authentic man deep inside, just as every woman has an authentic woman within, they just need encouragement and praise to come out. So when he's being confident, decisive, listening, validating you, showing equal respect, showing he cares or is thinking of you, or wanting to be better friends with you, praise and encourage him. Show him affection and support him as a provider and protector and he will show you more of the authentic man within.

Always speak well of the man. It can be hard to do, especially when you want to complain about him to your friends. It can be so easy just to blame all your unhappiness in the relationship – or a lot of it – on the fact he is a man, or worse, he is 'just' a man. To make matters worse the more you make him different and focus on what he doesn't do for you, rather than what he does, the more you make him the enemy and make it harder to be his close friend (see more on this in Step 3).

Just as what you do to one woman you do to the heart and spirit of every woman, what you do to one man, you do to the heart and spirit of every man.

If you want more Real Men then never speak poorly of any man.

When it comes to abuse and disrespect from men use the same basic approach that we applied to women. Our natural instinct is to bite back. This can easily lead to a tit for tat exchange, with each hurting the other more until someone submits. Don't just automatically bite back; keep your conversations to topic and never attack him personally. If he is abusing you stand your ground, get angry and point out when his behavior is unacceptable and he has crossed the line.

If he has threatened or used physical violence in the past don't try this, it can only inflame matters and he will be more likely to strike you again. Seek professional help. Perhaps you need to move somewhere you can feel safe.

If he can be reasoned with, unite with him, remind him you are friends and on his side too, you can work this out together. And don't keep ignoring any abuse or it will only get worse. If you need outside help, such as from police, women's refuges, or your friends, get it. And don't try to stop abuse or his neglecting you by abusing and disrespecting him. That will only lessen the man he is in your eyes, then you lose too, as he can never be the Real Man you need him to be.

The more you bring him down the less he will be able to satisfy your needs.

Be proud of your man and his authentic qualities. Don't let others talk badly of him or put men down in general either. They will only make it harder for your man to meet your real needs.

It's worthwhile pointing out a woman can feel more complete by having many of her authentic womanly needs met by an authentic man.

It can help her realize more of her authentic woman potential. The more complete she feels as an authentic woman, the more her Essence of Woman is raised – the higher the power of her ancient woman spirit.

Respect men who are true to themselves and, as we mentioned, they are more likely to respect you. The more men you respect the more authentic men you will have to choose from, and the more men will be available – and able – to help you realize your authentic woman potential.

◎

Ultimately it's worth remembering, with respect comes friendship, we can't be true friends with those we aren't prepared to respect. We choose if we respect someone or not. Choose to respect the Essence of Woman in women and Essence of Man in men and we will always have something to respect in each other, and our authentic selves will grow and emerge offering the potential for close and intimate friendships and more satisfying relationships.

It's worth reminding ourselves of two fundamental points:

Authentic men always respect women. Women who are true to themselves always respect men.

Lose the respect and we lose any chance of lasting relationship satisfaction. Try it. Start respecting your man or men and their authentic qualities and see how they respond. You might be surprised.

◎

Respect is a crucial and integral part of being true to yourself, but friendship is no less important. Get friendships wrong and they can ruin your relationships and leave you lonely and miserable, without family, and without supports. Understand what friendships want of you, and how they need to be different between men and women, and you can increase the closeness and satisfaction of your relationships, have more supportive friends, and increase your Essence of Woman at the same time.

Step 2: Grow friendship

> *It is not so much our friends' help that helps us as the confident knowledge that they will help us.*
>
> Epicurus

'How important is friendship to a healthy relationship?' I asked Eve, a well-dressed working mother of three delightful children aged nine, seven, and four years respectively.

'Very important,' she agreed.

'So before the kids came along how much time did you spend on your friendship, talking, going out together, having fun?'

'Almost every day. We always told each other everything.'

'So how close was your friendship back then?'

'Very close.' Tears welled in Eve's eyes.

'Now that you are a mother is your friendship with Kevin more important, less important, or about the same?'

'More important, much more important,' she emphasized.

'Great, so how much time do you give it? More time, the same, or less?'

'We hardly ever talk any more.' She wiped the tears from her eyes.

'So how would you describe your friendship with Kevin right now?'

'Terrible. I miss him.'

Chapter 8:
Types of friendships

As Eve's case demonstrates friendships are integral to living a fulfilling life. They make us feel more satisfied as human beings, and deeply enrich our lives. On a practical level they can help us work better together and bring us closer. They can also either raise or lower the Essence of Woman and the Essence of Man.

All friendships are not the same, and should never be the same. They need to be different so we better meet each other's basic human needs. The friendship you have with a woman for instance needs to be different to those you have with a man. If it isn't then you can all too easily lower your Essence of Woman and his Essence of Man in the process. You can make your partner less attractive, leaving you in an unfulfilling relationship that is set to fail. Understanding and building the right types of friendships is a crucial part of being an authentic woman. They are also an important skill that can transform all aspects of our life. Understand friendships and what types are most appropriate with different people and life can go from a competitive struggle to a shared and much safer comforting journey.

Our aim in this section will be to help you raise your Essence of Woman with friendship in all aspects of your life, including and especially in your relationship. At the same time ensuring we raise the Essence of Man so more authentic men will be available. We will focus on:

- friendships with women
- friendships with men
- friendships with family and community

In a moment you will learn about the basic desires that form the foundations of all friendships. By learning to understand what a person's needs are for friendship you can increase a sense of friendship with everyone you meet. As we shall soon see the core needs of every friendship are the same, no matter where we live, how old we are, our culture, or how intelligent we are; they are the basic needs at the heart of our humanity.

Friendships don't come naturally for many of us; many of us haven't been taught very well how to make them.

This can make it hard to build new friendships and keep the ones we have mutually satisfying. The following sections are designed to help make friendships more understandable, so they become easier to make and to keep.

So we develop the right types of friendships with different people, we will focus on the difference between a casual friendship and a close – or deep – friendship. Who we choose to have as a close or casual friend can profoundly affect the relationship we have with our partner. For example, you could risk a close and deep friendship with your partner by simply having a casual friendship with another man, it could be at work, or at regular social functions. This can all too easily happen before you realize it and can ruin your relationship, or taint it forever. Shortly we will describe what distinguishes a close friendship and a casual friendship and then see how they apply to the friendships you have with women, men, and to those in your community.

All friendships are important. The friendships you have with women, men, our family and community all have their own particular needs. We need to work on all of them and give them the attention they deserve if we are to get the most from them.

Let us begin by reminding you of the basic needs or desires at the core of every friendship. The Ten Basic Desires of Community Self we introduced earlier are the need to be:

1. valued
2. noticed
3. appreciated

4. heard
5. seen as the same (sameness)
6. validated/approved
7. respected
8. cared for
9. supported
10. protected.

No matter where we live, what religion or philosophy we live by, no matter our age, culture, our race or status in life, we all seek to be valued, appreciated, noticed, respected etc. Even a newborn has social needs the day it's born. Initially this is fulfilled by the bond met mostly by its mother, and soon by its family and their friends.

Why do we have these needs for friendship?

We mentioned it earlier. It's because they help us bond into a group with others so we feel safe and secure. We all have a drive inside us to find great comfort in the friendship of others like us. We are human; we survive better among those of our kind, we survive better in groups.

When we meet these Ten Basic Desires in people we indicate we're on their side; a friend not an enemy or potential threat. We indicate that we're trustworthy, and won't stab them in the back, or take what they need, and that we can work together rather than against each other. It feels great and puts us at ease, and stops us feeling vulnerable and alone. We all feel better around friends, especially close friends.

The basic desires behind friendships are the same in all human beings; they are qualities that make us human. The level of friendships however can differ; some friendships will not be as close as others.

What is the difference between a causal and close friendship?

Casual vs close friendship

Casual friendships are a luxury we take for granted. For some people in some cultures casual friendships are rarely considered, and not even an option. It's much easier to see the difference between casual and close friendships when we begin to understand why casual friendships can be considered so rare in some cultures compared to our own. One culture that highlights the difference between the two types of friendship is that of the highland people of Papua New Guinea (PNG).

In the thick rainforest and rugged mountains of the large island nation of PNG just north of Australia live a remote tribal people. It is so remote and rugged that to this day some people have rarely seen white people. In this lush tropical environment tribes-people mark out territories of land they protect for their tribe so they can grow enough for their families. According to author, Jared Diamond, in *The World Until Yesterday; What can we learn from traditional societies*? some tribes protect their land so vigorously that they place tall sentry towers to watch over their region. This is a dangerous place. To cross over into another person's land can mean certain death!

Why is it so dangerous?

One main reason is payback, or what we would call revenge.

In remote PNG there are no police, no judges or courthouses to deal with disputes or killings, accidental or otherwise. That means they have to deal with them by themselves. So if someone steals from another tribe the tribe they stole from seeks compensation, just as we would if someone stole from us. If the other tribe doesn't give it to them then they may end up fighting or go to war with the neighboring tribe. If someone in the other tribe kills someone in our tribe – even if it is an accident – our tribe again seeks compensation. If there's no compensation then our tribe would seek payback; kill one of them, or any of their relatives. Why seek compensation or payback? To make sure others won't come over and kill one of us when they please. It's like the pack of wolves we described earlier, you hurt me and I'll hurt you to stop you doing it again. Only this time hurting means someone dies. This fear of each other's tribes due to payback determines the quality or levels of friendships they can have.

To tribes-people in these remote areas the main friendships they have are those that help keep them alive. Close bonding friendships with family and their tribe – often their extended family pretty much is their tribe – means they can count on every person defending every other person, and even die for them if necessary. In these lands you rarely develop casual friendships because casual friendships would be with people from other tribes and those tribes could threaten our family at any time – we never know when there could be payback.

Our life in the 'civilized' western world is very different.

Thankfully we live in societies with police, laws, and judges who take care of disputes so we don't need to get involved in payback or revenge. The state will act on our behalf. The police will act as a deterrent against crime. This leaves us feeling safer. It means we can have a friendship with a person from another city for example, and feel joy in catching up, even if we barely know them. How many friends do you casually know in other towns or cities, or other places across the world? It is good to know we can trust strangers, recognizing they won't be out to get us for payback for which we may not even be aware. We can be 'friends' with so many more people as a result.

How does this clarify for us the difference between casual friendships versus close friendships?

A close or deep friendship can be said to be a trusting friendship so close that we would give our life to protect the other person, and we could expect they would protect us, if they were able. A casual friendship is all the other friendships.

A close friendship is a deep bond, often we might expect to find it within families; though these days many families in the modern world are so split and dysfunctional their members can be closer to enemies than friends. We can expect a close bond and friendship between parents and their children, between brothers and sisters, and between parents. If we are a close family we can expect a close friendship with cousins, nieces, and nephews.

A close friendship means we can absolutely count on the other person to be there for us.

It is as if we are one people, the type of close group nature wants us to develop so we survive, much like the bond of friendship among the tribes-people of remote PNG. Much like the bond we had as tribes-people when we were nomadic and spread over the world.

Casual friendships in contrast can be anything from just friendly acquaintances with people we know nothing about to deeper casual friendships, but not to the level where we can truly count on them.

There is a saying: until you are at your lowest, you won't know who your real friends are. You can guarantee close friends will be there for you. Casual friends on the other hand can't necessarily be counted on, when you need them most.

Clearly the most satisfying and fulfilling friendships will be close friendships, no other friendship will compare.

It is important to realize however we can't have deep or close friendships with everyone. No matter what we do or who we are not everyone is going to like us. Remember the advice of the wise counselor about bananas? Not everyone likes bananas, and we can't make people like them. Similarly we can't expect everyone to like us, as some just won't.

When it comes to close and casual friendships some friendships lean towards being close friendships, like you were friends for years but you only just met. Some we should definitely ensure stay as close as we can make them to being trusted and deep – they are good for us both. Others should never try to be close friendships – we are just not compatible. Most of our friendships will almost certainly be casual friendships.

You choose who becomes your close or casual friends. That choice will determine if your Essence of Woman is raised or lowered.

Which friendships will lower or raise your Essence of Woman?

The answers become apparent when we consider the three friendships we mentioned earlier.

Chapter 9: Friendships with women

Diane had decided to resign from work to see if it made her feel better. That was over six months ago and she still felt down. She had been in a highly paid manager's job in retail, the hours were long and pressures increasing. About a year into the job she stopped catching up with friends. It wasn't a plan; there just wasn't enough time. Soon she wasn't her usual confident and happy self, and those she occasionally caught up with were commenting on it. It made her self-conscious. She tried moving into a house with her new partner in a different suburb to see if that made her feel better – to see if settling down to a life together would stop her feeling so depressed. In the end it just left her alone every day struggling with her thoughts; she felt worse! Now she was too embarrassed to contact her friends; she felt such a failure. Besides, they now lived several suburbs away. It was all getting too hard. Her life was collapsing around her. Now her partner wasn't happy in her company either. She was losing it all. As her friendships faded she lost herself.

As Diane's case illustrates nothing can raise your Essence of Woman like being with other women, especially if they are true to themselves. Nature made women to be friends with other women. So a woman can't truly be herself unless she has other women as friends.

Traditionally, whom did women hang out with in their tribes? Other women.

Who did other men hang out with in their tribes? Other men.

It was basic, simple, and it worked. Men and women would come together among groups of men and groups of women, and then share each other's company in the evenings and at night. Hence the creation of woman's business and men's business mentioned earlier. Socializing with members of the same sex has great advantages. One of the biggest is it helps us remain true to ourselves.

How does that happen?

It is like respect we mentioned earlier. When you respect women for being women you help them feel confident to act as their authentic selves. The more women you respect and validate the more women feel comfortable being themselves. The more women you hang out with the more women you have around you who can validate you as a woman.

Who better than another woman to empathize and understand some of the troubles that you are facing as a woman? Who better to validate your womanly qualities than another woman who knows them too? Bring two women together and it is like two tribal women sharing what it is to be a tribal woman. It is the sharing of the Essence of Woman between you. Sharing this with another woman is like getting positive feedback, the more you give the more you get, each growing from being with the other.

The more you share time with other authentic women the more Essence of Woman is available to be shared.

No other friendships can do this, not even your bond with your child. Of course friendships with other women will have other advantages.

For example, being with other women also allows you to share your problems. It helps you feel less alone and vulnerable and offers a sense of safety. The more you share and talk with other women the closer you can bond until some – perhaps all – can be counted on as true and trusted friends. Close friendships with other women can be some of the most satisfying friendships you can find. Not only do they help meet basic social needs, but also they enhance your authentic self.

Talking is an important part of female friendship. Some people – men usually – may complain about women gossiping, but gossip – if done respectfully – can have many advantages, especially in a tribe.

The word 'gossip' gets a bad rap. But if women gossip about who is doing what and with whom then they share with each other what is expected of them in society. They will learn the rules. They will also make the rules, what men and women should and shouldn't do, what hurts other people and should be avoided. For instance if women notice some girls are being too close to men already in relationships they can check with each other, talk or chat about it. Soon everyone in the tribe will know if it is ok or not for young girls to get too familiar with older men already in relationships in the tribe – the women have spoken.

Through gossip women become the moral voice of society and spread their wisdom among us all.

That's right. Gossip can be good!

Of course gossip can be destructive if it involves malice or disrespect. Malicious rumors can do as much harm to a tribe as positive moral suggestions can improve it. Hence the need for respect – see Step 1.

Women can transform a society simply by having friendships with other women.
As they share their authenticity they can spread the great fulfillment to women and daughters everywhere.
In short women should spend lots of time with other women.
How can you create friendships with other women? How can you enhance or repair the friendships with women you already have, should you wish to do so?
By meeting their needs for friendship, and the Ten Basic Desires of Community Self of every woman you meet.
The following suggestions for enhancing and creating friendships with women are based on the Ten Basic Desires of Community Self. Being friends is simply about meeting someone else's basic human needs.

Enhance and create friendships

- **Make time, and be on time.** Nothing speaks of being valued more than when someone makes time for us. We can't be very important if they don't even make the time, or if they don't show up on time.

- **Respect, respect, respect.** See Step 1. An additional useful way of showing respect to those mentioned in Step 1 is to ask, but don't tell. Don't ever tell any woman what to do, ask them instead. If they say 'no' don't get angry, let them make their own choice. Treat them as though their life and what they do is as important as yours. If they actually take time from their life to help you then offer them honest and real gratitude. 'Please' and 'thank you' indicate respect if you mean them, use them often.
- **Listen.** Let someone tell their story, show interest, empathy, and understanding; that person is sharing their being. Truly listen, put yourself in their place and see how you would feel if you were them. Try to understand them; don't judge them. What would you have done if you were born into their shoes, or were in their predicament?
- **Notice her.** If you see your friend, acknowledge her, preferably by name. This helps people feel valued. Don't ignore friends. If you can't talk now say so, be polite, make another time.
- **Focus on similarities.** Notice and mention what you have in common. Never focus on the differences. Focus on people, events and topics you both like to talk about; even the weather be it miserable, or gorgeous. The more you show how much you are the same the more the friendship will grow.
- **Talk, gossip, discuss feelings.** Share what is happening, gossip. Ask with genuine interest how they feel. Share with each other your problems and lessen your burden. Respect each other's feelings and never invalidate someone else's experience. Never disrespect anyone you talk about.
- **Care for her.** Be the naturally caring person you are with your friends. Show you care by offering to help. Never promise help you don't intend providing.
- **Be supportive.** Be supportive of your friend's choices and decisions. Support of a good friend, especially if they are feeling down, can mean a lot.
- **Defend her.** Make sure your friends are safe. If police need to be called to protect her and her family then call them. Safety is

paramount. If she needs someone to stand up for her when she is weak, be that person.

⊙

The moment we meet someone new the first thing our brain thinks is: 'Is this person a friend or potential enemy?' It will then look at body language and how they behave. For example, if you don't look in their eye as you shake their hand to say hello that immediately says: 'I'm not interested in you', or 'I'm better than you', or 'I'm scared of you', none of which speak of being a friend. However if you look them in the eye, smile genuinely, don't seem afraid of them, and don't act like they are better than you, then you immediately put them at ease; you have told their brain you are a friend.

Keep in mind you have to allow for cultural differences. In many Asian cultures bowing the head is considered more respectful than looking in the eyes. The aim is to show respect according to culturally accepted norms; a form of body language familiar to them.

Try it.

Treat every new woman you meet as if you have known them for years and are old friends.

You might not always like each other but imagine you are friends none-the-less. Try to meet their desires of Community Self. Try to make them feel noticed, valued, appreciated, and heard. Help them to feel they are like you and you are like them and see how it changes how people react to you.

I once taught these techniques to a new father in his late twenties who looked like he was a member of a tough gang; he had tattoos from head to toe and body piercings to match. He always looked as if he could bash you, mostly because other people often abused him; they didn't like how he looked. He told me how when he went into the nightclub area in the city no one would let him in. It left him feeling angry and depressed. Then he tried a new approach, he acted like a friend in the ways we discussed.

Several weeks later he came back with a big smile on his face, everyone was treating him differently, he was even getting on better with his wife. I asked him what he did. He explained it simply, instead of looking with eyes down and being defensive wherever he went he actually approached the bouncers – security – at the clubs, started a conversation with them, about weather, football, about the type of night they were having, and shook their hands as if they were a good buddy. They all let him in! He never looked back.

People will react differently to you according to how you treat them. Treat them as a friend and even the people you thought might never accept you can end up also treating you like a friend.

Practical exercise

Each week pick one of the suggestions for 'Enhancing and creating friendships' and for that week devote your attentions to trying to meet that one need in every woman you meet.

- Week 1: Make time for at least three catch ups with friends. Make sure you're on time or early.
- Week 2: Make sure you don't order any woman around wherever possible for one whole week – even at work, unless you are in the armed forces. Ask them kindly instead. Say a genuine 'please' and 'thank you' to every woman who you wish something from, or to those who have made room for you, or have gotten out of your way. Treat every woman as an equal.
- Week 3: Focus on being a better listener. Let every woman who wants to tell her story share it with you. Try to understand her point of view and how you would feel if it happened to you. Don't judge or try to give solutions, just listen. Try to make the time to really listen, so they can have their full say.
- Week 4: Say a friendly hello by name to every woman you know when you see them. Let them know that you notice them.
- Week 5: For every woman you meet try to find things you have in common with them and mention them. If you both wear similar clothes, make up, or shoes let them know you like it too, and that it must be a good choice if you both like it. Don't focus on what is different.

- Week 6: Focus on validating and approving what other women do that you agree with. Validate their pains or fears in life. Let them know you would probably do or feel what they are doing or feeling if you were in their position.
- Week 7: Offer genuine help to the women you know. Ask if they need help. Show that you care, don't just say you care.
- Week 8: Focus on offering support to other women's endeavors. Show support for their decisions, even if it might not be how you would do it. Many an author, painter, artist, or businessperson wouldn't have succeeded without support. A show of support can be very powerful. Mothers especially need it.
- Week 9: Focus on helping women feel protected from harm or abuse. If you see a woman who might need help ask her what you can do. Let her know what services might be able to help. Don't judge her, protect her and her wise woman within, even if she may no longer be listening to her own inner wisdom.

It's up to us to meet other people's friendship needs, that is our job.

Trying to change someone else is disrespectful, as we mentioned in Step 1. We don't like it when others try to change us so we shouldn't do it to others, especially if we are trying to be friends. The good news is thanks to our strong desires for sameness (see Community Needs – we do what others do) our friends will likely do what we are doing soon enough and automatically meet our friendship needs as well. If they don't then perhaps they just don't want to be our friends. Or perhaps they don't yet know how to be, we should be patient, and give them time.

In our busy lives it's easy to neglect our friendships, like Diane did – as described at the beginning of the chapter – when her job became busy and stressful. This is a big mistake. You cannot be true to yourself without friendships with other women. To be alone is to lower your Essence of Woman. In the end this will threaten your relationship too, not just your friendships, as you are less able to satisfy your partner's needs.

And never expect a man to be your only friend; that will just lower the Essence of Woman – and the power of the Spirit of Woman – inside you. We will discuss how that can happen next.

Contact your female friends regularly. Make new female friends. Make at least some of them a priority so you can be more valued, appreciated and respected as a friend. Close friendships are the most worthwhile of all.

Contact your female friends today.

Catch up.

Talk.

Be the friend you want them to be.

Warning

If the woman you are trying to be friends with leaves you feeling worse after each meeting then keep it very casual.

If on the other hand that woman makes you feel good, and especially if they don't act like men but rather like an authentic woman, then consider spending more time with them. These can be the best women to be around to raise your Essence of Woman. Over time, and by you meeting more and more of her Ten Basic Desires, she can soon be one of your closest friends.

Try to never treat other women as the enemy, no matter how much they have slighted you. Either treat them as a friend or avoid them. If you can't avoid them then remember Step 1 and always try to respect them. If we don't then the Essence of Man will continue to dominate the world and every woman loses out.

Chapter 10:
Friendships with men

Steven was a registered nurse at a major public hospital, tall, dark, athletic, good looking, in his late twenties, and single, again. He couldn't understand it. He didn't fight with any of the women he had relationships with, or so he said. Actually he described quite the opposite. Steven was like one of the girls.

Did Steven have any homosexual leaning? Not at all, he said he was very attracted to women, especially good-looking women. He said he came across several really attractive women at work and would often hang out with a group of them and chat; he enjoyed their company. He found them more interesting than the average bloke; he wasn't into sports or drinking. What made it even more puzzling for Steven, he was everything he heard the women he spoke with said they wanted in a man. He was kind, considerate, loyal, cooked, would clean up after himself, could talk about feelings, he would even go shopping with his girlfriends as they tried on clothes or bought shoes. Apparently many of these good-looking women he met at work and elsewhere were attracted to him, at least initially. Then three months into all his past relationships – give or take a few months – the woman he was with would tell him she didn't love him anymore and break it off. Steven could make no sense of it. It wasn't like he was an abusive alcoholic or anything.

Steven was a kind and caring soft nice guy.

He made a great girlfriend.

⓪

Friendships with men can be dangerous. You can get hurt, really hurt. It can be like fire. On the one hand it can burn down homes, leave permanent scars, and destroy lives. Yet on the other it can also be a wonderful tool, keeping you warm when you are cold and miserable, and offering light when you can't see into the darkness.

Friendship with men can be broken down into two main types:
- Friendships with your partner
- Friendships with men who are not your partner.

If you want to feel fulfilled then it's important you know the differences between the two. We will consider each of them separately in a moment. It's also important to understand you cannot have a friendship with him as you would with a girlfriend if you want to raise your Essence of Woman and want to allow him to be true to himself.

Why can't you be friends with him like you would a girlfriend?

It is how our desires work.

We just noticed that the way to increase your Essence of Woman and be authentic is to spend time with more women who are true to themselves. This creates a virtuous cycle. Similarly, with men, when authentic men hang out together they raise their Essence of Man. Why does this work? For the reasons we outlined earlier; it shares our female or male essences among us, and because we are driven to do what others are doing thanks to the desire of sameness. If you are among authentic women you will be more likely to act and behave like them. The same goes for authentic men. Spend enough time with each other and we become like each other. This can work against us when men and women spend too much time together.

When women spend time with men they will take on traits of men.

They may be subtle at first, it may just be how you think that will change, and you might start to be more competitive and less sharing and caring for example. The more time you spend with men the more you will become like them. You may have noticed this in girls who grow up as the only girl in a family of boys.

If you are the only girl among brothers the boys will treat you like a boy and you can act like a boy to fit in – the desire for sameness. Soon you can talk, think, and act like a boy, get involved in playing rough games. I have counseled several women who have grown up in all-boy families; they tell me they tend to think and act more like a man, and often consider themselves a bit of a Tom Boy. Similarly the more time you spend with men – often just bigger boys – the more you can become like a man and think, talk, and act in ways that they do.

In terms of the Essence of Woman the more time you spend with men the more your Essence of Woman is lowered.

Spend long periods of time only with a man – make your partner your only real friend for example – and your Essence of Woman is going to be lowered. The longer you spend only with him and not with your girlfriends or other authentic women the more your Essence of Woman can fall. It's like you charge your Essence of Woman batteries by being with women. Spend too much time with men and they will deplete these batteries until they are empty. Then it can be very hard to locate the Essence of Woman within.

The same is true for men. The more time they spend with women the more their batteries run down until they too are empty. Much like Steven did as described at the beginning of the chapter. He spent so much time with the girls he became one of them and ultimately less attractive for it.

The longer men are with women friends the more their Essence of Man will be lowered.

Not intentionally. It will just happen. You will drive him to be like a woman and less of an authentic man. Make him into a girlfriend and he will not be able to satisfy your needs for an authentic man in your relationship.

Then what sort of friendship should you have with a man? How can you have a friendship that doesn't lower your Essence of Woman but still keeps him authentic to himself?

The best way is to understand the difference between the two types of male friendships, and know how to get the best from both.

Friendship with your partner

The most fulfilling relationship you can ever have with a man can be with your partner. He can meet both close friendship needs and authentic woman needs at the same time. A girlfriend can only meet your friendship needs. Just being with a man – even if he is not your partner – can meet some of your authentic woman needs for a man. But only a close and lasting relationship with a 'Real Man' has the potential to meet more desires for you as a woman than any relationship you can ever have.

How do we create the most fulfilling relationship you can with your partner, or with the man you want as a partner?

We focus on developing a close friendship in a way that helps him stay true to himself, while allowing you to stay true to yourself. And if the relationship is struggling we focus on making it close again by improving the closeness of the friendship, not only by ensuring we meet each other's friendship needs but also by building and maintaining trust. (We will discuss ways to do that soon.)

Close friendship keeps him real

Given the choice between a close friendship and a casual friendship you'll want to develop a very close and trusting friendship with your partner. You want to know and feel he is on your side, will be there for you when you need him most, to protect and keep you safe, no matter what! You want to know he is part of your closest of close family. This is also what nature needs you to do.

> **Nature needs you to develop a bond with your partner so close that nothing can break it.**

Your relationship needs to bind better than superglue. It needs to tackle the heat and the cold, and not crack under pressure. Why? So you will both be together – and stay together – to raise your children. Even if you decide never to have children nature will still drive your desires towards a bond so close that if you did have them you would stay together forever. Nature has made children the priority. It created the level of strength of bond we seek in our relationships to reflect this. Our children are less likely to survive in the natural world if their parents break up before the children are independent. Only a strong, close, lasting bond between a couple will do. Some of us may know this as searching for the 'the one'.

Many of us dream of meeting that one person who will fill our soul – a 'soul mate' – the one who will be with us forever, even after we pass away. In our heart we crave that one person, and we crave for them strongly for a reason. If we didn't it would be too easy to find an excuse to leave, and threaten our relationship and the survival of our children in the process.

What we actually crave when we seek 'the one' or our 'soul mate' is a partner who can meet our partnership needs, but who is also the embodiment of close friendship.

Imagine your perfect soul mate. Would you really want to be with them for eternity if you were not close friends? When nature wants us to stay together for the sake of our children it drives us to seek to bond as truly close friends.

A casual friendship won't do. We can't trust a casual friend to always be there for us, even if they did meet many of our other relationship needs. Casual friendships don't have the level of bond that will make us certain they would be prepared to lay their life down if needed, as a person would do in one of the remote tribes of Papua New Guinea. We cannot expect a casual friend to stay with us no matter how bad it gets. A casual friend would not stay around to help look after our children.

An example of such a casual friendship as opposed to a close one would be a couple primarily together because he has the money and she has the looks to compliment his status, yet they don't get along. Because they can't be close friends the couple will be casual friends at best. If he loses his money, or if her attractive looks fade, then most of the reasons for being together have gone. Since they don't have a close bond of friendship to fall back on they will almost certainly break up. If children are involved then they'll be caught in the middle. This relationship was always vulnerable and likely to fail.

We might try to fake many parts of our lives but close friendships are either genuine or they are not.

Unfortunately there's no magic way of testing the closeness of friendship. Sometimes nature tests it for us. It isn't until we are at our sickest or most vulnerable, until the other person has stuck by us when all our casual friends have gone, that we truly know we have a close friendship. Then we can be sure this is a person truly close to our heart.

(That doesn't mean we should intentionally test our friendships. This can make the other person want to leave, as it says you don't trust them. Better to stay together long enough to see if it lasts, and if you feel in your heart it's a close friendship then trust your instincts.)

Unfortunately there's no guarantee close friendships will stay close, especially if we no longer work to meet each other's friendship needs.

Close friendships are not like getting a diploma. You don't just study, put in the effort, and then stop once you have the piece of paper in your hand.

Nature needs us to show our commitment and prove our friendship regularly. It is true we can move to another part of the world, keep little contact for years, and still be close when we return, but unfortunately often that isn't how friendships work. Close friendships in a family, or childhood friendships can be steadfast, however close relationship friendships are more fragile and need regular upkeep. Nature needs us to continue to meet each other's friendship needs in many of our close friendships, especially in our relationships, or all too easily they will become casual, or worse still, fade.

Often couples wonder why their relationship and friendship drifts apart. They expect that once they have a bond it will just stay there forever, like a marriage certificate or diploma nailed to a wall. They expect their close friendship or relationship will survive even when they hardly see each other, talk, or share what's happening, and barely meet each other's friendship needs – love will keep it together, right? Unfortunately, no it won't.

Close friendship is like a tree; it needs care and nurturing not only from a seed, but throughout its life so it continues to flourish and grow.

The more care and nurturing we give it the greater the chance close friendship has to grow and strengthen. Even the biggest and sturdiest of trees still needs water and food from the earth. It still needs the right conditions to grow and flourish. So it is with close friendship, if we don't keep supplying it with what it needs to grow, flourish, and be strong it will wither and die.

So if we want to develop a lasting friendship with our partner – or prospective partner – the first step is to develop a close friendship – remembering not all of us are compatible, meaning this step might not be possible. Then once we have a close friendship then we need to remain close friends; we need to keep up the maintenance.

Following are some suggestions on developing a close friendship with your partner – or someone you want as a partner – and how to maintain it. Once again it's based on fulfilling needs of friendship, the Ten Basic Desires of Community Self. The suggestions are tailored to also help him be true to himself.

Close friendships with partner

Make time
We can't expect to be close friends and stay close if we barely see or talk to each other. Make time to be with each other regularly. If you value the friendship and relationship make the time.

Respect him
You cannot have a close friendship with a person you don't respect, and neither can he. If you think he is better than you or vice versa then you will have trouble being close friends. Close friends respect each other as equals. Respect him as a man – see Step 1 – if you want him to be the 'Real Man' nature intended.

Listen
If he wants to share something listen, try to see his point of view. Don't judge him, don't disagree with him, listen.

Notice him
Notice when he is near you; acknowledge that he is there. Say hello, give a hug, or a gentle touch; they all say to him 'you are important and not ignored'.

Focus on similarities
Discuss dreams, goals, and ambitions you have in common and how you can achieve them together, such as having a family, or about the family, building a home, travelling; whatever you can share that is similar. Focus on what is different and you drive the friendship apart.

Validate him
Validate him as a man. Validate and approve his activities and behaviors, especially those involving providing and protecting. Tell him how important his role is, and how much you appreciate his efforts. Validate and approve of his need to be with his mates – encourage this time – so they can help him be true to himself.

Talk
Talk regularly about issues that need to be discussed. Don't assume you know what he's thinking. Ask and discuss matters before you come to any conclusions on what you each think is going on.

But don't push him to talk if he doesn't want to. Often many men don't want to talk much. For these men you can become closer to him by how you treat him. (See 'Make time', 'Respect him', 'Notice him', 'Care for him', 'Validate him', 'Be supportive'.) If you make him feel good by validating him when he does talk he will probably open up more to you with time.

Don't engage in much gossip with him though. Men have their own gossip, women have theirs; the two are often different. Don't mix the two or you will be making him into a woman.

Care for him
Care for him when he is sick. Show you care for how he thinks and feels. Share your naturally caring nature with him.

Be supportive
Men can take on the world when they feel the close support of a woman by their side. The more you support his decisions and choices the closer he will feel to you. If you especially support any activities you need of him as an authentic man, such as work, then he will become more true to himself. Many men I have met have rated this as the one thing they want most from their partner.

Allow him to protect you
If you fight his battles for him you are usurping his role and will lessen the authentic man within him. Let him provide for and protect you and show your appreciation for it and you will validate him and it can bring you closer. Fight against him and you become the enemy.

The key here is don't try to make him like you. Appreciate, support, and validate his differences. Allow him to have opinions that are different to yours. He will want to be closer to you if you make him feel better as a man. The more he wants to be with you the more he is likely to protect you and the closer the bond you will have together. That includes having fun.

Make time for fun

> **Friends have fun together, they play together, and they enjoy sharing a good laugh.**

If you want to be and remain close friends make fun time. If you can't have fun together you may have to ask if you are actually compatible.

Build closeness with trust
What do we do if we have lost the closeness in the relationship, perhaps want to build a level of friendship and closeness we have never had? You work to meet his needs of friendship, as outlined above, but you also build the closeness with trust.

You can't have a close bond with your partner if you don't trust them. If they break our trust of friendship, or we break theirs, we may never be close again. Trust is like a warm and cosy house. Build it, maintain it, keep it in good condition and it can house a wonderful closeness and intimacy. Damage it; neglect it, dishonor it, infest it with doubt, and it may never recover, and all too easily just fall apart.

How do we increase and build trust? By doing what we say, and sharing secrets.

How can I trust you if you never do what you say you'll do? If I ever choose to tell you a secret how will I know you will keep it if you never do what you say? You have to prove trust if you want someone to trust you by doing what you say. You must also say what you do; be honest and not deceive or intentionally mislead. Stick to your word. The moment you lie, or don't do what you say you will do, trust is weakened or destroyed.

Do you tell your partner you will do something for them but never get around to it? Perhaps you say you will cook a nice dinner, arrange a good night out, organize a babysitter so you can have an intimate evening together, but never get around to it? Then you have just lessened the level of trust your partner now has in you. You have lessened the closeness of your friendship.

If you want to build a close friendship, even make a friendship closer, then you need to prove you are the most trusted person on earth; you need to show them you only make promises you keep; you always do what you say. Another way to build trust and develop a closer bond is to share secrets.

Share secrets
To share a secret with a partner is to share something you both value and will protect.

Sharing secrets means you are working as a team to keep something between you that no one else will ever know. How important, trusted, and special must we be if someone is prepared to share their most trusted secret with us?

The deeper the secret and the more secrets you share together the closer you can become. Sharing a deep secret often means making ourselves emotionally vulnerable. Many of our deepest secrets are often the most embarrassing and most personal. We never share them because we can feel humiliated, or worse. When we share such a secret we are giving the other person our heart and soul and putting it into their custody to protect. If they fail to protect it the most valuable level of trust we can ever have will be broken, and they will be breaking many of the friendship needs we mentioned earlier that bond us together.

It's worth pointing out that only when you trust your partner enough should you share your most precious secrets. If you share your deepest secrets too early, as if to prove you have a close friendship when you haven't had time to build one yet, you are making yourself vulnerable. If the relationship goes sour – you realize you are actually not compatible after all – then you have given him many ways to deeply hurt you.

Similarly don't expect him to just share his deepest secrets with you. This indicates you don't really value them and you expect him to share them with anyone who he is trying to be close with. It can easily drive him away as you are not showing him the respect to decide when he's ready. Once he trusts you enough he may tell you that one thing he never told anyone else. It is then up to you to treat this secret, even if it doesn't seem a big deal, as a precious and fragile thing. If he learns you don't take his secrets seriously he will be unlikely to share with you ever again.

We can also increase the bond of friendship by creating new secrets.

Do things together others will never know about. In the bedroom for example, or when you have fun together. The more secrets you create and store forever between you, the closer the bond you create.

A warning though. Don't make the secret about something illegal. Firstly, that's disrespectful to the rules society has agreed to live by; effectively you're committing a crime against all of us. Secondly, it puts an unnecessary burden on our partner that they should never have to bear – are we really respecting them if we expect them to keep a secret that could get them in serious trouble? The secrets to create and share together should rest well with each of your consciences.

Don't break trust

Once trust is lost often it can never be recovered.

Breaking trust is like infesting a house with termites; it destroys the foundations and is very difficult to fix. Once you break a trust you cannot take it back. The damage is done. The closeness of the relationship has been poisoned forever. Our brain works by using the past to predict the future. Once someone has broken our trust it will constantly remind us it can happen again and prevent a truly close bond ever forming. Once that happens we need to decide if we want to stay in a relationship; do we want a life-partner who can never meet all our relationship needs?

Many relationships and friendships can be made close, even if they were once casual.

Close friendships can be made stronger and rebuilt, even if we become more distant, even if they have become casual. The key is to build and maintain precious trust. Break the trust and the foundations are damaged, sometimes irreparably.

Ⓜ

If you want a close friendship with your partner work every day to meet his friendship needs in a way that enhances his authentic self. But don't try to make him your girlfriend; enjoy him as a 'Real Man' friend, and never make him your only friend. Build and maintain trust; do what you say and create and share secrets to help develop a deep and close bond.

But what about casual or close friendships with other men who are not – and will never be – our partner? Should you have those? Unfortunately these types of friendships can be the most damaging of all.

Friendships with other men

It seems harmless enough, spending some time chatting with guys, perhaps flirting, maybe just getting a male opinion. Besides, it can be fun. What harm can there be? That depends on how fulfilled you want to feel in your relationships, whether you want a truly close relationship with a partner, and whether you want to remain satisfied in a close and lasting relationship. It also depends on whether you want to remain true to yourself, raising your Essence of Woman in the process.

Consider the following two scenarios and the impact they can have on the closeness of your friendship with your partner and the impact on you as a woman:

- You are in a close relationship and you have a casual or close friendship with another man.
- You are not in a close relationship and you have a casual or close friendship with a man you are not attracted to enough to be in a relationship with him.

Each scenario holds its own dangers and can prevent you meeting important relationship needs, and each one can affect your Essence of Woman.

Having friendships with men who are not your partner can have consequences you never intended or didn't expect.

Friendship with another man with relationship

You are in a close relationship, you are close friends and he fills your heart, but something may be missing. Perhaps he doesn't meet a need, which leaves you feeling a bit restless. Perhaps he doesn't make you feel validated or as supported as you would like. Or he barely notices you anymore and makes you feel unappreciated and you are slowly drifting apart. So you develop a casual friendship with another guy at work, or some other man you know socially. It makes you feel better to be around him. It seems to fulfill desires in you that were being ignored. What harm can there be? More than we might immediately imagine.

Think of your friendship with your partner as being like a tall sacred temple held up by ten precious marble pillars. Each pillar gives it strength. The temple is at its strongest and most impressive when all ten pillars are doing what they can to support the temple. That is when your friendship has everything it needs, when all ten pillars of friendship are strong and keeping up the sacred temple you have built together.

Now suppose your temple is not as strong as you'd like. Suppose it's missing a few pillars to keep up its beautiful roof. Then someone comes along and offers you some of their pillars, making your sacred temple complete! There's only one problem. The pillars don't fit the sacred friendship temple you have with your partner, they're a different rock and shape. These pillars make a different type of temple of friendship between you and the person offering to give them to you. You might try to make them fit the temple of friendship between you and your partner, but they won't. They actually make the temple of friendship with your partner unstable.

When you develop a friendship with a man other than your partner you are offering him some of your current relationship's pillars of friendship, those that are not being met. Each pillar you offer him takes one away from the sacred temple you have with your partner and reduces it in strength and beauty. Each one makes it less and less stable.

The friendships between women and men are not like friendships you have with girlfriends; many women can meet many of your friendship needs at any time and it's good to have many girlfriends as it helps meet many social needs. The friendship you have with any man is different; it is as if you are being driven to build one sacred strong temple together with every man you meet. You can try to build a sacred temple so your needs of friendship with men are met using many different parts from different places – different men – but in the end that will just contribute to an unstable disjointed mess. Only one man can fulfill the satisfaction of building a complete and strong scared temple of close friendship with you. Only building and then maintaining that one friendship with that one man will help keep it stable and complete.

This is a mistake we often make. We think we can have our needs of friendship met wherever and with whomever we like. But when it comes to long-term partners nature needs us to develop a close bond with just one person. The closer the bond, the more fulfilled we feel. In the context of a relationship with a man the list of friendship needs inside you can only be met by a man. Meet these needs and no other man will be able to meet them. Have many men meet these needs and then no one partner can ever meet enough of these male-dependent friendship needs to make your relationship truly close, satisfying, and stable.

The ten pillars of friendship your relationship needs to be strong and stable are the Ten Basic Desires of Friendship – the Ten Desires of Community Self in the Balance of Self (BOS) Model. Try to have many men meet these needs and you lessen your ability to develop the one close friendship you feel you need within.

Think of it this way. For every friendship need another man satisfies for you, whether it is respect, feeling valued, appreciated, or supported, that is one desire you will not seek to have met by your partner. As your partner meets less of your friendship needs, your close bond of friendship is weakened.

In other words if you have what seems a casual friendship with another man you threaten the closeness of your already existing close relationship. If you have a close friendship – in contrast to a casual friendship – with another man you tear away the foundations of the close friendship of your current relationship. You tear down the beautiful temple you had previously built and cared for. The close relationship you once had may crumble at its foundations.

Consider an all too familiar scenario. Suppose you don't feel your partner is noticing, validating or appreciating you as much as you'd like – he isn't meeting these friendship needs. You find a guy at work who gives you attention, notices and validates you in your job, and appreciates you as a friend. This makes him great to be around, he makes you feel better about yourself; he meets friendship needs in you that your partner isn't currently meeting. Then you get home, you don't need your partner to meet these needs as much so you dismiss that he isn't noticing and validating you. Rather than discuss it with him so he can actually meet your needs you spend less time with him and talk less together. You start to become more distant. The more friendship needs the other man meets in you the less you feel pressed to have met by your partner and you spend even less time with him, less time sharing intimate stories or experiences, and less time validating each other. Why should you spend time with him meeting needs you are having met elsewhere? Soon you spend such little time meeting each other's friendship needs you don't even meet enough to be called close friends, and your relationship is now unstable. If this continues it will likely fail.

Satisfaction in relationships comes down to meeting basic human needs. If you don't let your man exclusively meet your needs of friendship that only a man can meet you lessen the closeness and success of your relationship.

So if you want to build a stronger and closer friendship with your man then work to ensure he exclusively meets your needs for male friendship. Don't spend time with other men, chat and flirt with them, don't get involved in too much casual chitchat. Keep it distant. If you're at work keep it professional and clinical, don't try to strike up close or casual friendships with other men. You can still be friendly; respectful, courteous, appreciative, and validate their good work; just don't spend much time being casual friends with them. The more you do the more they will meet male friendship needs for you and will affect the satisfaction of your close relationship.

Casual friendships with men also reduce your Essence of Woman, for many of the reasons we have already discussed. The more you spend time with him the less of a woman you become as you take on male traits and behaviors.

If you want to have your needs met in a close relationship and keep your Essence of Woman raised then avoid casual and close friendships with other men. The only men you should be working on having a close friendship with should be your partner or your prospective partner. Casual and close friendships with men aren't as benign as they might seem.

It also goes without saying if you don't meet his needs for friendship that only a woman can meet he will be open to having these needs met by other women. If you don't make him feel supported, appreciated, valued, or respected for instance then when other women offer this he is more likely to want to spend more time with them. This will mean the friendship of your relationship will likely deteriorate further and the woman he has the new friendship with could easily become his new primary relationship; he could easily leave you for her as she meets more needs than you do.

Friendship with a man without relationship

We now know even a casual friendship with a man other than your partner can reduce the closeness of your current relationship. What about having friendships with guys when you are not in a relationship yourself and have no intention of ever having a relationship with them? Surely that must be ok; there is no close relationship to destabilize or break?

Unfortunately these types of relationships can be also be very damaging to your Essence of Woman, and your ability to find and maintain the close relationship you need.

Suppose the casual friendship you are having and never intend on developing is with a man already in a relationship. Then by you having even a casual relationship with him you threaten to destabilize his relationship with his partner.

You will meet womanly needs in him that his own partner should be meeting and lessen their bond.

By doing this you also set an example and other women will be driven to do the same. Soon many women will be destabilizing close relationships and risk, some day, destabilizing yours.

What about a casual friendship with a man not in a relationship – a single guy – but you never intend to have a relationship with him? Is that ok?

Firstly it will lower your Essence of Woman for reasons already outlined.

Secondly it will start to meet his friendship needs that can only be met by a woman. He can easily begin to believe there will be something more, and it can build false hope. It will also prevent him developing friendships with women who might actually want a close relationship with him.

The more needs of friendship you meet for him the less he will want met by other women and the less he will be looking elsewhere to find it.

If you don't want a close relationship with him give him a chance to find one, don't spoilt it for him and other women by being his friend.

Similarly it goes without saying that if you develop a close friendship with a man you have no intention of having a relationship with then you ruin both of your chances of having a close relationship. He will meet many of your needs for friendship with a man and you will meet many of his friendship needs with a woman. The motivation to find a real relationship is then less for both of you and so you both stop looking elsewhere and may not even recognize the opportunity when it arises, as you have no motivation to try another person out.

I recall a friend telling me about a young beautiful woman whose best friend was a gay guy. Her bond with this guy was so strong that she would make catching up with this guy a priority. My friend found it impossible to develop a close friendship with her because the gay guy was in the way. It wasn't long before my friend's attempt at a relationship with her ended. She then wondered why.

It doesn't have to be a casual or close friendship with a gay man, a casual or close friendship with any man can put you at risk. Clearly the more guys you hang out with on a casual basis the more they will lower your Essence of Woman, so trying to fit in with the guys can seriously backfire.

If you ever want to know the joy of a close relationship with an authentic man avoid casual or close friendships with any man who cannot be your close friend *and* partner.

We may consider tribes to be primitive but many tribes had this worked out rather well. They recognized the great value of a close friendship with just one member of the opposite sex, their partner. Their solution was simple. The men hung out with the men, and the women hung out with the women. It helped them stay true to their authentic selves, and not threaten the strength and bond of their relationships.

Three NEVERS of friendship with a man

NEVER:
- share what is emotionally important to you with a man who isn't your partner or you want to be your partner – share it with a girlfriend instead
- share intimate secrets with a man who isn't your partner, or you want to be your partner again, share it with a girlfriend instead
- try to have your relationship needs met with someone outside of your relationship – you may as well throw your relationship off a cliff.

If you want your relationship to be satisfying and last the test of time, then learn what needs aren't being met and work to fix them. Don't do that by having them met by someone else. And unless you want to be a man, don't hang around them. You know it will lower your Essence of Woman and the satisfaction of your relationships. Is that really what you want?

Friendships with men can be wonderfully fulfilling and help you realize more desires than in any other relationship. Understand friendships enough and you can not only build and increase a close and lasting intimate bond with a partner, but also raise and maintain a raised Essence of Woman in the process. By helping you fulfill your desires for an authentic man these friendships can help you realize your potential as a woman who is true to herself.

Other friendships that can help in this regard include those you have with family and the community.

Chapter 11:
Friendships with family and community

Amelia had only been in her new nursing job at a major hospital for less than three months and was already unhappy. It wasn't the work; she loved it, and sounded like she was very good at it too. The problem was she was young, in her early to mid-twenties, and she was promoted to head of her department ahead of many older more experienced nurses. Going from a well-liked sociable young nurse who would hang out with the girls, enjoying chats with her colleagues, suddenly no one talked to her, she wasn't invited to any functions, and her colleagues spread malicious rumors about her. We spoke at length about her style of leadership. Perhaps her one fault was she was too soft with her staff, she wanted to be liked. Now she felt unable to care for her patients as she would like, and would come home at the end of a very long day and cry.

Trying to be an authentic woman without friendships in family and community – work included – is like trying to be a functioning hand without any fingers. It won't feel right, and it won't be complete, or work to its potential. Friendships with family and friends help make a woman more complete.

What type of friendships should we have with our family and community? Should the friendship we have with our brother or sister be the same as we would have with a colleague at work, or a neighbor? Should they be casual or close friendships? Which friendships should you work to build so they can help you raise your Essence of Woman and be true to yourself?

Let's consider family friendships and community friendships in turn.

Once again if we want to have our needs met we can't expect the friendships we have with family or members of our community, including those at work, to be the same.

Family friendships

Clearly the best friendships to have in a family should be close friendships. Close friendships in a family help us feel warm, safe, and secure; they help our family to be a comforting refuge on a troubled planet. A close family becomes a strong foundation for us to go out and take on the world. Unfortunately many of us don't live in families we would call close any more. In fact many of them can be easily classed as downright dysfunctional.

Why is that?

There can be many reasons why our families are so unsupportive, dysfunctional, and even hostile towards their own members. Some we alluded to earlier. For example, the effect of chronic threat and the devaluing and disrespect of women will make a family dysfunctional. It will lead to women being more likely to be abused, and dominated. It will lead to a lack of functional role models such as mothers and fathers who can show us how to be friends. Chronic threat plays an important role in our family being dysfunctional. Some of it just comes down to modern living.

As was previously mentioned we live in a competitive modern society. We are encouraged to make it on our own. Today we use wealth, power, and status as a substitute for a supportive family and community. Unlike ancient tribes, or even the remote tribes of Papua New Guinea we mentioned earlier, we don't need to be a close-knit group to survive anymore; we just need enough money and status. The state now keeps us safe. This allows us to move away from our families into new suburbs, cities, states, and even new countries. Our families can be scattered to the four winds. This will then affect family friendships.

How close can you be to your brothers and sisters if you never see them? How close are we going to be to parents if we hardly talk or visit? How can we develop close friendships with any of our family if they are scattered across a country, or around the world?

The side effect of using money and status rather than family for security means we reduce the closeness of family friendships.

This then affects your ability to be whole.

As we previously mentioned you can't realize all the joy and fulfillment that motherhood can bring by doing it on your own. A mother needs other women to help her. The women that provide the best supports are usually family. This is how it was before civilizations developed, when we were still tribal.

In a tribal family caring for children is shared. Women are supported as mothers and helped to fulfill their most important role. Sisters and aunts offer support and care. They are also there to be close friends. A woman in a tribe knows what it is to be true to herself thanks to the close friendships of the family, and those of other women in the society. It would have been much easier for the women of the Cherokee, Iroquois, and many other North American native tribes for instance, not living under threat, to be true to themselves thanks to the close friendships of their families. That is before white man came, of course.

It is hard to build close family friendships in a community that uses wealth and status as a substitute for close family support. It can be harder still to be a fulfilled and satisfied mother without female family friendships and supports.

Nothing can substitute for a close and functional family.

Suppose we are no longer close, how can we build friendships in a family so it can become closer and better help meet your needs? Here are some suggestions:

- **Live close by.** Keep the family nearby and they can be close. Keep them scattered and the family can become shattered. Closeness means knowing they will be there for us in our hour of need. They can't do that as effectively if they aren't close by.
- **Meet regularly as an extended family.** You value your family by meeting regularly. Many Italian, Greek, Irish, Portuguese, and Chinese families still do. Try the same. Getting together once a month as a family or extended family should be a minimum.

- **Become a matriarch.** If the family won't organize themselves to come together and support each other help them by organizing it yourself. Be the leading woman and mother, help settle disputes, help them learn to be friends.
- **Mend friendships.** Don't let disagreements turn into feuds. Show you still care for each other. Apologize as a sign of respect. Make the family greater than any problem that might divide it. You are all of the same blood after all.
- **Respect each other.** Respect everyone! Treat all family as equal contributing members. Never put someone else down. Offer real choices whenever you can; being a dictator does not show respect (see Step 1). Make 'respect' a basic necessity for all family events at all times. Never abuse another member of your family, and don't tolerate abuse from others either towards you or other members of the family.
- **Listen.** Everyone in the family has something to say and share. Listen, without judging them. Better still let them have their say and share experiences and stories with all the family, as we used to do in our tribes.
- **Notice each other.** Never ignore anyone in the family, whether as punishment, or out of laziness. It's the one sure way to destroy closeness in a family.
- **Focus on similarities.** Share what you all have in common, the children, the weather, financial struggles, and car problems, anything others may have experience with too. The more you show each other how similar you are the more they will want to be close to you and won't feel threatened by you.
- **Care for each other.** Nothing shows closeness more than caring for others in their hour of need. Be there for each other, on call, no matter what. If caring for someone is getting too much ask for help from the rest of the family, or seek professional help. Help everyone to feel they are under the warm blanket of care of their family.
- **Be supportive.** Offer support and help each other. That is what families are for. Help each other often, without expectations

or rewards. The more we give without expectation or reward the more the family appreciates us and draws us closer. Never punish someone for not helping you, that's a sign of disrespect. That doesn't mean being the family doormat.

- **Protect each other.** Don't let abuse ruin a family. Protect the members being abused at all times, whether from inside the family or from outside it. Separate the parties involved if necessary, and help them sort out their differences. Don't punish them. Seek professional help early if you need it. Be a mediator and teach everyone how friendship works and the needs we all have of friendship (see the Ten Basic Desires).

Family should never be our enemy they should be our friends.

By building close friendships in your family you can help ensure your family stays close and doesn't ever become enemies. Then you create the best environment to realize your personal truth and establish a role model for your daughter, granddaughter, and their daughters to come, and ultimately all women in society. Money, wealth, power, and status can never be a substitute for close family. It is up to you to determine which is most important.

Warning

Beware of family members with addictions to alcohol, drugs, and gambling, or any other addiction. Addictions are insatiable. If you keep giving them what they want you will make their addictions worse. I have sadly seen all too many families broken by addiction. Addictions call for tough-love: don't give them anything until they have quit the substance or habit for at least six months. Offer to support them with their treatment and rehabilitation. Ensure they know you're not abandoning them and that they will always be a valued family member. But they can't enjoy the benefits of the family until they have overcome their poison. The family is too important to be destroyed by that poison.

Community friendships

Friendships in the community – including both paid and volunteer work – are just as important to you as a woman as any other. You should make friends and not enemies in your community for two very good reasons:
- so you can feel happier among friends
- to reduce chronic threat.

It's impossible to be close friends with everyone, simply because of the numbers involved; we may meet a thousand or more people a week. But we don't have to be close friends with them to feel safe and have fulfilling interactions and relationships with them; we can have casual friendships, or be friendly acquaintances instead. Remember, all we need to know is that the other person is on our side. Make them a friend, even a casual friend or friendly acquaintance, and we do that.

How do we make casual friendships or friendly acquaintances?

By following how to make friendships with women and men as outlined above – by meeting their Ten Basic Desires of Community Self. You have already seen several examples of how to do that. For example, choosing to see their similarities to us – as opposed to their differences – can go a long way towards making others feel we are their friends, as it did with the chap with all those tattoos.

The more casual friends and friendly acquaintances we make the less enemies we have, the less anxious we are, and the happier we feel. This is as true with our neighbors as it is at work.

Unfortunately workplaces can be the antithesis of friendliness, bullying might be more the order of the day. Bullying is about status and power, neither of which helps us meet our Community Self needs at work.

Don't have your Community Self needs met at work and it will be a horrible place to be, and we won't be as effective as a team.

If you want an effective business you need an effective community to be the business. How do you do that?

Try for one week to meet your colleagues' Ten Basic Needs of Friendship. Listen more, recognize people by name, validate them and the job they are doing, and see how they behave differently to you. We all want friends; we just don't all know how to make them.

A friend who works for a large car manufacturer told me how his company has a set of rules in place regarding how to relate to other people. If a customer is at the counter they are immediately noticed and acknowledged. If a colleague walks within a few feet of them they are acknowledged. They are taught how to listen to customers and validate their concerns. He told me that the workplace tends to fall apart and be less effective when a manager doesn't make sure the rules for interacting with people are maintained. What they have learnt to do is meet many of the Ten Basic Desires of Friendship such as to help people to feel noticed, and it helps them run an effective and happier business.

When work is happier, the neighbors are happier, our friends are happier then we are happier.

The other great benefit of making more friends is you raise the Essence of Women by reducing chronic threat.

The more you show community how to be friends, leading by example, the fewer people will fear each other and the lower the level of threat in our community.

We don't all have to be rivals. We can live as friends. We don't need to feel we have to fight each other to have enough for our family and us. Unfortunately the wealth is being horded – for reasons we outlined earlier – and now the few are letting the many suffer and go without. Learning to be friends can go a long way towards remedying that.

Friends share. Friends make sure each other are well, cared for, and safe. They offer help; they don't restrict it or hold it back so they can feel they are better or safer than everyone else. So if you want to make a hugely positive impact on the world spread your skills and knowledge of friendship to as many people as you can. The more you share it and the more people learn how to meet each other's needs the less threat there will be in your town, city, state, country, and the world. With less threat once again the Essence of Woman can be raised and balance finally restored between the Essence of Woman and the Essence of Man.

Make friends in your community and you increase the true power of women everywhere.

All friendships are different; they have to be if our needs are to be met. Be aware of the similarities and differences and you can raise your Essence of Woman and increase the number of authentic men. You can also work to improve the quality of your relationships and life for everyone as your influence and understanding spreads. Friendships are a powerful way to raise the Essence of Woman and help you realize the fulfillment of being an authentic woman.

An even more powerful and self-empowering way to raise your Essence of Woman is to learn to listen more to your heart. The Essence of Woman, and nature itself, is talking to you in your feelings. Want to know what it really is to be an authentic woman? Don't just read a book; learn to truly listen to, and communicate with a part of you that really knows!

Step 3: Listen to you

Pay attention to the whispers, so we don't have to listen to the screams.
Cherokee Proverb

In the depths of your heart lays the source of what it is to be human; the blueprint of the authentic woman within. In those depths you'll find the spirit of ancient woman talking to you from across the ages with an insight and awareness you have barely begun to know. It sees far more than you're consciously privileged to see. Yet it knows what you need, and your place among all things. Many occasionally listen to it; give it names such as intuition, a gut feeling, or instinct. None of these names do it justice, none encompass the scope of truth and insight it can reveal, despite the fact that it is the most useful tool we can ever learn to use. Call it by whatever name you choose; I call it Inner Self.

Chapter 12:
Communicate with the Inner Self

Intimately knowing and learning to communicate directly with your Inner Self can be a personal breakthrough. It can help you discover and resolve your deepest emotional pains and fears, and give your life direction and a deep feeling of hope, purpose, and meaning. Better still, communicating with your Inner Self can grant you direct access to the Essence of Woman and the spirit of ancient woman within. No part of you knows the honesty of the Essence of Woman within more than your Inner Self.

Communicating with your Inner Self will help reveal the truth of your womanly nature.

Our society may want you to be the woman it thinks you should be. Men may try to control you to be the woman they think they want. Your Inner Self knows the woman nature needs you to be. Learning to intimately know and communicate with your Inner Self is the most powerful and pure way for you to realize your true nature.

What is our Inner Self? How can we be so certain it represents the truth of whom we are?

The Inner Self is largely represented by our limbic system. What is the limbic system?

In simple terms it is the part of the brain that drives our desires to eat, drink, care for our health, have families, and form groups and communities (as described in the Balance of Self Model). It is a part of the inner and central part of the brain, often referred to as the reptilian brain, as it has structures in common with those of reptiles, such as alligators, turtles, and lizards.

Think of the limbic system like your own personal manager. It decides what's important or relevant. Is that tree important to us, is that smell something we should react to, should we get to know that guy?

The limbic system is aware of far more than we realize. Most of what happens to us we don't consciously notice.

We don't pay attention to every sight, sound, change in temperature, and every other change in the world or inside us that our body can notice – such as the movement of blood through our kidneys, sights, sounds, smells, and tastes, subtle shifts in hormones. The reason is obvious; we don't need to consciously notice them to get on with our lives.

Not only can our limbic system notice those subtle changes, it also contains a manual of how we should react to what is happening.

Can the limbic system and our Inner Self be trusted?

It most definitely can be trusted, especially in comparison to some other parts of our brain.

Part of our brain that is connected to our limbic system creates stories, the ideas and beliefs we have about the world and ourselves. This mostly takes place in the outer parts of the brain and is especially co-ordinated by the prefrontal cortex – near the front of the brain – which is used for planning. This dynamic part of the brain is constantly changing, always developing new theories, ideas, and opinions of the world from day to day and minute to minute. It prepares us for what might happen next; constantly considering possible futures. Importantly it creates our delusions and fantasies.

We can all believe in fantasies and delusions because our brain can easily create them. It can even make them seem real.

As we will later see our brain is built to create delusions and fantasies, many of these we know as ideas, beliefs, and theories. We want to believe them because then our world is predictable. If it is predictable it is safer.

We also want to believe them if others do. The more others believe it the more likely we will too (see the desire for sameness, one of the Ten Basic Desires of Community Self). We can create all manner of constantly changing ideas, stories, and beliefs about the universe and ourselves. We have believed in spirits, gods, and monsters, even that the world was flat. Our ideas, beliefs and opinions will always change, but part of us remains relatively unchanged and certain. It is the manual of what we need to do to survive and be human. It is our limbic system, what we can recognize as a physical representation of our Inner Self.

Can our Inner Self be trusted? What can be more trustworthy than a part of us that cannot be fooled and always remains true?

The best part is we've all evolved to directly communicate with it.

Yes, you and I can learn to access the most insightful manual we can ever know. We can bypass all our fantasies, lies, and delusions about ourselves, all the stories others tell us about who we should be, and access the source, the blueprint and truth of who we are.

How do we access this amazing source of great knowledge?

With something we have access to every day: our feelings.

Feelings can offer us insights we never thought available. They can help guide us and change our lives.

But how do we listen to and understand our Inner Self? Below are three practical and simple steps that will help calm and settle your noisy chattering and often-anxious mind, so you can make a clearer connection. They'll help you learn to communicate with your Inner Self directly in ways you would have never believed you could.

So far you may have learnt to listen to your gut-feeling or intuition, you have just barely learnt to focus on your Inner Self. But true communication is more than just listening, it's being able to speak and ask questions too. Asking questions of a representation of your inner truth takes communication and self-knowledge to a whole new level.

You can use questions to communicate with your Inner Self in several ways; we will explore four types of questioning:

- Questions to help overcome and reduce emotional pain.
- Questions to help resolve and overcome your past and future fears.
- Questions to offer guidance and direction, so that life has the best chance of being meaningful and fulfilling to you.
- And questions to help you directly connect with your Essence of Woman and the spirit of ancient woman within.

We all suffer emotional pains, and fears that limit us and prevent us being the most fulfilled human beings we can be. We all like to choose a direction that offers us hope, purpose, and meaning. Learning to ask questions of your Inner Self can help you achieve these. Asking slightly different questions can also help you connect directly with the spirit and Essence of Woman within.

For communication with our Inner Self to work at its best it must be honest.

Simply touching the truth of our Inner Self can transform our lives.

The three practical activities that will help you communicate with your Inner Self are:
- right place
- right mind
- right question.

Before we start we need to begin with the most important step of all: making time.

Make time: The most important activity

We can't communicate properly with anyone if we don't make the time. We can't get to know them; can't get to understand what they mean, or where they are coming from if we aren't with them enough to find out. The same is true with communicating with our Inner Self. If we don't make quality time in our busy lives to have a meaningful conversation with our Inner Self then we are wasting our time. A word here and there is not real conversation. If you truly valued your friendship with your partner for example, wouldn't you give them your time so you could really talk?

How much time should we set aside so we can communicate properly with our Inner Self and get the maximum benefit?

Enough for it to work and help improve our lives, but not so much that it stops us living life.

If you are doing it every day, hour after hour, for months then you are probably overdoing it a little. But let's be realistic, most of us aren't going to have a problem spending too much time communicating with our Inner Self. Most of us struggle making enough time.

Generally speaking the more time you spend getting to know and communicate with your Inner Self the better.

My personal recommendation is: start slow and keep it simple. Put aside regular time in your days and see how you go. You can make great progress simply by making this time just once a day. If you are really serious you can put aside more time and really get to know yourself well.

Practical exercise

Set aside thirty to sixty minutes every day in your diary as you would any other activity. Try to make it a routine. Tick it off once you have done it. If you feel you need more time, make it. Think of it like learning a new language. When you do this you often set aside time for lessons or practice. You can do the same here. Only this time you're setting aside time that can transform what you think and feel, and can raise your Essence of Woman like no other activity you'll ever try. I'll let you decide how important you think this is and how much time you think it's worth making in your day. Once you have made the time then apply the three practice steps.

Practice activity 1: Right place

Once you've made the time you need an appropriate place. You wouldn't try to have a deep conversation with your best friend at a loud concert, or worse still, at the bottom of a swimming pool. Finding the most appropriate or right place to communicate effectively with your Inner Self is important. It must be a safe place, and free of distraction.

Find a safe place

Firstly, we need a mind free of fear. Fear blocks internal communication, it prevents us noticing what we feel deep inside. We need to know what we really feel in the depths of our heart so we can hear what our Inner Self has to say. So if you are in a place, or choose a place, and it is not safe, your mind will be so consumed with fear and will block all meaningful and deep communication with your Inner Self. So wherever you choose to be to communicate with your Inner Self it must feel safe. *You* must feel safe.

Clearly what this means is if you live in a suburb, country, or village ravaged by violence then unless you can find a safe and quiet place away from this horror you can forget about really knowing your true Inner Self. Work to solve the violence first, and then look to working on yourself after that. Your brain won't let you communicate with your heart until you have convinced it you are safe.

Similarly if you are in an abusive relationship unless you can find a safe and quiet retreat, a place where you can feel you will not be disturbed or threatened in any way, you will have almost no chance of deep and meaningful communication with your Inner Self. Your mind will have enormous trouble trying to settle. You can make it settle with practice – and we will learn some techniques to do that next – but it will be so much harder than if you are in a safe and quiet place from the start.

> **First find a safe place to be quiet and still. Then your mind can reveal the truth of what you feel inside.**

Clear all distractions

Have you ever tried having a deep and meaningful conversation with a friend and been distracted by them texting on the phone? It doesn't work. Distractions are the enemy of good communication.

Possible distractions are the enemy too. If we are expecting a phone call or a knock at the door then our mind will be thinking about that. This will also block good communication.

Find a place where you won't be disturbed.

It may be an office, in the bedroom, the garden, or by the sea. It means switching off all forms of communication such as your computer, phone, the TV or any games devices – anything that may interest or distract us.

Better still, create a quiet place, a personal retreat. You can give it a calm feel, some soft colors, perhaps even burn some incense if that helps calm you. No music though, no matter how soothing, the changes in melody can be distracting.

As we shall soon see the way we communicate in a meaningful way with our Inner Self is to not just notice our feelings but be able to hold them, to keep them in our focus so we can ask questions of them and better understand them. We can't do that if we are either distracted, or think we will lose focus.

Ideally, the place you choose should be one you use regularly. Your mind will get used to it and allow you to calm more quickly. This will mean you can get further towards the truth in each session.

With practice, as these activities become second-nature, the place won't be as important. You'll be able to listen to your heart in all places, provided you are not too afraid, and not too distracted.

Exercise tips

- Switch off anything that might distract you.
- Put a note outside the door if you need to 'Do Not Disturb!'
- Make sure everyone knows this is your quiet time.
- No one is to disturb you unless the house is on fire, there is a zombie invasion, or a nuclear war.
- Try to use the same place over and over again.

Once we have our right place we are in a great position to create right mind. It's worth pointing out, creating right mind can have benefits that go well beyond helping you communicate with your Inner Self.

Have you ever felt like your mind needed a rest? Perhaps you wanted a way to switch it off from life's worries? Our mind can drive us a little crazy it can be so distracting and annoying at times. Maybe you want a greater sense of calmness and tranquility within yourself, techniques that can help calm you when you are angry, and settle you when you are distressed? Could be that you want a way to give your mind a boost, give it a sense of clarity in your busy life? The skills you are about to learn you can use in many aspects of your life. Creating a right mind is a very useful skill to have.

Practice activity 2: Right mind

To communicate with the feelings deep in our heart – our Inner Self – we need a mind that is ready. It is like tuning a radio to the right frequency, or turning to the right TV channel. Our mind needs to be 'tuned' to the right channel too. It is tuned when it is in a right mind. A right mind is a calm and tranquil mind. This is a mind best suited to honest and meaningful communication with your deepest feelings.

How do we calm and settle our mind?

There are many well-tried and tested ways to calm a turbulent mind. Two methods that you may be familiar with are using breathing, and mindfulness. We will use both.

Breathing

Try it now.
- Focus on your breathing, just notice each breath in and each breath out.
- Now control the breathing. Breathe in as you count silently to three, then breathe out slowly – at the same rate – as you count silently to six
- In for three … out for six.
- In for three … out for six.
- Do this at least three or four times in a row, without taking any breaths in between.
- Focus on each breath as you breathe. Take your time; there is no hurry.

- As you breathe out imagine any tension or stress as if it's a mist. With every breath out this tension mist leaves you.
- Every breath in is clean and crisp.
- In and out.
- Just focus on the breathing.

Controlled breathing is a great way to begin to calm the mind. It is used a lot to help people who suffer panic attacks and feel suddenly severely anxious. Many people under stress use it to calm the mind just enough so they can start thinking more clearly and rationally again. Do it slowly and it calms you.

Start any session where you want to communicate with your Inner Self with these simple breathing exercises.

Mindfulness

When you focused on your breathing a moment ago you were using a form of mindfulness. It isn't magical, but it is powerful, and it works. It is a great way to settle a troubled mind and offers many health benefits too.

When the mind is in the present, noticing all that's here and now, it doesn't have anything to be scared about – it isn't considering all the bad things that might happen – and it settles right down.

That is all mindfulness is, bringing the mind out of the future and the past and focusing it clearly on the present. People have known its benefits for thousands of years. Many of today's mindfulness techniques are based on types of meditation that have been around for millennia.

If you already use mindfulness or meditation to focus your mind in the present use that. If not, you might like to consider the following three techniques. Try them, find the one that works best for you, even develop your own technique, and practice it. Even if you never use mindfulness to help you communicate with your Inner Self, it will still have enormous benefits; helping you manage stress, addictions, or recover from just being mentally tired. Mindfulness allows our mind to take a well-earned break.

Before trying any of the following methods be in your right place and let your body and mind begin to settle using the breathing technique described above.

Technique 1: Zen meditation

The first technique is based on an old Zen meditation. Let's go through the steps.

- Sit comfortably, in a chair or on a cushion, just make sure you aren't too comfortable that you will fall asleep.
- Find an object to look at; a pattern on the floor or a light switch on the wall. Whatever you choose make sure it doesn't move – such as the flame of a candle, or the smoke of incense – or has too much detail that you start analyzing it.
- Now keep your eyes on the object – and don't let your eyes wander!
- Stare at that object. You can blink, just don't stop looking at it. Keep your eyes still.
- Now try to keep the rest of your body still too. You can breathe – obviously – or you will pass out, but try to keep your body perfectly still for as long as you can.
- Continue to keep your eyes strictly on the object you are looking at, and remain perfectly still.

It isn't easy initially. Our brain is used to us moving our eyes and looking around. It is used to us always moving. Being still can be very strange at first, but if you hold it long enough it can be very soothing. It also settles the mind.

Think about a problem and you will notice your eyes wander, as if searching for a solution and thinking it might see it. Walk around and your brain is working on what you might encounter next. In both cases your mind is not present here and now, it is somewhere else, considering possibilities; considering the future. This isn't where we want our mind to be.

When we are still our mind has permission to be still.

When our body is still our mind doesn't need to anticipate as much. If we keep our eyes still our mind won't be working on solving complex problems. The quieter our body becomes, the less we move, the quieter our mind becomes, at least initially. Now let's take this simple exercise a few steps further:

- Focus all your attention on the object you were looking at before.
- Focus on as much detail about the object as you can, such as its color or shape. But don't interpret it. Don't try to understand it, or comment on how nice or horrible it is. That takes the mind elsewhere. Just notice it. Notice as much about the detail as you possibly can.

If you try to interpret something you're attempting to give it meaning, you wonder what it is for example, or how you might use it. This takes your mind into the future and how things might happen, how you might use the object, or what someone else might think about it if you showed them.

Our aim here is not to interpret, just notice whatever details you can.

Do not try to count anything either. That is interpreting too and we don't want that. Just notice.

Soon you might begin to notice your thoughts. Like a background chatter of noisy images. Many often show up. Often it includes what you have done or what you need to do. It can also include matters you are worried about – they often make an appearance. For now just recognize the thoughts are there and return your focus to the details of the object you are looking at. Try to keep that focus and attention, remaining perfectly still, for as many minutes as you can. Try to go for at least five minutes to begin with, but don't look at your watch or clock.

If you worry about the time then your mind will not be present. So make sure you have set aside enough time to practice your mindfulness so you don't have to worry about when you have to finish and distract your mind.

Technique 2: Toy boats on a stream

Technique 2 uses a different strategy to deal with our thoughts so we can remain in the present and disconnect ourselves emotionally from them.

Begin by using Technique 1. Do the breathing then keep still. Then:
- Let your thoughts flow by as if they are floating past you in a stream.
- Don't drag them in or give them any attention, just notice them flow by. Don't emotionally engage with them.
- If a thought grabs your attention then imagine it's a toy boat, just let it back onto the stream so it floats by.

After explaining these techniques to a patient she told me she found visualizing a conveyor belt worked best for her. When a thought grabbed her attention she imagined putting it on a fast conveyor belt – the type you see in a post office or a factory – and watched it speed away. Visualize whatever you like, just don't get emotionally involved in your thoughts.

For instance, if thoughts of shopping come up then don't start thinking about what you are going to buy. If a friend pops into your thoughts then don't start imagining what you might say and how they might feel talking to them. The brain's job is to consider possibilities. It's ok to let scenarios arise, but when being mindful we don't let ourselves get emotionally involved, we just let thoughts float away.

Practice it, be still, and let your thoughts float by. Some find it useful to think of their thoughts on the other side of frosted glass so they aren't attached to them. Some think of it as if they are a pilot of a plane, passengers keep coming forward asking them to take another course or direction. You can hear them, but you don't have to pay any real attention; you most certainly don't have to do what they want and divert your course or attention. Keep the plane on course, keep your mind just noticing, and learn to let your thoughts just pass by.

The more you practice the easier it gets.

Technique 3: Feeling the breath

Technique 3 uses feelings to bring our mind into the present.
- Start with Technique 1.
- Now close your eyes and notice your breathing, each breath in and each one out.
- Focus on the detail of the breathing, notice your stomach move as you breathe, notice your chest, the air moving through your nose and your throat and upper chest.
- Focus on how it feels. Feel what the breath in the back of the throat feels like. Examine that feeling – the sensation – in as much detail as you can.
- Focus on what your chest *feels* like as you breathe. You choose what part of the body you want to focus on and feel your breath. Focus on as much detail as possible.
- Just notice the detail of the feeling of breathing. Not on your emotional state, just the detail of the physical sensation of breathing.
- Do this for at least five minutes. Longer if you can. You shouldn't need to do it for more than half an hour.

When you focus on feelings the part of the brain that does the interpreting and takes our mind to another place isn't working.

Focusing on a sensation in great detail is like switching the interpretation part of our brain off, which is our intention.

I taught this to a businessman recently. He was under enormous stress with work and had many intense and important meetings. He would often get flustered, nervous, and couldn't think clearly by the time he had to give a speech or presentation. Now he has learnt just before his meetings if he closes his eyes, focuses on the feeling in his chest of him breathing, he calms right down and can think more clearly and be more effective in meetings.

Try these simple techniques. Let your mind and your feelings be present in the here and now. Experiment for yourself and find the technique that works best for you. The aim is to bring your mind into the present, to not name, count, or interpret anything. The aim is to just notice, but notice in as much detail as possible.

How will you know if it's working?

You'll feel much more relaxed and less anxious than when you started.

Use these techniques daily to get the greatest life benefit. Master them and you will find it easy to connect with your Inner Self and create a clear connection with your heart any time you choose.

Mindfulness to Inner Self

Now let's begin to communicate with our Inner Self. We'll start by using our memories.

Think of a memory that has great emotion or feeling for you. Preferably choose one that isn't scary. Maybe a heated discussion with someone at work, or with your partner about money, or about the kids. Or something you regret. It could be a really lovely memory. Notice what you did, and remember how you felt. Try to remember the feeling in great detail. Choose a memory where what you felt was fairly clear and is easy to remember.

- As you had that heated discussion what were you feeling?
- As you worked on the money problems what did you feel? What was that like?
- As you spoke with a close friend about your kids or your relationship how did you feel?

Memories and feelings are always linked; every memory has a unique feeling coupled with the events of that memory.

Access the feeling and the memory can appear clearer, you can remember more of what actually happened. It is like noticing a smell and then getting a vivid recall of some time in your past when you last noticed that smell. Have you ever noticed a smell of perfume for example, and suddenly had a flashback to another time in your life? Feelings may not trigger the sudden flashbacks a smell can but the more you focus on what you felt the clearer and more detailed your memory can become. It works the other way around too. Access the memory, try to recall what happened in as much detail as you can, and you can also access and notice what you felt like at the time.

Now replay the memory as if it just happened; remember the detail. But do NOT under any circumstances make the memory up. It must be as it was. If you can't recall it as it was then try to remember something you can remember that was as it actually happened.

Do you have that memory? How did that memory make you feel?

In other words, what was your Inner Self trying to tell you? Remember, our Inner Self communicates to us in our feelings.

Our Inner Self can tell us many things in our feelings but one of the easiest for us to read is if it approved of what was happening or it didn't. If it approved then it liked what was happening, or what we thought was going to happen. If it disapproved it didn't like what happened, or we thought was going to happen, and doesn't want it to happen again. How do we know if it approved or disapproved? By whether the feelings were pleasant or unpleasant.

Go back to your memory. Did you have pleasant feelings or unpleasant feelings? What did you feel?

If you felt pleasant then your Inner Self was sending you a reward or incentive. It wanted you to do more of what you had just done or were planning on doing. If it felt great talking about the kids for example, your Inner Self could be rewarding you for being a mother, and for being social and sharing with a friend – we won't worry about just what it was rewarding you for just yet.

Did the memory have unpleasant feelings? Then your Inner Self is telling you not to do whatever you did – or were planning on doing – again.

Try another memory. Do the same. Remember it as it was. Just notice it, and ask what did your Inner Self think about that? How did it make you feel? Was it pleasant or unpleasant?

Choose a memory from earlier in the day, perhaps a clear memory of an event earlier in the week. Try this for as many memories as you like. Was the message from your Inner Self useful for you or not? Were the memories pleasant or unpleasant?

What did it feel like the first time you met your partner, for example? Was it a pleasant feeling? We'd hope so.

Congratulations. You have just been communicating with your Inner Self. You have achieved an important but significant first step.

As we mentioned, effective communication works both ways; we don't just listen we also talk. In the past you may have just listened to your intuition or your gut feeling. In this case you also learnt to speak to your Inner Self and listened for a reply.

How did you speak to your Inner Self?

By communicating with it in the language it knows, scenarios and feelings.

By you re-exploring a memory you gave it an image of what happened – a scenario of your past – to consider. It then gave you a feeling in response. That feeling told you something about what your Inner Self thought about the scenario you gave it. It gave you either a pleasant feeling or an unpleasant one, perhaps a mix of both. Every time you decide to evoke a memory you are giving your Inner Self a scenario to consider. Listen to your feelings and it will tell you what it thinks.

Why did we learn mindfulness before we tried this?

Firstly, so your mind could more easily focus on your memory and not be so distracted by other thoughts. And secondly so you can have a clearer more honest discussion with your Inner Self.

If our mind isn't calm and emotionally able to detach we won't hear messages from deep in our Inner Self. Instead we will simply be reacting to the events around us, and the feelings associated with these, which will cloud the message with our current feelings and thoughts.

For example, imagine looking at the original Mona Lisa painting and trying to work out how you feel about it whilst at the same time being in a heated angry discussion on the phone. The anger will cover any other feelings you have and it will be hard to know what feelings such a classic picture can evoke. It isn't until you put down the phone, let the anger of the call settle, that you'll notice the feelings such a painting will give you. It isn't until the emotions of our life are allowed to disappear and no longer distract us that we can notice the message – the feelings – from our Inner Self.

Similarly emotions can cloud what we see and can prevent us feeling what our Inner Self is trying to tell us.

All of us have emotions and feelings that disturb us. Some are so strong we completely avoid them. For instance, they can be powerful emotions from trauma of our past, or stomach churning fears we have for our future. We might not like to face or see many feelings and scenarios, but how can we have a heart-to-heart with a part of us that communicates with feelings if we aren't prepared to see some things it tells us? Learning mindfulness allows us to detach emotionally from traumatic memories and disturbing feelings we normally avoid. It allows us to just observe them. So if our Inner Self shows us images and feelings that disturb us we can now be more confident we won't be pulled into that memory and feeling, remain in control, not be forced to avoid it, and just observe what our Inner Self wants us to see.

Communicating with our Inner Self is about facing the truth of things we might not like to see.

One of the best things about communicating with our Inner Self is it can help us work out what really troubles us, not what we think the problem is, but what our heart knows the problem is. We often lie to ourselves so we don't have to face our deepest pains. Our Inner Self can help us see the truth of our pain. Once it has helped us see the truth it can then be used to help give us an honest path so we can change it. Without being able to detach emotionally like we learnt to do with mindfulness none of this level of personal change and deep insight will be possible.

Practice your mindfulness every day, learn to just notice what you feel, let thoughts just float by, then you will be able to communicate with your Inner Self in a much clearer and honest way and get much more out of it.

Practice activity 3: Right question

We realize our greatest insights from our Inner Self by learning to ask it questions. Often we have many fears, emotional pains we don't understand or cripple us, we can be unsure of our way, we can be uncertain of ourselves, and our life can lose a sense of purpose or meaning. Asking questions of our Inner Self can give us the clarification we need. The trick is to ask the right questions.

What are the right questions?

They're the questions that matter most to your heart. The ones that help transform you into a satisfied and balanced human being.

In a moment we will consider four of the most useful types of questions you can ask your Inner Self. The aim is two-fold. Firstly to help you gain skills to communicate with your Inner Self. Secondly to help you personally resolve issues and help improve the quality of your life. The following questions will be explored with these goals in mind:
- How do we resolve emotional pains?
- How do we resolve fears?
- How do we make the right choices?
- How can I be true to my Essence of Woman?

Amazing as it may seem, and we hinted at it earlier, your emotional pains can be resolved. Communication with your Inner Self can help resolve these emotionally painful issues. Fears that still bother you, even childhood ones, past traumas or abuse, can be understood and resolved. So can the fears of the future. Rather than flip a coin for important choices we'll learn to ask the one person who knows your needs better than anyone: your Inner Self. No better or purer source can teach you how to be true to yourself. Ask the right questions and you begin to connect with your purest form.

Having learnt how to ask questions of your Inner Self you will cultivate a remarkable resource to help you explore and understand anything that troubles you. If it hurts you can resolve or come to terms with it. If you are uncertain you can find the best course of action to take. If you are unsure of yourself as a woman, you can know the truth of the woman within with the greater confidence.

The truth is within. You just need to ask the right questions to reveal it.

Let's start to learn different ways of asking questions of our Inner Self.

Chapter 13:
Questions to resolve emotional pains

Elise seemed troubled as she sat quietly waiting for her routine prescription. Slim, intelligent, in her early twenties, this was her first year at university. After a short chat she admitted to being terribly depressed for several months. She didn't know why, she was social, well liked, didn't do drugs, and was doing ok with subjects she enjoyed. Her future seemed bright and promising; she should have felt on top of the world. As we chatted more the reason for her melancholy soon became obvious, it had to do with a boy.

Elise had been in a relationship with a guy she really liked. Then she dumped him. She felt she had to, her father made it clear she had to do well with her marks or he would no longer financially support her. She reasoned her father was right, her head had told her she had said her goodbye, which was over a month ago. Her heart was telling her differently. She cried deeply when I mentioned that perhaps in her heart she hadn't yet broken up with him. She had finally let herself realize what her heart felt to be true.

Like Elise we all suffer emotional pain. Sometimes the cause isn't obvious. Communicating with our Inner Self can help reduce and resolve many of the emotional pains that hurt us. It can even help resolve dissatisfactions that go back to childhood, such as feelings of being different, an outcast, and of being abused and not respected. How do we use our Inner Self to help us resolve, understand, and eliminate the pains that define our lives and reduce our happiness? We begin by asking our Inner Self what the emotional pain wants.

In this method we will use the Balance of Self (BOS) Model as our guide. Understandings we have already attained will help us find the most useful questions to ask of our Inner Self. As you will recall the BOS Model represents all our human desires. It also represents the source of all emotional pain.

We feel emotional pain when our needs are not met or we expect – or imagine – they won't be.

This makes the BOS Model a useful guide around which to ask questions of our Inner Self. For example, if we are feeling emotional pain and dissatisfaction in our relationship we can ask our Inner Self what – in our heart – is missing? Knowing that our needs in a relationship include those of close friendship we can ask our Inner Self what does it feel about our friendship? Is the friendship we have with our partner satisfactory? Is that the cause of our pain and dissatisfaction?

Try it. If you are in a relationship explore how you feel about your current friendship. Visualize your friendship and what it feels like. Create a clear image of the feeling that represents your friendship. Now ask your heart, put it to your Inner Self, what does it feel about the friendship you have? What is the truth deep inside? What is your gut feeling about the friendship?

If there is a pain we feel in our relationship and our friendship seems ok then perhaps some other need in the relationship is causing the pain. If your relationship is not as happy and fulfilling as it should be then put whatever you think is missing to your Inner Self and see if you are right.

For example, you can ask you Inner Self: am I unsatisfied with my relationship because he doesn't earn enough, isn't wealthy enough, isn't ambitious enough and doesn't have enough status or power? Don't assume you know. Ask your Inner Self and see.

How do you ask your Inner Self?

You talk to it in a way you have already begun to. You present it with scenarios and see what you feel. For instance, create an image of what it would feel like if he did earn more, or had more status, or more ambition. Visualize what that would be like. Imagine the detail, how he would behave, how others might treat you, how you would act and behave. Imagine it like a movie with you as the star, only this movie has lots of detail and feels real. Then see in each case how you would really feel. How does that new image make you feel deep inside? Does it resolve the pain or discomfort? Not just if it makes you feel better, search for if it truly resolves the actual pain you feel, not just suppressing it, and or covering it with something that feels better.

Explore your heart for the truth of what you feel.

Every emotional pain has a scenario that can resolve it; it has a need your Inner Self wants you to satisfy, even the emotional pains of our past. It's like finding the right key to the right lock. Every emotional pain is a different lock. You need to find the key that fits it so it is opened, resolved, and goes away. Sometimes an emotional pain can be filled with many needs that seek to be met; needs all wrapped up into one that represent many locks that need their individual key. Find the right key for the right lock and you unlock your pain. Think of the BOS Model as a collection of keys. Sometimes we have to try many before we discover which one fits.

We all suffer emotional pains. We can all face them and find what they want from us.

Will it be easy?
Not really, how many of us are prepared, or have been taught, to face something so raw and painful as the agony we can know in our heart? Pain hurts, that's why we call it pain. We don't put our hand in a fire. We take it out. Facing our pain doesn't come naturally, and yet it's the one thing that can offer our greatest salvation.
Up until now looking at our pain may have seemed pointless, all that would happen is we would feel worse for it. Our pains didn't make sense; there seemed no point in facing what we couldn't understand and couldn't change. The BOS Model helps us make practical sense of our emotional suffering, so that looking at our emotional pains is far from pointless, indeed it can be liberating and transform our lives. The

BOS Model can help guide us towards the true and honest causes of our discomforts.

Give it a try. Notice your pain; bring it to the surface, if it isn't already there. It can be a pain of the past, or a concern of the future, whatever image or concerns bring you emotional pain. Perhaps it is pain you noticed in a dream, perhaps it makes you cry as you go to sleep. Grab it. Hold it. Then try a key. One at a time present a scenario to your Inner Self and finally see what your emotional pain needs to be resolved and go away.

It can seem hard at first. You will want to dismiss the pain and step back. Be prepared to cry. Let it happen. The more you can access the true thoughts or memories of the pain the more you can understand and change it. Once you have the clear pain in your presence ask your Inner Self the types of questions we mentioned before, ask it what it needs to truly resolve it. Ask it to help you see the true nature of your emotional pain and what it wants from you.

This is a method that I learnt – through experimentation and necessity – to face and understand my own emotional pains. Initially I had no guide such as the BOS Model to help me, I was just searching to understand and find the truth of the deep emotional pain I was feeling. My pains were so strong I considered ending my life to escape them. With persistence however, as if convincing my Inner Self I was serious and that I really wanted to know, it eventually showed me. It didn't reveal the answers in words. It revealed them in images, memories, and feelings. Now if I feel sad or notice an emotional pain I use a slightly different approach, closer to the one I have described to you.

The first step to resolving a pain is to understand what need is missing, or we expect will be missing.

We can use questioning our Inner Self to help us better understand any emotional pain's cause. Try it.

Practice tip

Write down three things that currently cause you emotional pain or you are deeply upset about.

1. ....
2. ....
3. ....

In your 'right place' and with 'right mind' tackle each cause one at a time. Ask your Inner Self what's causing the pain, what's missing, or what you expect will be missing – search inside the pain. Use the BOS Model as your guide and test what need or needs you feel are missing. Put scenarios to your Inner Self; explore what it would feel like if that need were actually met. See if that truthfully and honestly resolves the pain. Search in your heart for the key.

A word of caution

Don't start feeling sorry for yourself. Don't dwell on how horrible the pain is or how bad you think the situation is. This is you letting your brain only see an unpromising future where many needs will never be met. This will only block you from being able to see the cause of the pain in the first place and will cloud your feelings so you won't be able to use your Inner Self to help you. If you find yourself distressed and dwelling on your pain then go back and practice more mindfulness. If that doesn't help, have a sleep and try it again at another time. Better still imagine what it would be like when the pain is actually gone and how your life will be so much better for it. Our aim is not to create a sense of hopelessness, simply to explore the causes of what is missing, or what we expect will be missing, that we need.

Don't stress if you don't find your answer straight away. Often the truth takes time to reveal itself. Usually it has been hidden a long time or we would have addressed it and faced it sooner. Learn to simply face the causes of your emotional pains and you have made a great step forward towards greater fulfillment and lasting happiness.

The more persistent and honest you are with yourself the better the results. Persistence and determination go a long way to emotional liberation.

The first step to resolving an emotional pain is to face it and work out what it represents. You have begun to do just that. The next step is to develop a plan or approach so the needs that arise will be met. We will work on how to use questioning to do just that. First we will learn new ways of questioning that can help you communicate with your Inner Self to help resolve your fears.

Chapter 14:
Questions to resolve fears

Over ten years ago Alison was physically assaulted by a man she had trusted, who had been her friend. The emotional echo of one moment had spread a web of fear into all aspects of her life. Today she was scared to be alone, to be with others, to be abandoned, and too scared to be confident and succeed. Her three-year-old daughter was also anxious, and to make matters worse Alison was also depressed. Her husband had been given a lifetime opportunity to make great money up north, to help the family get ahead, but it meant she would be left without her closest support while he was working away for up to six weeks. Her anxiety now left her terrified; it had raised so much she was struggling just to cope. Then we had a breakthrough.

Resolving this one original fear from just one event transformed her life. She said she couldn't believe the relief. Her confidence improved, she found it easier to make friends, and she was even ok for her husband to take his work trips, so long as he called her at night. Finally she felt less afraid and more trusting. Even her daughter seemed calmer and better behaved. From a life that had left her feeling depressed suddenly there was hope. Resolving just one fear had helped her be born into a happier life.

As we can see from Alison's case fear is one of the most powerful and influential emotions we have. Fears learnt or taught in our childhood, or traumas of our past, can flow on down the years and prevent us ever feeling safe, or make us incapable or unable to meet our needs. Fears of the future can stop us making life-changing decisions we know are for the better but feel unable or not strong enough to face. Fears can make us run away and hide, from ourselves and the world. They make us want to escape from a deep-seated agitation that grows and interminably persists. They can make it next to impossible, or too traumatic, to sleep. Fear is the one emotion, either subtle or extreme, that is inside us all; it never leaves. Yet just as with any other emotion or feeling it can be both understood and mastered. One way is by asking questions of our Inner Self to help us better understand and resolve our fears.

We all have many types of fears. Some are fears of the unfamiliar, situations or circumstances we have never been in before such as giving a speech, or moving to a new and unfamiliar place. Some of our fears are taught. Parents teach us some of our fears, to be anxious or afraid for no apparent reason and we can remain anxious about people or many situations as a result – we are afraid because they were afraid – we pick up common fears like being afraid of what others think about us. Most of our fears however are fears of the future – of what hasn't even happened yet – or fears from our past – traumas that still affect our lives today. The fears we have of the past or future are types of fear where asking questions of our Inner Self can help us the most. The reason asking questions of our Inner Self can help us with fears of the past and future is because of what our brain wants of us to resolve these fears.

What does our brain need to resolve or overcome a fear of the past or future? It wants to know our plan, or if there is absolutely nothing we can do about it – what we call acceptance.

Why a plan or acceptance?

It has to do with how our brain uses pathways.

Our brain is made up of billions of nerves, small cells that have many connections with other nerve cells that communicate with each other using a combination of electrical impulses and brain chemicals. Many of these cells connect with many others cells into what we call pathways. Nervous system pathways determine what we do, think, and feel.

Suppose you want to throw a ball. The brain pathways that deal with sight will recognize where you want to throw it. The brain pathways dealing with making your arm move – called motor pathways – will throw the ball. And the pathways used to keep you standing – more motor pathways – will make sure you keep your balance as you fling the ball into the air. If the ball breaks a window then the pathways that make you feel afraid will likely kick in and soon the pathways you use for running will get you moving. Pathways control everything that involves an action, thought, or feeling. Some of the most useful pathways our brain creates are those that represent possible future scenarios, so we know what we should do in those scenarios, so we have a better chance of staying alive.

Knowing what to do when we are in danger gives us a better chance of surviving. If you know to stop when the traffic light turns red you have a better chance of not being hit by a car. If you are a pilot and you have practiced what to do when both engines fail then you have a better chance of surviving the inevitable crash. Like the pilot who knew what to do when birds took out both the engines of his Airbus A320 in New York and then successfully landed – crashed – on the Hudson River. If our brain pathways tell us what to do in any given situation we have a much better chance of surviving. Fear is one of our body's ways of making sure we have such pathways, what we would call a plan. If your brain has a plan against what might kill it, injure it, or see it not have important human needs met – the needs summarized in the Balance of Self (BOS) Model – then it is prepared and more likely to survive. If it doesn't have a plan we could be in a lot of trouble, or dead meat.

Our brain comes up with worst-case scenarios to help prepare us and keep us alive. It makes these so it knows it has a plan for what can threaten us the most. It uses our past experiences and what we may have seen that has harmed other people – such as killings or violence on TV – to come up with whatever worst-case scenarios it can make. Then it uses fear to bring to our attention that we need to make a plan for that scenario. Through fear our brain is letting us know its worst-case scenario and it is asking us – with urgency – to give it a plan of what to do.

The fear simply brings the scenario to our attention: saying 'this is important, NOW!' I will keep bugging you with the fear until you give me the plan I need!

Of course at times nothing we do will make a difference. Such as if we are the passengers in a plane that is about to crash. Many of us aren't afraid of flying because we have considered this worst-case scenario. We know there's nothing we can do – no plan we can make – that will make a difference. As a result our brain doesn't bother us with bringing the scenario to our attention by using fear to make us create a plan. It doesn't make us feel afraid of it because that would be a waste of time. When we know there's nothing we can do, that no plan will make a difference, we know that as acceptance. When we have acceptance our fear levels go right down and don't bother us.

In other words to resolve a fear all our brain wants to know is what we will do, or do differently next time – how things can be different. Or it wants to know nothing would make – or would have made – a difference.

All of those most troubling fears of traumas of our past are still there simply because we haven't shown our brain what we would do different next time – a plan – or that it was beyond our control, and we could have done nothing about it – acceptance. The fears we still have of the future are present because we haven't given our brain enough of a detailed plan of what we will do about it, or haven't accepted we can do nothing that will make a difference anyway.

Yes, even the most traumatic fears of our past, the traumas that give us nightmares or flashbacks only want a plan or acceptance. Once we give it what it needs it goes away. So too our most troubling imaginings of the future simply want to know what we will do, or that we can do nothing that will make a difference.

Where does asking questions of our Inner Self help us with fears of the past or fears of the future?

Our Inner Self can help us work out what we are actually afraid of – it can help us face the truth of our fear – and access our fear on an emotional level so we can resolve it – create the plan or acceptance. It's hard to change a fear we aren't prepared to face and recognize. As we are about to see, unless we engage with the fear emotionally – much as we did with our emotional pains – it too will remain and continue to bother us. Unfortunately there isn't a list of fears to test and see what fear is affecting us – like the list of desires we could check against from the BOS Model a moment ago. Fears can be many and varied; any one of us can have thousands of them. So we use a slightly different approach than we used when resolving emotional pains earlier.

What are you afraid of?

What are you afraid of? What makes your heart race, your stomach churn, and your palms sweat uncontrollably? Thankfully most fears are obvious; straight in our face and easy to imagine or recall. Sometimes we can hide from them, not want to see them, suppress them because we don't like how they make us feel. Sometimes we can have trouble working out exactly what the fear is about and what it wants of us. That is where communicating with our Inner Self can help. It can help us get to the truth behind even our deepest fears. It can help us step inside to see the secret to resolving the fear, a secret that so far we haven't been able to find.

The first step in using our Inner Self to help work out what we're afraid of is to face the fear.

It is much like we did a moment ago when we faced our emotional pain; we access the feeling – this time fear – in all its detail. Then we hold the fear, we keep that fear present, we don't let it fade away, we don't try to step back or avoid it, we hold it in all its clarity and strength. Holding and keeping our fear in our presence is a critical step. Once we hold it then we can search inside it and ask our Inner Self to help us see where it comes from and what it wants from us – ask it questions. We let our Inner Self help to show us the truth behind the fear.

This sounds hard and goes against everything most of us are taught to do with our fears. Most are taught to ignore fears – just as we have been taught to ignore or run away from our emotional pains. Even more of us are taught to run away or avoid them. All the fiber of our being tells us to keep away from fears. But face them and hold them and you can understand and master them. Like being able to tame a wild stallion. Face it, know it, and it can do your bidding.

Why does facing and reliving a fear in our mind help you overcome it?

Overcoming fears is not a logical or emotionless process, we can't just rationalize them away. We can't just say, I shouldn't be afraid of the bullying I had as a child; I'm an adult now! I shouldn't be afraid of giving a speech; I don't even know the people. I'm sure you have tried it, tried to rationalize your fears away; we all do. However we have to emotionally engage with the fear to access and change it. Why is that?

You will recall a moment ago we noted that our memories are laid down with our emotions; access one and you can tap into the other. This is especially true of our fears; the stronger the fear the more powerful and clearer the memory. For example many combat soldiers suffer what are called 'flashbacks' where a simple event like a soda can hitting the floor can make a sudden loud noise that can take them back to the terror and images of fighting the enemy. Since strong memories such as fears are laid down by emotions – the emotions make the memory strong – we need to use emotions to change them. By accessing a fear on an emotional level we can tap into the memory and its associated feeling and replace it with a strong new memory. By trying to change it rationally we aren't accessing any emotions so the memory and its associated emotions won't change. To change a fear we need to shift the memory and the emotion that laid it down and made it strong in the first place.

People often ask, what is the point of bringing up the past; we can't change it. This is true, we can't, but we can change how our brain interprets it.

We have to remember our brain loves to generalize about what happens to it. If we are told we are hopeless enough times our brain will believe we are hopeless or useless, it will expect others to treat us this way in the future. When a past trauma happens, our brain also generalizes. It can generalize and believe it is weak or vulnerable, it can believe it is someone who is abused; it can believe the world is never safe and that one belief can rule and destroy our lives. No, we can't change the past, what we can change are the brain's generalizations, how it interpreted the events. We can change how the trauma changed us and how we saw the world and ourselves differently, and how it left us continuing to often feel afraid. We can change the generalization by accessing the feeling and memory of the event and reinterpreting it in a more realistic way. Alison, at the beginning of the chapter for example, resolved her fear by accessing it and changing it so she no longer told herself she was weak and unsafe. As a result, her fear no longer bothered her and her life changed forever.

Warning

Fears are not to be taken lightly. Some fears can be so strong they need professional help to work through, such as those from trauma that leads to conditions such as Post Traumatic Stress Disorder suffered by combat soldiers. If you have memories such as these and you access them and don't resolve them, then by simply remembering them, you make them stronger. So unless you are truly prepared to face and resolve a fear don't try to present it to your Inner Self. You will only find it a stronger fear next time. Don't try to remember a fear you aren't prepared to change. If you are having trouble resolving traumatic fears and memories seek the help of a specialist in trauma therapy.

This is how I learnt to overcome many of my fears. I still use these techniques today. As a result I often describe fears to patients now as if they are big balloon monsters, only we don't know they are balloons, as they look so big, real, and scary. Our natural instincts when we see one of these balloon monsters is to turn and run like crazy. Like the good balloon monster it is it chases us. Next time we look around it is even bigger and scarier. So what do we do? We turn and run like crazy! Eventually we are too exhausted to run any more; we are forced to face it. Face it, step inside it, call its bluff and let it give you its best shot, let yourself feel the consequences of the great fear, let yourself know it and explore it, see it in ways you haven't seen it before, and soon something amazing happens. It just fades away, as if it was always just full of hot air and had no real substance.

Fears have to appear real or we don't take them seriously. If we don't take them seriously we can be harmed or even die. But most of what we are afraid of will not kill us, most fears we can survive quite well. Unfortunately, by ignoring these fears we let them grow. Soon we have so many big and hard to manage fears they cripple our lives. At some point we have to learn to stop and face them. They are not at all as they appear.

This is where communicating with our Inner Self becomes useful.

It can help us face our fears, step inside them, and see what we need to resolve them.

How do we do that?

Resolve the fears

The first step in communicating with our Inner Self to resolve our fears is to make sure we are in the 'right place' and the 'right mind'. We cannot overcome a fear if we are in a place that brings it on. There are methods of exposing ourselves to fear to overcome them but that isn't the approach we are using here. Here we need to be away from what scares us.

Once you are settled and feel safe then search for what scares you. Search out a fear inside you and face it. Search with your heart.

Now step inside it, and use your heart to ask questions of the balloon monster – a monster that appears real but is actually full of hot air and has no real substance.

If it is a fear you have of something happening in the future present the scenario in detail to your Inner Self to consider. Then begin to ask your Inner Self questions about the fear you are holding and examining.

What questions should you ask?

To weed out fears that are probably never going to happen ask your Inner Self if this fear is realistic. Is it truly likely to happen? If it doesn't feel in your heart it will happen your Inner Self will let you know by letting the fear go away. If it is realistic then present plans – imagined scenarios – for your Inner Self to consider.

In other words, call the fear's bluff, imagine it happened, imagine what it would feel like, then visualize and feel what you would do. What would you do? Would you survive? Would life go on? Would you eventually get over the event you are most afraid of – such as your partner leaving you? Imagine how you would continue to eat, drink, survive, and even thrive and what it would feel like. Imagine for instance you are with a new partner and have a better sense of self to boot. Explore the fear. Explore alternative outcomes. Give your Inner Self a plan and see what it thinks. Explore in your heart if there really isn't anything you can do that will make a difference. Perhaps all we need to show our Inner Self is that we will do the best we can in the circumstances. Help our Inner Self see our plan or help it develop acceptance and our fears of the future can be much less powerful or almost completely go away. That said, some fears of the future are fears of our past resurfacing – such as a fear or failure or being humiliated as you once were in your past. We are afraid it will happen again. Fears of the past can be dealt with in a similar way to how we deal with those of the future.

Fears of our past can be like a tree of fears. One root fear can develop several branches leaving us afraid of many scenarios and things. Like the fear Alison suffered that affected her career and social life; it basically affected her whole life, all from one event, and one basic fear. The key to getting rid of fears from our past is to trace them back to when they first began – to the initial incident. Overcome the fear associated with that initial incident and then all the branches that stem from it become weak and much easier to manage. How do we find the root fear? We search with our heart. We ask questions of our fear using our Inner Self to help us.

Access the memory of the fear or traumatic event of your past that still scares or traumatizes you. Then step inside it; immerse yourself in the feeling and memory as if stepping into a dark house with a torch. Search inside the feeling and the memory to find when you first felt this fear. Present the memory to your Inner Self and see if it feels like this is the source, or if it can sense something deeper. Don't think maybe there's a deeper memory – whatever you do don't make a memory up – search only for what actually happened and see if you can access it. With a little practice once you recall a fear and hold that feeling other memories associated with that fear will reveal themselves to you. Persist and you can find the source.

Once you have the root fear hold onto it as a memory and a feeling and explore it and see what your Inner Self requires to finally resolve it. For example, often it simply requires us to access the fear and ask if we did the best we could under the circumstances. If no other course of action was available, and our Inner Self agrees, then acceptance will come and the fear will leave us. If the fear remains we can help our Inner Self see other points of view and see if that resolves it.

For instance I had many traumatic memories of high school and being ostracized. As I embraced the fear of others abusing me, and started to explore why, I began to wonder what other children must go through for them to treat me like this. If I had similar beliefs or views as them for instance would they still have treated me as different and abused me? As I explored this in my heart and presented this image to my Inner Self, I realized they probably wouldn't. Then I saw that other children were simply a reflection of their parents' beliefs. Since my immigrant parents' approaches and beliefs were different I was always – to some extent – going to be different and therefore abused. By exploring the trauma and fear from other points of view – in this case from those of other children and their parents – I could see how this could all happen. My searching for the truth of the fear and trying to understand it led me to ask useful questions of the fear that helped me resolve it. Many of the traumas and fears of my past no longer bother me now that I've stepped inside them and explored and found their truth.

Is facing our traumatic past easy? No. And yet if we simply step back and never delve inside it the pathways that create trauma remain intact and our fears remain and control us. It is useful to take courage from knowing our Inner Self can help us find what will resolve even our most troubling fears, if we ask questions and present them to our Inner Self and let it show us what to do to resolve them.

How do we know if a fear is resolved?

It's like a great weight has been lifted from our shoulders; a great feeling of relief. Persist with searching your heart to face and resolve your fears and you can feel lots of this relief.

The key to resolving a fear by asking questions of our Inner Self is to persist. Don't let the fear escape unchanged, don't let it wear you down or try to convince you resolving it is impossible. It isn't. Sometimes our fears seem impossible to resolve and conquer, but as you explore them you will soon learn even our biggest fears are made of smaller ones. Every fear can be broken into smaller fears more easily conquered – often fears we already had that we added to later. Go back and conquer the smaller fears first and when you return later to conquer the bigger fear it will crumble. Persist using questioning of your Inner Self to conquer your fears and all of them can be mastered. Your Inner Self is a truthful, insightful and powerful ally.

Try it. Practice it. Face your fears one by one. Work on that one troubling fear until it is resolved and learn to communicate more deeply with your Inner Self in the process.

Practice tip

Simply rehearsing in your mind what you would do in a future scary situation can go a long way to reducing your fear of the future. Practice, rehearse, and go through your options as if they actually happened then see how you feel. If you are still afraid do more research so you know more about what might happen and feel prepared, then rehearse what you will do and once again see how you feel. Your Inner Self will let you know when you have a plan that works.

If you find yourself getting too overwhelmed by the emotion of your fear, stop. When a fear gets too strong it shuts down the parts of the brain that do the planning and thinking. Until your fear levels go down you will not be able to ask any questions of your fear so you can change it. Be curious about your fear, don't treat it as if it has any power and you can avoid getting consumed by it. If emotion does overrun you, stop and practice mindfulness as described earlier. If that doesn't work have a sleep and try again later. If you still struggle to manage your fears get professional help so you can improve your confidence and learn how to master the fears that still afflict you.

What you have just learnt is a different way of communicating with your Inner Self. Instead of presenting it with a list of options we learnt to hold a feeling and memory in front of our Inner Self so we could question it and offer it scenarios.

Next we explore another form of questioning that will help you communicate more closely and effectively with the ancient woman wisdom within. It involves questioning your Inner Self so it offers you direction and guidance, so you can access choices and decisions with greater confidence, and live a life with more purpose and meaning.

Chapter 15:
Questions to help with future choices

We all have questions about the future. Is he the right man for me? Should I take the job? Should I work or stay at home with the kids? Questions such as these regarding our future happiness are always very important. Our Inner Self is well placed to help us answer any questions about our future.

Why? Once again the answer has to do with how our brain works. One part of our brain is very good at looking beyond logic and helping us with problems regarding the future, and our Inner Self has direct access to it.

Parts of our brain deal with day-to-day activities and help us plan for the next minutes, hours, and weeks. We often consider these parts to be the logical or rational segments of the brain. They deal with specifics, like counting numbers, and whether we eat or don't eat and so on. You couldn't buy food, or make day-to-day decisions without them. These rational parts were thought to be in the left hemisphere – the left half – of the brain. Now we know they are scattered in other parts as well, often depending on if you are right- or left-handed.

Then there are parts of the brain considered the artistic or creative parts. If you felt creative, inspired, had vague notions of what you wanted to express, this was thought to happen in the right hemisphere. Once again we have since learnt these less well-defined or less logical human qualities happen in many parts of the brain, not just the right hemisphere. What we have also learnt is that the parts of the brain that deal with less of the day-to-day matters tend to consider the distant future.

It makes sense. There are times when we have to make decisions that affect us right here and now, we need to be precise and decide. We either stop at the traffic lights or we don't, we put the food in our mouth or we don't, we find something to drink or we don't. We wouldn't kind of put food in our mouth or we would starve, or kind of stop at traffic lights or we might be hit by another car. Some activities need us to be precise. But sometimes we don't need to be so precise, such as when we consider the future.

The further we look to the future the less we can be sure what might happen. The future is vague. So many possibilities all seem to blend together. Our brain still considers these many possibilities but it doesn't have time to show them all; it might have hundreds of possible futures that could take anything from minutes to hours to make us aware of them. Those minutes and hours could be better spent doing what we need to do right now, like eating, getting warm, or avoiding other cars. Therefore, much of what our brain considers and sees regarding the future often goes without our conscious awareness.

Our Inner Self is directly connected to the parts of the brain looking far into the future. It can see possibilities – of which we aren't consciously aware – way into the future.

Since we don't have time to see all the future possibilities we are often left with our Inner Self's impression of what it was shown. It presents as a gut-feeling, an intuition, and even an inspiration. We can have a vague feeling something might happen and be right. We can't say exactly how it will unfold but somehow we know. Our Inner Self has a direct connection to that part of the brain; it's therefore the best part of us to ask when it comes to deciding matters of the future.

If you have an important question involving your future happiness ask your Inner Self.

How do we do that?
We present it with options or scenarios of the future and see what it tells us, much like we have already done when we were working to resolve our emotional pains and fears.

For example, if you want to know if he is the man for you then put the scenario to your Inner Self and see what your intuition and heart tell you. Mind you, it has probably already let you know.

Within a few minutes of meeting a potential partner for the first time you would have had a first impression, a feeling about him. That feeling was from your Inner Self. The number of times we tend to ignore these feelings then find they were justified later is amazing. Many of us still think we know better than a part of us that sees more than we consciously see.

Try it. If you don't know what choice to make or what path to take, put the scenario to your Inner Self. Make it a detailed and realistic scenario, like you did earlier to help you resolve your fear. Notice what the scenario feels like, and ask your Inner Self what it thinks about it. Should you take the option or shouldn't you? Do you marry the guy or don't you? Search for the truth within.

Practice exercise

Write down at least five questions you want answered about your future. Questions where you don't know what to do.

1. ....
2. ....
3. ....
4. ....
5. ....

Tackle one question at a time and present it to your Inner Self as a scenario. Make sure you have a clear and calm mind so you see what your Inner Self has to say and not what you want to hear.

If you attempt the exercise and still haven't a clear feeling about what you should do it's probably because you haven't given your Inner Self enough information to be swayed either way.

Our Inner Self doesn't see everything. At times, it doesn't have enough information to make an accurate prediction or give us a clear vision of the future. In that case we need to research the topic more.

For example, if the question is about what job to take or career path to follow then research the options, get a realistic view of what it would be like, then put that scenario to your Inner Self and see what you feel in your heart. Is that really the career for you? Research what lifestyle you would lead, how long it will take, what recognition and appreciation you can realistically expect. Ask people in the industry. The more information you have the more realistic you will be and the more accurate impression will be delivered by your Inner Self. Do you still really want to follow that career? Only you can know that. Only your Inner Self can give you an indication as to whether it will meet enough of your basic human needs to feel truly satisfied with your choice.

Whenever you have to make a potentially life-changing choice always ask your Inner Self. Always listen to the depths of your heart.

Trust in your Inner Self's decisions and never look back. It will always help you make the best decision in the circumstances.

Is your life lacking a sense of hope, something to really look forward to? Perhaps it all seems useless? Your Inner Self can also help you create a future full of hope, life-purpose, and meaning.

Create realistic hope

We mentioned earlier that to resolve our emotional pains we need to recognize the cause of the pain – what is missing, or what we expect to be missing in the future – then develop a plan, a vision of how our needs will be met. We need to be able to create hope. Asking questions of our Inner Self can be a very useful way of creating realistic hope, and giving our life a sense of purpose and meaning.

We can build realistic hope by creating plans to deal with the causes of our emotional pains. Go back to the emotional pains you explored a moment ago. Focus on one. Present it to your Inner Self and see what it needs to feel fulfilled, so the pain actually goes away. Perhaps it needs you to have more close friends so you don't feel lonely? Perhaps you need to be closer friends with your partner, or to get on better with the people at work? Maybe you need to move to a neighborhood with more supportive people? Put the scenario to your Inner Self and see. Does the plan in your mind feel like it will resolve the issue? Great, put it into place. If it doesn't then do more research and present your Inner Self with other options.

Don't just consider the easy choices, dream up the hard ones too. Often our brain will trick us into believing we can't do anything because all our options look too hard. And yet often by seeing past the hard choices, the more difficult path, we find the joy for which we search. Consider the hard choices and put them to your Inner Self. Perhaps you have to sell up and move? Perhaps you need to talk with your partner about difficult matters you have dreaded talking about? Perhaps your lifestyle needs to change? Let your Inner Self guide and help you create realistic plans of hope for your future.

Practice tip

Write down your emotional pain. Then write down three things you can do to resolve each of your emotional pains.
Emotional pain:
Options:

1. ....
2. ....
3. ....

Now break down each option into smaller tasks or steps, the things you need to do to make them happen – such as contacting a new social group, checking out a new venue, taking up a group sport or activity. Plan your steps. Be creative. Look past what you would normally do. Imagine how you will be successful in each step. Seek professional help if you are still struggling.

The best future we can create is one of realistic hope. By rehearsing how it will happen we prepare ourselves to succeed. When the opportunities arrive we will grab them. Imagine a realistic hope that feels honest and we ensure we are creating a life with the best chance of satisfying our desires.

How do we use Inner Self questioning to give our future a sense of real purpose and meaning?

We begin by giving it something worth caring about and striving for.

Create a future of purpose

A businessman in his mid-fifties came into my office recently complaining his life seemed hollow and had no meaning. He had achieved all his career goals, his two children had grown up, one lived overseas, and the other was successful in his own work in another city. He had no grandchildren and travel didn't interest him, even though he could afford it. He spent little time with any friends, the one guy he talked to liked to analyze the world like he did. He had no hobbies, and nothing excited him. His wife pointed out he had emotionally detached from life. She was right. His life had nothing he would emotionally engage in. We both agreed he needed a cause, something to work for that held meaning. But what was the point of doing anything if he wasn't emotionally connected to anyone or anything enough that it would make whatever he did worthwhile? If he had grandchildren he was emotionally close to for instance he would work to make the world a better place just for them. Then his life would have a purpose; it would mean something. If he was to find a cause to strive for, to find meaning and purpose, first he would have to get emotionally involved with the world and people.

Do you have people you deeply care about? People you would work towards making life happier for? It could be children, or grandchildren, nieces, nephews, or children of friends. What about your partner? It could even be the land if you deeply care about it, or the earth. If you don't have a deep emotional connection to anything then that will need to change. Modern lives often don't feel like they have purpose and meaning. What drives us – money, possessions – can make it seem meaningless once we have those things and realize they do not buy happiness.

Suppose you cared about the survival of the natural world because you truly felt for it, then your life would have a sense of purpose as you tried to protect it. Suppose you kept in close and emotional contact with your children and grandchildren, your partner; then you could find purpose and meaning in helping to create a better world for them. It is next to impossible to find purpose and meaning without emotionally connecting and caring for something or someone in the world. Once we have something to care about then we can ask our Inner Self to help us find the long-term purpose and meaning we need.

How do we do that?

By creating an image in our mind of the world and/or people we most care about and how we feel about them. Then we put the question to our Inner Self, 'how can I help them most?' Search in your heart, feel how you can make a difference. Even the smallest effort can be hugely significant. Search your heart for the goal or cause that gives you the most passion. How can you help the world and people you care about most in a way that gives you greatest personal satisfaction? Put scenarios to your Inner Self and let it help you see how best to use your unique set of talents and abilities. Once you find it you will be driven every day to achieve it. Suddenly life will have a sense of real purpose and meaning.

As you are beginning to see your Inner Self can be a most useful and insightful tool. Learning to communicate with it can resolve our deepest emotional pains and fears. It can give us great hope, purpose, and meaning. As we are about to see it can also help provide an insight into yourself as a woman in a way no one else can. Some of the most powerful questions and insights of all come from using your Inner Self to connect with and reveal your Essence and Spirit of Woman. Want to know who you are as a woman? Why not ask the source?

Chapter 16:
Questions to understand Essence of Woman

Understanding your heart and what you truly feel as a woman is within your grasp. You don't need anyone to impose their view of what the Essence of Woman is, or what the spirit of ancient woman represents for you, you can know it for yourself. How do you do it? One way is to listen more to your instincts, your intuition, and be true to your deep authentic womanly feelings, as we have been learning to do. The other is to take communication with your Inner Self even further to get a much clearer understanding of what drives and defines you.

We have already used communication with our Inner Self to better understand our emotions, our fears, and to help guide us into the future. We have been communicating with our Inner Self by presenting it with simple scenarios such as, 'will becoming more of a friend with my partner help relieve some of my emotional pain?' Or 'what do I need to do to resolve my fear, what plan will help me feel less afraid of the future?'

But let's delve a bit further. We can communicate with our Inner Self and gain much more from it by asking it more complicated questions. In this chapter we present it with more detailed hypothetical scenarios and see what we feel back. This approach can help you more clearly see what desires define you as a woman.

We have assumed that women are the carers and nurturers. So let's put some scenarios to your Inner Self and see if what you feel fits with this assumption.

Consider some of the following scenarios. Imagine them actually happening – as vividly as you can – then ask your Inner Self what you feel. Don't second-guess or look for what seems logical, explore what feels true in your heart.

Your Essence of Woman

You are walking down the street of your safe neighborhood. You know your neighbors; they are good people. The five-year-old girl from next door is sitting on the footpath with her hand covering her face, crying. Do you say hello and walk on past, or stop and see if you can help?

Your four-year-old son wakes up crying at 2 am. You have a busy day with lots of meetings and work – you need your sleep now more than ever. Do you try to go back to sleep and hope he settles, maybe seeing if your husband gets up, or do you immediately check on him to see if he's ok?

You see people suffering on the TV, children starving, and women huddled together in fear. What does your heart tell you to do?

A baby bird falls out of its nest, do you leave it on the ground or find a way to put it back, or take it into your care?

How did your heart react in each scenario? How did it make you feel? What did it make you want to do? Would you help the helpless girl? Would you put your son's needs ahead of work? How did you react to the starving children and scared women on TV? Or the baby bird on the ground? What do these scenarios tell you about how important caring is for you? How important is it to your Inner Self? Ultimately you do care don't you, about children, your own child, nature and others in distress? If you are being true to yourself your heart tells you caring is part of who you are as a woman.

You have two children, both under five. You have a husband – father of the children – who meets all your womanly needs; you are very close. In the next three years you can only see your husband, or your children, but not both. Both will be safe in that time when they are not with you. Who would you choose?

What does your heart tell you about the strength and power of your desires as a mother if you prefer to care for your children over being with your partner? Does your heart tell you to care for your children first? The desires of a woman to care for children she is strongly emotionally attached to are very powerful. We know they have to be or our children won't survive. Now you can begin to see how powerful these desires are inside you as a woman and a mother to put the needs of the children first. Would you really give your children up to strangers just to live with your partner?

A being of great power offers you two choices:
- You can never be friends with a man you are attracted to, but have sex with him as you please. He will never truly value or respect you.
- You can be his friend but never have sex with him. He will both respect and value you and be there for you no matter what.

Which would you choose?

How important is friendship in your relationship with men? How much is about sex for you? Would you choose friendship over sex if you had to? Which desires seem strongest for you? Ideally you want to have sex and friendship with the man you are attracted to, but what if you had to choose? Would your heart really want you to stay with a man who could not respect you? We mentioned earlier that friendships, including friendships with a man, are important for you as an authentic woman. Search your heart, do you feel this to be true?

You grew up in a family where your parents knew how to fulfill each other's needs, and your mother adored being a mother. How would you feel in your heart about having children and being a mother?

Now imagine your parents were always fighting, your mother resented her children, especially having you. Would that change your desires to be a mother? Would it change what you feel in your heart?

How were your desires to be a mother affected by experiences with your mother? We know some desires will be written inside us but can they be overridden or suppressed by our childhood? Can desires be altered by the type of role models you have in life? Are you listening to your heart or simply doing what your mother did?

⓪

Imagine you have never been taught how to react or respond to a man.

Now you meet a man you are deeply attracted to who can definitely meet your needs. No one will ever know what you will do next. What do you feel in your heart you want to do with him, and want from him, now, and in the long term? Try to be specific.

If you could only listen to your heart would you know how to be the woman he needs you to be? How much of your behavior towards the men you are attracted to is about raw womanly desire and what you physically need to do? What does your physical desire feel like? How powerful is it for you?

⓪

Imagine being part of a small community where everyone adores mothers and holds women in the highest regard. They are more than respected – they are the pinnacle of their community; the best it has to offer in every way. In your heart would you want to be like other women, or like the less favored and insignificant men?

How much of your womanly behavior is determined by those around you? Is part of being an authentic woman about also being part of a community and doing what others expect us to do? Would you really want to be anything other than authentic if this was what everyone around you thought was the best anyone could be?

⓪

You meet a man all your friends don't like. No women seem to like him. You are single, looking for the right man. He has qualities you once recognized in your father; you and your father were very close. Would you consider a long-term relationship with him?

How much of your experience with your father affects your heart's desires for a man? It makes sense that if you lived with a man who knew how to keep you alive he would have proven what he did as a man worked. As a result you would want to find such a man. But is that what you feel? How many of the qualities you seek in a man, how many of your desires for a man, are molded by your experiences with your father? How much of being a woman and having womanly desires are defined by the men close to you in your life? Take away the men and what is left of your essence as a woman?

Questioning our heart is a great way to help us understand the priorities and details of the desires that define us. Every question helps us piece together a more detailed picture of our heart. Every question can help you see the woman you are and the desires that define you. Every scenario helps you ask and explore for yourself how true you are being to these deep inner feelings. Hard questioning of our heart and feelings peels away what we have been taught. It removes who we think we should be, and leads us to our true being.

I find the most useful questions that help define our desires and how powerful they are in comparison to each other are those that give us a stark choice. The ones that ask us what we choose if we had to, if life or nature put us in a horrible position where we had to make a decision we would rather never make. Like choosing our children over our caring partner, or choosing friendship or sex but being unable to have both. The more stark and difficult the choice the more we can learn about our priorities and what part these desires play in our lives. The more you ask the more you learn, not from reading books but simply listening to your heart.

The truth of who you are is within. The scenarios you present to your Inner Self can help you unlock that truth.

The next step to helping you be more true to yourself, raise your Essence of Woman is to be, and remain, attractive, but not in a way many of us think.

Step 4: Be attractive

> *The women's chief told them: Over there near the corral are the men sitting in sight. All these women are cutting the meat. Their chief did not take off the clothes she was wearing while cutting the meat. They were told by her: I shall go up there first. I shall take my choice. When I come back, you will go up one by one. Now we will take husbands. Then she started up. Then she went to all those men. She asked them: Which is your chief? The men said: This one here, Wolf-robe (Napi). She told him: Now we will take you for husbands. And then she walked to that Wolf-robe. She caught him. Then she started to pull him. Then he pulled back. Then she let him loose. He did not like her clothes. While the other women were picking out their husbands, the chief of the women put on her best costume. When she came out, she looked very fine, and, as soon as Old Man saw her, he thought. Oh! there is the chief of the women. I wish to be her husband.*
> Story of the first marriage, told by Joseph Tatsey, Blackfeet[9]

We see a lot of 'attractive' women on TV. Boobs, booties, slim bodies seem all the rage. But being and staying attractive is far more than just about looks. As we are about to see the qualities we find attractive in other people are the same traits that promise to satisfy basic human needs. The more needs we can satisfy the more attractive we become. One quality in particular – strong Personal Self – can be very attractive to both men and women. We need to keep and maintain this quality if our relationships are to be and remain satisfying. It is a quality we can all learn to increase and that also raises the Essence of Woman within.

What are the qualities that make us attractive? And why do we need to remain attractive?

The key lies in being authentic.

Nature made us search for certain qualities in others so we can fulfill being a human being. We can recognize these as the qualities that make us authentic. For example as a whole woman you promise to meet the needs authentic men have been programmed by nature to seek out and find. The more authentic you become the more you will be able to satisfy his true needs for a woman and the more he will want to know and be with you. Similarly the more he is true to being an authentic man the more you can find him attractive as he promises to meet many needs nature made you search for in a man.

Being friendly is also a very attractive quality. If you are friendly and have friends then you are promising that you will be able to meet his friendship needs – the Ten Needs of Friendship we discussed earlier. As we recognized a moment ago meeting close friendship needs plays a huge role in creating a deep and lasting bond in a relationship. The closer we can be friends the more we want to be with them. The closer we maintain the bond the more we are going to stay. Yes, looks may get each other's attention, but we have all experienced at some time a person who looks great but isn't very attractive at all. We can read the qualities nature made us seek out in a partner often within seconds or minutes and see if they are attractive to us. Eventually we look beyond mere looks to find what is truly attractive.

Yes, certain physical features and even body odor will also determine if we want to get to know them better or not – being biologically compatible does play a role. But at the heart of attraction are men and women searching for a promise of a future together, a future that truly satisfies. The more needs you can promise to satisfy the more attractive you can be.

Why do we need to remain attractive? To continue to promise and meet each other's relationship needs.

As we just noted developing a close friendship and bond isn't like earning a diploma and nailing it to a wall. Friendships require maintenance. We need to continue to meet each other's needs so we can feel safe and secure. If you stop being friends you will be less attractive. If you stop being authentic you will stop meeting his needs to be

Step 4: Be attractive

with someone who is true to herself. Stop meeting each other's needs and why should we stay? We are made to search for people who will continue to satisfy the basic needs inside us.

By being true to yourself you are naturally meeting and promising to meet many Family Self needs. By being friendly and developing a close friendship you are meeting and promising to meet many Community Self needs. This makes you very attractive. But by meeting Personal Self needs your attractiveness can shoot through to a whole new level.

You can be far more attractive to an authentic man if you can also promise to meet his Personal Self needs.

In the process you become even more of an authentic woman.

Chapter 17:
Enhance your Personal Self

Personal Self, you will recall, is one of the Three Human Essences in the Balance of Self (BOS) Model. It represents desires that help keep you alive as an individual. It reflects your development of a strong sense of individual self, knowing what you think and feel in your own right.

Hold on a moment. How can we promise to meet Personal Self needs in someone else? Aren't Personal Self needs something we have to meet ourselves?

Yes, only you can know what your needs are and ultimately know how to meet them. Only you can develop a true and genuinely unique sense of self. But by you having a strong sense of Personal Self you also help your partner – or prospective partner – meet their Personal Self needs. Have and maintain a strong Personal Self and you are promoting, allowing, and encouraging your partner – or prospective partner – to be true to themselves and live a more fulfilling life. You are also giving them permission to be themselves.

Ultimately we all want to be individuals. By having a strong Personal Self you are saying you respect individuality. A person who respects his or her own individuality is more likely to respect it in someone else. They are less likely to try to change someone else. By having a strong Personal Self you will give a partner – or prospective partner – a nurturing environment to develop and maintain their own sense of self. You will not be putting them down but rather allowing and encouraging them to develop a strong Personal Self for themselves. You won't be getting upset with their individuality you will be more likely to embrace it. The promise of being accepted for whom we really are and of living a more fulfilling life simply by being around you makes you very attractive.

Look around you. Don't you find people who know themselves, who don't want to change you, who are comfortable in their own skin and confident in whom they are more attractive? We all do. These are qualities that represent a strong Personal Self.

Not having a strong Personal Self and maintaining it in a relationship can be catastrophic.

Relationships are about compromise; we need to compromise so the relationship can work. However, all too easily we can compromise so much of ourselves we don't know who we are anymore. We can completely change. Then we are no longer the person they were attracted to, and our relationship is more likely to fail as a result. Increase and maintain a strong Personal Self and you remain you, strengthening your relationship.

The most important attractive qualities radiate from inside us and people will read them in our appearance and behaviors.

For example, your level of Personal Self will show in your level of confidence, and your pretentiousness – how much you have to pretend to be someone you are not. People with a strong Personal Self show they respect themselves. They show it by keeping fit, by taking pride in their appearance because they value themselves, not to try to impress others, and not to try to fit in. They do not try to be glamorous because they know they don't need to; they don't feel so insecure they need to be that noticed. They are not overweight because being overweight indicates they don't value or respect themselves. You can read if a person has a strong Personal Self very quickly.

Can you fake having a strong Personal Self to make yourself seem more attractive?

You can, but how long can you keep up the lie? And why bother? If you are attracting your man with a lie you are attracting the type of men who are attracted to your lie. Then you either have to keep it up or wait for the relationship to eventually fail, as you are unable to continue to meet each other's needs. Why not just be genuine and have a strong Personal Self in the first place?

It's worth pointing out that a strong Personal Self will also enhance your attractiveness to authentic men.

Because a strong Personal Self is about listening to your individual desires and needs independently of others in many ways it is akin to being in contact with your Inner Self. We know communication with your Inner Self increases your Essence of Woman. So too does increasing your Personal Self; it helps you be true to the desires nature wrote inside you. When you have a strong Personal Self you are being true to the inner you. You are being truly authentic.

Learning to build and maintain a strong sense of Personal Self greatly increases the chance of you developing and maintaining lasting and satisfying relationships.

Time will pass and looks will fade, but no matter our age we will always be more attractive with a strong Personal Self.

How do we increase and maintain a strong Personal Self?

Follow these six simple and practical steps. Everything from writing poetry, to art, dance, music, cooking, and going for a walk in nature can have remarkable benefits. However how we use them will determine if they increase our Personal Self or not.

Six steps to increase Personal Self

Chris came in a shattered man. Embarrassed he was crying he couldn't hold back the tears. 'They left me,' he said. 'I don't know what to do.'

In his own time he told me of his teenage children, a daughter fifteen and his son seventeen. For over ten years – since their mother abandoned them – he was devoted to his precious children. He worked long hours in low paying laboring jobs, kept them well-fed, clothed, and in a house he cleaned and maintained that he wanted to be able to call a home. He had few friends; he never had time for them. He had few dates; again he rarely found the time. He enjoyed caring for his children and his whole life was devoted to it. Then they both decided to leave him.

Where did they decide to go? To live with their now wealthy mother in a nearby city.

Suddenly everything that he lived for, everything that gave his life meaning had just gone. Why? His son told him he thought his father was weak. His daughter followed her bigger brother, but was also enticed by the many things her wealthy mother could buy for her.

In trying to help this man develop a sense of self and successfully reclaim himself over many months I developed the following methods. I would later be able to help other people increase their sense of self in similar ways. Now I successfully use these methods to help people overcome and prevent depression.

Today Chris has a much stronger sense of self. He takes time to enjoy what he likes for a change. He has regular contact with friends. Chris's son no longer thinks he is weak and they have regular contact. His daughter moved back in with him once she realized her mother could not be counted on to offer her the support and care she needed – her mother's partner was abusive, that didn't help. Chris still devotes much of his time to help his children and those around him. The difference now is he feels stronger inside. He is no longer just a father, he is Chris, an individual deserving of having his needs met as much as any of us.

The story of Chris is an unusual one. It is usually women I find that devote themselves so completely to their children that they lose who they really are.

Regardless of your gender, the process of growing and maintaining a strong Personal Self is simply about increasing a sense of you, of knowing who you are away from the influence of others. I often ask a question to help people learn their level of Personal Self. Don't worry if you can't answer it, many people can take a lifetime to find an answer that truly satisfies them. Many others may not find one at all. Only when you have a strong Personal Self will you know the answer that is true for you.

What is the question?

'If you were the only person on the planet, and you didn't have to answer to anybody, what would you do?'

This is not about imagining a horrible apocalypse. The aim of the question is to ask what you would do if no one was watching, and no one knew what you did or didn't do. What would you choose to do?

What would you feel like doing that would truly satisfy just you? What would you wear if no one ever saw it? What would you eat if it were just for your taste and/or wellbeing? Where would you go? How would you spend your time? There is no one else to please or impress, remember. What would fulfill your heart, just for you?

It isn't an easy question is it? Yet all it does is strip away the influence of others – the influence of the desires of Community Self – and lets you see what is left. What is left? Who is that person inside you when you aren't being influenced to do, think, and behave like others?

A person with a strong Personal Self can answer these questions easily. They know who they are away from others; they have an identity all their own. Because they have a separate sense of self they are less influenced by others to change. It is easier for them to stay true to themselves in any relationship and make sure they have their personal needs met.

Isn't increasing a strong Personal Self being selfish? Should we really be working to just have our individual needs met? Shouldn't we be working to make sure other people's needs are met instead?

When you have a strong Personal Self you listen to all your innermost desires. If you were being true to these desires – as you would if you had a strong Personal Self – would you still want to help people? Would you still want to help your children, your family, and those close to you? Of course you would. How is this selfish?

Spending time to have our needs met goes against the ideals of our community. Our community wants us to put other people's needs ahead of our own; it wants us to think of the community ahead of us. Why? Nature ensured we survived better in groups. We won't work together in groups if we only look after our own needs. But if we only work to ensure other people's needs are met what happens to our own fulfillment? How will we feel? We know we feel emotional pain if our own needs don't get met. Developing a strong Personal Self is not being selfish; it is about living true to ourselves as human beings.

Selfishness is disrespecting other people's needs.

A good example of selfishness would be to tread over other people and their needs to achieve wealth and status.

Respect other people's needs and we respect their humanity, the desires they need to satisfy in their lifetime so they can be at their very best. Respect humanity and we must also respect our own. All our desires are important, not just ours personally, not just the community's, not just our family's. We can all have our needs met if we work to respect everyone's needs in the process. We can also still work as a community or group thanks to us respecting and satisfying our desires of Community Self.

Developing a strong Personal Self is not about neglecting the needs of others. It is recognizing and respecting everyone's needs, including your own.

Personal Self is considered the core or foundation of the BOS Model. If it is low then Community Self and Family Self will also be low. If you aren't being you in a community or family you won't have your needs met in your family and society. The stronger your level of Personal Self the more satisfied you can be with friends, community, and family.

Yes, a strong Personal Self will make you more attractive than you could otherwise be. It will even help you be more of a woman. Most of all it will help you to be the true and genuine you and live a fulfilling and satisfying life because it helps you to have your personal needs met.

The following steps are designed to help you increase and maintain a strong Personal Self. The more you apply them the more your Personal Self will grow, even under the great power of the influence of others – the often overpowering desires of Community Self. Increasing and maintaining a strong Personal Self isn't hard, but we won't develop one if we don't make it a priority. Once we give it the attention it deserves a strong Personal Self will develop naturally.

How do we begin to increase and maintain a strong Personal Self?

By applying the most important step of all: making time.

Chapter 18:
Make self time

Two different types of self time increase Personal Self: quiet time and personal enjoyment time.

Quiet time

We have touched on quiet time as part of preparing to communicate with your Inner Self. The more time you spend alone in a quiet and undisturbed place the more you can get to know what you think and feel; the better you get to know your true self. Not until we get away from the influence of others do we get to see and know ourselves as individuals. Make the following your priority:
- Set aside some quiet time in your busy schedule every day.
- Take longer quiet time on weekends.
- Make sure you will not be disturbed.

Think of it like getting to know a close friend.

Sometimes it's great to spend time alone with just that one friend. It helps us get to really know and appreciate them. This time the friend is you.

Personal enjoyment time

Personal enjoyment time is essential. It gives our brain hope. It tells it we can have our needs met too, we don't always have to sacrifice of ourselves and miss out. We all need to do things we personally enjoy, and we need to do them regularly.

One of the quickest ways to lower our Personal Self is to take away what we personally enjoy. Don't let ourselves enjoy what we like for long enough and we won't know what we like anymore. Then we most definitely have a low Personal Self.

I remember a young mother once telling me she was so busy at home with the children she forgot what it was like to have fun. 'What's that?', she asked. She was seeing me for counseling regarding depression. She became more and more depressed as she found she had less and less time to do what she personally enjoyed. Her depression improved once she gave herself permission to enjoy life.

Making personal enjoyment time doesn't mean we should always put our needs above everyone else's. That doesn't work either; our family, our friends, and the community still need us. What it does mean is not putting ourselves last. Worse still, not making ourselves a priority at all. So to increase your Personal Self using enjoyment time try the following:

- Do things you like, just for you, every day. It doesn't have to be big, just a nice quiet warm bath can be good. It could be a walk, or run, or gardening. Do what YOU enjoy!
- Explore things to enjoy. The more you like the more you get to know yourself.
- Plan enjoyment time, for the morning, the afternoon, or the week.
- Make time for others too so you don't feel guilty and sacrifice all your other needs for Personal Self needs. Life needs a balance of our needs (see Balance of Self Model).

Personal enjoyment time is the key to unlocking Personal Self. If we have lost our sense of self, personal enjoyment time can help us find it again. If we never had our own sense of self it can help us find it.

Personal enjoyment time is not selfish. It's a human necessity.

People who can genuinely enjoy themselves also become genuinely more attractive. Don't you like to be around people who know how to have fun?

Chapter 19:
Increase contact with Land

If you want a powerful and effective way to increase and maintain a strong Personal Self you need look no further than using Land.

Land, you will recall from the Balance of Self Model, is everything that is not human. Nature can be a great resource but also a wonderful guide to being true to our inner nature. It can be a potent force to increase Personal Self.

As previously mentioned using Land as a way to increase a sense of self is not new. Traditional tribal cultures have used it – and many may use it still – to help guide them and give them a strong sense of self. The key to using Land to increase Personal Self is to connect with it personally, like the Aboriginal Australians did. That doesn't necessarily mean a walkabout so the Land can truly teach you your place, but it can mean just spending more time away from other people and being in contact with part of the natural world.

How does increasing our contact with Land increase our Personal Self?

The more time we spend with Land on our own the more we are away from the influence of others. That means the powerful urge to be like others and think like others – due to Community Self desires – is much less. You can be a completely different person when you're on your own in the natural world. Others aren't telling you what to do, what to say, or what's important. It gives you a rest from the pressures of a hectic life.

Nature helps you see who you are when others aren't around.

Who are you when others don't affect your life? Who does nature think you are? How does it treat you? Does it treat you differently if you are rich or poor? Do the trees or ants care if you're a man or a woman? Do the hills and streams stand in judgement of you? Do they think you are any more or less than any other human? They don't, do they?

We are so much more than each other's friends, family, workers, mothers, and fathers. If we are always with other people we can lose sight of this. We can lose perspective of our place among all things and what it is to be a human in the natural world and universe. We can lose our sense of self.

We will discuss ways of connecting with nature on a deeply personal level more in Step 7 as we increase our spirituality. For now just spending any time in contact with the Land can be highly beneficial.

It is beyond the scope of this book to explore all the ways you can use Land to help increase your Personal Self. Following are a few suggestions:

- Go bushwalking.
- Spend time sitting under a tree.
- Be in the natural world and feel it, sense what's there, notice the friendship and connection.
- Help restore damaged creeks and waterways.
- Grow a garden, keep herbs, sculpt a bonsai tree – keep nature close to you.
- Sit listening to birds and watching the sky.
- Spend time near natural water such as creeks, lakes, and the sea.

To use the Land to increase Personal Self we ideally want to spend more time with what isn't manmade – such as being away from buildings, technology, and the like. Manmade objects bring us back under the influence of others; the people who made them have left their mark and we notice that. If people made a building for example, we respond to the vibe or impression of the building, the ideas and influence of the people who made it.

The less contact we have with manmade objects the less other people influence us and we can find a clearer connection with who we are when no one's around.

So go out walking in nature. Go a short way on your own, but make sure others know where you are. Walking in nature by yourself can be dangerous, and we don't want to get into danger.

There is another way we can use Land to increase Personal Self no matter where we live. By using culture.

Use culture

Culture; what we eat, wear, the songs we sing, the art, the sculpture, the pots and utensils we use, all reflect the land they come from. If we are on a Pacific island for example, our food, stories, painting, and utensils will be different to if we lived in a desert. On an island we probably wouldn't make pots, just baskets. We would eat fish rather than goat or camel. We would tell stories of fishing rather than of long journeys to find water. We would paint pictures of fish and nets on an island, whereas we would paint pictures on rocks and caves of animals we hunt if we lived in a forest or desert. The land affects how we express our humanity. We know this expression as culture.

Culture can be personal and used to increase Personal Self.

Any time you write, create a story, paint, sculpt, cook, sing, or dance just for you, just as an expression of what you feel inside, you are creating your own personal culture. This is a reflection of what you feel and your interaction with your environment; your Land. As you touch these inner feelings that inspire you, which don't come from the influence of others, then you increase your Personal Self.

So write stories from your heart, poems that touch you, songs that are just for you. Paint from the depths of your soul as if no one will ever see it. Dance as if dancing to feel the world. Cook to express the inner you. Express your Inner Self in your personal culture regularly and your Personal Self will rise like never before.

The aim here is simple: express yourself in the physical world, but not to impress or influence others.

Many of us want to not feel so pressured by those around us. Once you achieve this by developing that personal identity and connection with the Land others will be far more attracted to you; like the spirit of the land radiates from you. Many will want to know your secret.

Chapter 20:
Take back choices

Every choice connects you emotionally to the world. It helps motivate you to have your desires met. It tells your brain to believe in hope and promise. Without a sense of choice we give up on being who we can be and become less of ourselves. Every choice we give away lessens our sense of self.

When we take away choice we are telling our brain nothing we do will make a difference. You might like the salmon and goats cheese sandwich but if I take away your choice that's too bad.

As we have seen our brain works on creating plans for the future. It's always dreaming and the plans and dreams it comes up with determine how we feel. If they are promising – such as having that gourmet sandwich – we feel great. If they aren't promising – we are going to be overworked all day for instance – they can make us feel truly miserable. But our brain isn't stupid, it knows better than to create plans that make no difference. Why make a plan it can never put in place and actually get to work? Take away choice and we are telling our brain that the promise and hopes it has for the future are irrelevant. If the plan is irrelevant or useless then so are the feelings that go with it. Why have feelings such as hope that will motivate us to do what will feel great if there's no chance of change and therefore motivation? Why feel great about having the sandwich if there's only horrible dry bread on offer?

The more choices we give away or decide not to make the more we emotionally detach from the world.

Why feel the great promise if nothing we do will make a difference? Why build up our hopes? Why build the hope of having a caring partner if you can do nothing about it? Every choice we decide not to make dashes potential hopes, feelings, emotions and experiences against the rocks. Take away enough choices and we can lose all emotional connection to other people and the world. We can lose our self.

To have a strong Personal Self is to have a strong sense of choice. It's about having our individual needs met. We can't do that if we don't have hope; if we don't feel anything will make a difference.

To increase and maintain a strong Personal Self we must claim our choices and take them back. We must not give them away lightly, if at all.

Suggestions to increase choice

- **Don't give away your choices.** Don't let others make decisions for you. Make as many as you can that affect your life. You choose how you live.
- **Own your choices.** Take responsibility for them. You make an important difference with every choice you make. They affect everyone and the world. You are more powerful than you think.
- **Recognize your choices.** If you feel trapped make a list of five options. If you can't find five you're not looking at the more difficult choices that can actually see you out of your problem. Choices always exist; some may be very hard choices but they are choices none-the-less.
- **Notice four choices you make in your day.** Write them down so you can recognize them and see that you do actually make many choices. Such as how you care for your hair, how you dress, what you eat and when. You make thousands of choices in a day – notice them.
- **Act on your choices.** Don't just think you have choices, show your brain you do by following through. Choose to do it, and then do it!

Make those who represent you accountable, get actively involved in the choices they make that affect your life. Don't let them make any more choices for you than is necessary. Take specialists' advice; let them share their experience, but always – wherever you can – make the choices yourself.

The same applies to the home and relationships. Wherever possible don't let others make choices for you. If you are a couple, make decisions together.

The more you let him make decisions for you the more you lower your Personal Self and become less attractive to him. And vice versa!

Recognize your choices in life. Make it a choice that you pick up the children, don't make it something you have to do. Make your life a choice. Choose and you increase and maintain a strong Personal Self.

Exercise

Ask yourself: 'Would I still do it if it was optional?' Would you still care for your kids, if you didn't have to? Would you still work? Search for the benefits in what you do; this will help you see it as a good choice. Once you see it this way it feels like a choice.

Choices are precious; more so than an arm or a leg. They make you whole; an individual self and they're critical to increasing and maintaining your Personal Self.

Chapter 21:
Increase self-worth and self-respect

Self-worth and self-respect are at the core of a strong Personal Self; we are more likely to look after our individual needs if we respect and value ourselves. A large part of our self-worth and self-respect comes from how we are treated by our family and community. If they value and respect us we are more likely to value and respect ourselves. Even if our family and/or society don't value us we can still increase self-worth and self-respect in several ways.

Increase self-worth

There are three simple ways to increase our self-worth:
- be deserving
- don't put yourself last
- learn to say no.

Be deserving

We all deserve to be happy and live lastingly fulfilling lives. But others can make us feel we have to earn it. Chris, the father whose teenage children left him, was a classic case in point (see page 146).

When I was trying to help Chris out of his depression I noticed every time he started to feel happy he would sabotage it; he'd stop doing the exercises to increase Personal Self that were working for him, such as making sure he had enjoyment time. Over many weeks of this continuing we explored his past. He grew up being told by his father he had to earn being happy, he had to suffer to succeed. He told me he felt he was a failure in life, and as a father. He said that his father would be disappointed with him. He truly believed he wasn't worthy of happiness; he actually told me this.

If you feel undeserving of happiness you have been taught it.

Many of us are still taught we have to earn our happiness, it has to be our reward for suffering, and if we don't suffer we shouldn't be happy. It sounds absurd, and it is. However, this one simple belief can make our self-worth plummet and stay low. If you want to raise your self-worth you need to change that belief about yourself. You may need to see a therapist but below are some suggestions.

How to feel more deserving

- Do things that make you feel valuable to your family and community. Get active, help others to help themselves.
- Treat others as worthwhile and valuable so you feel more deserving of feeling it too.
- Be with close friends who know you deserve to live a fulfilling life.
- Set standards for yourself; maintain your integrity so you never doubt you are deserving and worthwhile.
- Get to know who you are in the natural world – see increasing contact with land. The land does not judge whether you deserve happiness or not, it already knows you deserve it; it needs you to be happy so you can play your part as a human being. You are happy when you do what nature asks of you.
- Always remember you are as deserving of happiness as much as any human or creature on the planet. Don't let anyone tell you otherwise.

Treat us as if we all deserve to be satisfied human beings, living in a balanced, sustainable, and respectful way with each other and we are all more likely to live that way. We must begin to realize we all deserve to be happy – we all should strive to have a strong Personal Self no matter who we are or what we have done, and whether we think what we have done deserves punishment or not. If we don't then fewer and fewer of us will be living truly satisfying lives. And fewer of us will respect each other.

Don't put yourself last

Low self-worth is putting our needs last so our individual needs aren't met. We can counter this with practical steps:
- Keep a diary or daily planner. Put aside time for your needs – such as self time, quiet time, and enjoyment time – in the planner, then make sure you take the time to satisfy them.
- Don't let others convince you your needs are not worthwhile. Stick to your plan unless there's an emergency.
- Make a time to help others that better suits you; don't just work to someone else's timetable by ignoring your own plans – unless it's an emergency. That way you get to do what you need to do too.
- Never, ever, tell yourself you aren't worth it, or 'why bother, it's only for me'.
- Don't earn feeling good deep in your heart; just do what works to make it happen!
- If you still have doubts write it in your mirror or refrigerator, 'I am worthwhile, I deserve to be happy!' Repeat it a thousand times if you need to!

If you are a parent you will almost always put yourself last; it goes with the job. The first person's needs you sacrifice are your own. The second person's needs you sacrifice are your partner's. The last person's needs to be sacrificed are the children's. If it weren't this way our kids wouldn't survive. But if you always put yourself last how will you ever feel satisfied and fulfilled? The key is to create the right balance. Always putting you on the bottom of the list isn't the right balance.

I offer a table of how you can balance your needs as a parent in Appendix 1. It is from an earlier book *A Balance of Self*, published in 2011. We can all have our needs met even in a busy family, if we make the time and make it a priority.

Learn to say no

If you are someone who can't say no to other people's requests for help, even at the expense of yourself, then you need to learn the magic word: 'No.'

Children begin to say it when they are around two years old. It allows them to see how much control they have in the world as a person. Saying no can be a powerful way to increase your individuality too.

Saying no enables balance in our lives by allowing us to have our needs met as well as helping us meet the needs of everyone else.

We have to be careful how often we say no though. If we always say no then others won't be there for us either.

If you have trouble saying no, try the following:
- Don't automatically say yes. Say you'll get back to them. Then check carefully and realistically if it's something you can do.
- If you can't say no say 'I really would like to help but I can't right now.'
- Agree that what they want sounds important, and politely refuse.
- 'No' is not a dirty word. Your needs are as worthwhile as anyone else's.

Increase self-respect

We have already discussed ways to increase respect among men and women. We can add to these to raise our self-respect in simple ways:
- Take care of your health and wellbeing to the best of your ability. Never do anything that will deliberately harm your health such as smoking, abusing alcohol, or using recreational drugs. Eat well, exercise, care for yourself as if your body was sacred.
- Never harm yourself physically in any way for anyone.
- Never abuse yourself.
- Never punish yourself, no matter the reason.
- Never put yourself down.
- Respect others at all times.

If you are obese, don't exercise, don't take your medications, smoke, drink excessively, take recreational drugs, party for long hours, work excessively, or even drink too much coffee, we can guarantee you have a low Personal Self. Obesity is becoming an epidemic in our western world, in the USA and UK alone over two-thirds of the population is overweight or obese and the levels are rising. If we truly respected ourselves would we let this unhealthy behavior continue? With obesity on the rise what does that say about the levels of Personal Self in our society?

The more we show ourselves respect the more others will treat us with the respect we deserve; the higher our level of self-respect will rise.

The higher our self-respect the more our Personal Self rises. To show that you truly respect yourself you should take proper care of yourself, as you know you should. If you can't do this then it suggests someone at some time taught you that you weren't worthwhile or weren't worthy of respect. If you can't change that belief then you will struggle to respect yourself. If you can't do it on your own then I recommend you seek professional help.

Sometimes women ask why they are attracted to the so-called bad-boys, the guys who don't respect themselves, and who don't respect their partners. The bad-boys can seem attractive for many reasons. For one thing, they have many authentic man features; they appear confident, don't care what others think, have some leadership qualities. On the other hand, they also validate low self-worth and low self-respect in women.

If the bad-boys don't respect themselves they validate that you don't have to respect yourself either. If you feel you deserve to be treated badly they will also validate it; treating you badly. You will feel uncomfortable and as if something isn't right if someone is actually nice and always respectful to you.

You choose your partner according to what you believe about yourself.

That's why many women keep getting into abusive relationships; they find the men who can validate their low self-worth and low self-image.

As a general rule women who respect themselves aren't attracted to men who don't respect themselves. Same goes for men who respect themselves; they aren't attracted to women who have no self-respect.

If you want to increase and maintain a strong Personal Self you need to make sure you have a strong sense of self-worth and self-respect. Increase yours and you ensure it is raised in your daughter too – she will learn from your example. Then she too will avoid being attracted to a man who will abuse her. You will increase your chances and her chances of living a satisfying life. The same goes for women in your social circle and your community.

Chapter 22:
Treat yourself as a best friend

Dee was a divorced single mother living with her fifteen-year-old son. She had been working as a secretary and came in one day telling me she felt quite depressed. Dee was great at negative self-talk. Over many consultations she would put herself down telling me how she should be tougher and stronger. She even cussed herself in front of me; she really gave herself a hard time. She agreed to do four things a day a best friend might do for herself. For instance, if she needed a break she would take it. If she needed a coffee as a treat or to clear her head, she would take one. If a best friend might recommend she have a nice therapeutic massage, foot massage, or facial, she would have them. Often a best friend would want us to treat ourselves well. She agreed to try to do this for a week. It started ok, and then as stresses in her life increased she started to be hard on herself again.

Would we abuse a best friend as we abuse ourselves?

If we did they wouldn't be our friends any more, not if they had any self-respect. So why are we so quick to abuse ourselves?

One thing we can say with reasonable certainty is we weren't born to abuse ourselves; that would reduce our chance of survival. It's hard enough to survive without each of us being our own mortal enemy. That means if we are abusive to ourselves it is because we are taught.

So who taught us? We learn from role models as we grow up. We also learn from those around us in our community.

If you are hard on yourself then a parent or someone close to you as you grew up was probably also highly critical of themselves. They then became critical of you, perhaps nothing was ever good enough, or you could never get it right. This criticism then became part of your image of yourself. Who am I? I am the person who can never get it right, I am the one who isn't smart enough, isn't strong enough, I'm just not good enough! Once you believe it then you treat yourself this way. You will get upset with yourself every time you make even the slightest mistake. You will treat yourself as your parents treated you.

Unfortunately this self-abuse can go on for generations. We can teach it to our children without even being aware of it. We are critical of our children because we are still critical of ourselves. We expect more of them just as we have been taught to expect more from ourselves. Soon they also develop critical self-talk and self-abuse and no longer talk or treat themselves as a good friends but as a person who is never good enough.

The same rule applies to how others treat us in the community.

As we have seen the influence of community in our lives is very powerful thanks to the desires of Community Self. If others are highly critical or unforgiving of us they will teach us to be the same.

We live in critical societies that seem to expect us to be perfect and never make mistakes. Everyone wants it done right first time. It is part of the competitive society we choose to live in. So if others are critical of us we will expect it even when they are not there, much like Dee did. Even when there was no one to criticize her she was so used to being criticized and so scared of making a mistake her mind treated her as she was used to and spoke to her in a very critical way.

How do we fix this so we treat ourselves as friends rather than inadequate children or imperfect members of a community?

The ideal cure is to live in a caring and supportive family and community, where a strong Personal Self is valued and encouraged, and friendships are truly valued. Since many of us don't, what is the next alternative?

Learn to be our own best friend.

If others won't treat us with the respect we deserve and be kind to us, or don't have our interests at heart, then we have to take up that challenge, be bigger than them, and do it ourselves.

We might not be kind to ourselves. We might not even care for ourselves very much. But we would be kind to a best friend; we would often support and care for them. Since the desires of Community Self – our social desires – are more powerful than our desires of Personal Self we can fool the brain into treating us well by making us our own best friend. We can use how we would treat a best friend as our standard for how we treat ourselves.

The following are suggestions of how to treat yourself as a best friend. The idea is to do it regularly, make it a habit.

Exercise: How to be your own best friend

- If you wouldn't do it to a best friend don't do it to yourself.
- If your best friends wouldn't let themselves be treated that way then don't treat yourself that way.
- If in doubt, ask the best friend inside you. What would your best friend recommend if they were in the same situation?
- A best friend would compliment you and pat you on the back for a job well done. Do the same. If you achieved something hard, or that you have strived for, acknowledge it, as a best friend would.
- Set a task of doing three things a day a best friend would recommend. If that's a tea break, a therapeutic massage or a facial, have one. If you need more time in your day just to gather your thoughts do it.

The way to gauge how you should talk to yourself, treat yourself, and enjoy yourself is to use the idea of a best friend as your guide.

If you don't have a best friend, imagine you did. Imagine they really like you and care for you. How would they treat you right now? What would they say to you to support you? What would your best friend say if you did something wrong? How would a best friend make your day better? Your inner best friend wants to support you, so let them.

Make being your best friend your homework for three days every week. Better still do it every day for a month. Keep doing it until it becomes a habit. As you become a better friend to yourself you will also be a better friend to others and more people will want to be around you. You will become more attractive to others. Be your own close and best friend and you will make sure your individual needs are met by having a strong Personal Self.

Chapter 23:
Increase Personal Self in children

There's no better time to instill the basics of a strong Personal Self than when girls are young. This not only provides many benefits for them, but also for us, and for our society. As we become their example our own Personal Self rises.

Teach a child how to increase their Personal Self and they can find it easier to maintain this lesson as adults. The more children we have taught how to increase their Personal Self the more people we will have in society who respect themselves and each other. Children who grow up learning to have and maintain a strong Personal Self will find it easier to be attractive, stay attractive, and have and maintain lasting and fulfilling relationships. They will be more likely to find a life balance so that their family is more stable and their own children will live more satisfying lives. They will also be true to themselves as they prioritize their inner desires over the expectations of others.

Exercise: How to increase Personal Self in children

- Teach them early that it is ok to just sit quietly. Show them. Lead by example as you introduce them to quiet time.
- When they are around six or seven years old teach them to meditate to help them create a quiet mind. Simple mindfulness techniques like those in Step 3 will do.
- Teach them it is ok to have fun time – self-enjoyment time – and work or study time as well; they can do both. Work or study without fun time, will reduce their Personal Self.
- Take them walking in nature, a park, forest, nature reserve and teach them to feel and connect with the natural world.

- Encourage them to express themselves in art, music, dance, and writing.
- Teach them to grow their own garden and how to care for it.
- Give them choices when you can, don't always dictate to them, especially when they are adolescents.
- Show them how to treat their body with respect and care for it as if it is sacred. Be the example; treat your own body as a sacred vessel.
- Give them tasks to do that make them feel valued. Give them genuine praise.
- Teach them the basics of friendship and how to be friends with themselves and each other. See Step 2.
- Ask them regularly for their opinion and listen to them without judgement.

The strongest way to increase Personal Self in children is by example, by creating it in ourselves.

Children do what we do, no matter what we say. If you want your daughter, son, niece, or nephew, to have a strong Personal Self, show them. As you raise your Personal Self as an example to your children you will – of course – raise it in yourself as well.

Mindfulness and meditation can be taught from a very young age. I know of a GP colleague – a mother – whose family does meditation together, often in the mornings. She found it improved their mood, their attitude at home and at school, and their concentration. It is also a great way to help reduce anxiety. Some teachers are now teaching and practicing mindfulness techniques in class and also finding impressive results.

It's also important to show children how to balance work and play. If they have to focus on work the whole time – making study and marks their greatest priority –they will lose a sense of themselves. Seeing themselves as a worker or studier above all things can make it hard to maintain a strong Personal Self in adulthood.

Creative play is great for children on many levels. It allows them to express what they think and feel. It naturally increases Personal Self. Creativity helps them connect with their feelings and express them. Just playing computer games or simulations is more about following someone else's rules not listening to what you feel and expressing it. These games might help with co-ordination but they won't enhance or increase Personal Self. Try to stick with games and activities that require imagination and creativity, away from computers.

Teach them to be friends with themselves and you are also teaching them to be social with other children. Friendly people become popular; they are attractive to other people. If you want your child to have a lasting close relationship later in life then it begins by learning about friendship when they're young.

Never underestimate the influence of being in nature. As a young boy I had the privilege of being in forests and bushland regularly. Nature holds deep and warm memories; it helped me in troubled times, and still does today.

Teach your child to enjoy nature and it can help guide them for the rest of their lives.

Try to give your children three choices rather than telling them what to do, one being the best option and the one you want them to follow. By creating choices and consequences and letting them choose you go a long way to helping them develop a sense of choice, control and individuality.

Children are the hope for the future. The more we can help them to be authentic early the happier and more satisfying their lives can be. When they also learn there is more to attraction then as they grow up they too will look deeper into the hearts of each other and search for those with a stronger authentic self. The more we demand of each other to be authentic the more we can spread greater balance and harmony – natural qualities that emerge when we are living true to ourselves.

Being and remaining attractive plays a critical role in being authentic and creating stable and fulfilling relationships. Sex is a vital part of being human too. The choices we make regarding sex can have profound consequences in our lives. Not only will it determine if we have lasting and satisfying relationships, it will also define the levels of the Essence of Woman in you and in society. Part of being true to yourself is to learn how to make wise choices about sex so the Spirit of Woman inside you will rise. It means learning to be sex-wise.

Step 5: Be sex-wise

Concerning fidelity, human frailty must be taken into consideration, but the Indian woman was a true wife and the Indian man a true husband. The vows on both sides were taken seriously and both man and woman looked upon their marriage contract as something extremely vital to their position in the tribe. The integrity of the home was revered, and a man known as a good husband and woman known as a good wife were honored members of society. Polygamy was never extensively practiced among the Lakotas, comparatively few men-chiefs or men of special note – taking more than one wife. But this arrangement was not assigned to divine instruction nor given a religious hue: it was wholly and solely an adjustment with the social plans of the tribe. A chief would have considered it much more dishonorable to have one overworked wife than to have two or three to share the duties of his household, and the women were of the same opinion. But fidelity was another Indian virtue to become weakened by the disruption of his society, for white man was wont to take the things that pleased him.

Luther Standing Bear, Oglala Lakota[10]

Let's be honest, sex can be confusing. Having sex too early in a relationship can ruin it. Having sex too freely – depending on the society you keep – might give you a reputation and wreck your chances of finding a long-term partner. Not having sex when your partner needs it can strain or even break a promising relationship. It's often hard to know what choices to make when it comes to sex, but these choices are very important. They can leave us feeling satisfied and lastingly happy, or miserable and lonely, and anything in between. How you choose to have sex can also either raise your Essence of Woman or lower it.

How can we see past the confusion?

One way is to see sex in terms of the desires we use sex to fulfill.

As we are about to see sex does far more for us as human beings than just make babies. We use it to satisfy many basic human desires. Understand what these desires are and our choices become clearer. The consequences of our sexual choices will make more sense.

In the following chapters you can examine what basic human needs and desires you are using sex to satisfy. One type of sex for instance can lead to us having lasting and satisfying relationships and stable families. Another type can do the opposite. Don't know what type of sex to have and we can get hurt, even devastated, and ensure our relationships are sure to fail.

Sex should leave us feeling satisfied; ideally feeling more complete.

Unfortunately, sex can easily leave us feeling far less satisfied than we would like. Mostly this happens due to sexual desire mismatches; between the type of sex we are having and the outcomes we want. Sex seems hollow and isn't satisfying your desires? Chances are you are suffering from one or more of the types of sexual desire mismatch. Practical recommendations follow.

The aim here is simple: to give us the best chance of creating stable and lastingly satisfying relationships.

It is not for me to tell you – or anyone else – what type of sex you should or shouldn't have, how often, and with whom. That's your choice. Hopefully after considering this approach to how we view sex, it will be a wiser choice, and one that will help you feel more complete as an empowered authentic woman.

Chapter 24:
Sex and basic human needs

What basic human needs or desires can we use sex to satisfy?

At some point human beings didn't just use sex to make babies any more, sex took on many other roles. We weren't the only primates to use sex for more than just procreation, consider one of our close primate cousins: the bonobo chimpanzees.

In the Southern Congo of remote Africa lives a small black group of primates called the bonobo chimpanzee. A slightly smaller cousin of the chimpanzees we often see in movies or on TV these mostly peaceful creatures live in a matriarchal society; their leader and most dominant member is a female. Food is plentiful and threats rare so the strength of males to protect the group doesn't tend to come into play. The bonobo society is a freely sexually expressive society.

When the bonobos find new food and are happy and excited they all have sex. If there are tensions and disagreements in the group, they all have sex. Yes, all of them have sex; age and gender are not boundaries. Males may have genital rubbing with other males. Females can have genital stimulation with other females. Adults with infants, all ages, all together, with one apparent exception. The bonobo son cannot engage in sex with their mother; sexual contact can otherwise be with anybody. Once they have sex they all seem to settle. Clearly they are using sex for more than procreation. For the bonobos sex also has a social function.

The bonobos have learnt to use sex to help them fulfill what we can now recognize as Community Self needs – it helps them bond, and feel safe and secure among each other in the group. We too have evolved to use sex to fulfill social desires. We have also evolved to use it for many of our Personal Self and Family Self desires. In other words, we can use sex to satisfy desires of Personal Self, Family Self, or Community Self – all the desires of the Balance of Self (BOS) Model. Which of these desires we use sex to fulfill can have important consequences.

We can break sex into three sexual desire types:
- Self Sex (Personal-Self Sex)
- Social Sex (Community-Self Sex)
- Family-Positive Sex (Family-Self Sex)

As you can see each desire type reflects the three desire groups of the BOS Model. Each of these types of sex will meet Personal Self, Community Self, or Family Self desires respectively. As we are about to see not all of these sexual desire types will necessarily leave us feeling truly satisfied in a long-term and stable relationship.

What do the three basic sexual desire types represent?

Self Sex

Self Sex, as the name implies, is engaging in sexual activities with the sole intention of pleasure, but only for ourselves. You can have this sex either alone or with someone else you *use* to help satisfy you. Having Self Sex alone is usually in the form of masturbation and can have many benefits or uses from relieving stress, treating migraine headaches, to helping enhance a better understanding of your own sexual responses so you can teach your partner what works for you and share greater pleasure together. We can even have Self Sex because we are bored. Often sexual aids or toys can be involved. When we have Self Sex with someone else we are basically using someone else to replace the toy or toys. We are having sex with them just for our own physical pleasure; they are nothing more than a physical object for us.

Social Sex

Social Sex is engaging in sex for the main purpose of making friends and influencing people outside our relationship, such as to impress them, gain attention, and be noticed. We are using sex to fulfill the Ten Basic Desires of Friendship so we can feel better about ourselves among them. We can use sex for example to feel noticed by having sex with a celebrity or someone who is popular. We can have sex with people in power or influence so we can feel better about our own social status. We can have sex to feel supported by building alliances and social structure, for example, having sex with a colleague at work to climb the corporate ladder. It helps us feel more valued and important. They will be more likely to support us in our ambitions if we have sex with them. In simple terms Social Sex is every type of sex that isn't Self Sex or Family-Positive Sex, since inevitably if it isn't for self-pleasure or to build a stable relationship and family – what we use Family-Positive Sex primarily for – we are having sex for social reasons.

Social Sex is very common in our society. We can find examples all around us. We may have even used Social Sex ourselves.

For example, when you have sex with a guy with whom you don't want a serious relationship that is Social Sex. When a guy has sex with you merely to impress his mates, that is a clear example of Social Sex. When you have an affair with a work colleague but know they will never leave their wife, that is Social Sex. When you have sex with other women, the vast majority of the time that is Social Sex. When you pick a guy up at a bar and take him home to have sex, that is Social Sex. Of course, if you treat him as an object then it is Self Sex, or a mixture of the two.

Family-Positive Sex

Family-Positive Sex can arguably be the most important type of sex of the three. It's the closest we can have to an ideal use for sex if we want lasting and satisfying relationships. Family-Positive Sex is to have sex to fulfill your Family Self desires, including your authentic desires as a woman or man. These desires enhance and build a strong bond so we can have a stable relationship and family. Family-Positive Sex is about having sex with someone with whom we are working towards developing and maintaining a close friendship.

It isn't Family-Positive Sex unless working towards, or maintaining, a close friendship is involved.

Family-Positive Sex helps satisfy the Ten Basic Desires of Friendship. For example, we make the other person feel valued by making time to enjoy sex together, especially if they desire it. We feel more valued when someone makes the time. We help our partner feel noticed by not ignoring their gestures that they want sexual intimacy. We help them feel heard by listening to what pleases them. We help them feel validated and respected by giving them the sexual pleasures they desire. Every one of the Ten Basic Desires can be applied to sex to help us build a closer friendship and bond.

Ideally if we are having Family-Positive Sex together we're working to maintain the needs of a close friendship and each other's authentic needs. He is being the man you need him to be sexually. You are being the woman he sexually needs. If we continue to increasingly satisfy each other's needs we are more likely to want to stay. We will build strong, stable, and mutually satisfying relationships that meet our emotional and physical needs.

Can we have sex that meets more than one desire type? Sure we can.

For example, women have been shown to be more attracted to men who other women find attractive. To have sex with such a man can help you meet Community Self desires – to help you feel like you fit in, that you aren't too different to other women – desires of sameness. At the same time, you might be so attracted and get on so well with him you want him to be the father of your children – to satisfy Family Self desires. In this case when you have sex with him you are not only meeting Social Sex desires but also fulfilling Family-Positive Sex desires.

To keep it simple it is easier to simply think of what we are mostly using sex for. Are we using it primarily as Self Sex, Social Sex, or Family-Positive Sex?

Most of the time it can seem obvious what type of sex we are having. Sometimes it isn't. How can we tell what desires we are using sex to satisfy?

One of the ways to know is by examining your intent, and what dreams you are using sex to fulfill.

It can be hard to know what drives two people to have sex. Using someone for Self Sex can look the same as Social Sex, some Social Sex can look the same as Family-Positive Sex, and so on. It isn't the physical act of sex and how we have it that defines it as Self, Social, or Family-Positive Sex, it is the intention behind it, and the dreams we are trying to validate or satisfy.

For example, do you use sex to build a lasting relationship, to fulfill a dream of being together for a long time and possibly having a family together? Then for you it is Family-Positive Sex. Do you intend to have sex as exercise, like stress relief? That is Self Sex. Do you intend to have sex as a path to corporate success, a promotion, or to feel more valued or desirable as a woman? Then it is Social Sex. What heart's desires are you intending to satisfy? That determines your sexual desire type.

Of course your partner can be having sex to satisfy any one of the three types of desires with you too. Just because you are having Family-Positive Sex with him doesn't mean he will be having the same with you. He could be using you for Social Sex, to feel better about himself, or to impress his mates. He could even be using you for Self Sex, as if you are a sexual toy. And this is one of the major hurdles we can run into when it comes to sex: the potential for a sexual desire mismatch.

Whenever we have sex with someone else there's always the potential for a sexual desire mismatch. The desires we seek to have satisfied may not be mutual, leaving either one or both of us deeply dissatisfied with the sex and even our relationship. One of the main reasons I was compelled to write this book was because sexual desire mismatch seems so common. An obvious reason will be explained shortly.

So what exactly is sexual desire mismatch, and how can we overcome it to avoid or prevent sexual dissatisfaction and disappointment?

Chapter 25:
Sexual desire mismatch

Anita was out every weekend wearing designer clothes, her hair just right (she had spent hours perfecting). Her perfume was exclusive and her shoes were especially chosen to match the designer handbag. She was dressed for attention, attractive and seductive. Anita was in her early thirties. She considered herself a fun-loving party girl.

Anita would have sex with at least one new guy every week. The wealthier he looked the more she was attracted to him. Even if he wasn't great looking, wealth made him especially appealing. This had gone on since she was at least fifteen years old, where she would fake her ID to get into nightclubs and bars. She had known – briefly – many men.

Relationships of more than a few weeks or months were rare indeed, yet her girlfriends would tell you the long-term fairy tale of a proper relationship weighed heavily on her mind. The problem was once she was in a relationship she became restless. Unless the man she was with garnered enough attention and praise from her friends, or she felt not enough men in general still noticed her, she started to get angry. The first person she would get angry with was her current love interest.

It had become a habit; party, take recreational drugs, have sex, have short relationships, and keep searching for Mr Right. She was getting tired of it all but what else could she do? Worse still many of her friends had babies and she wanted one too. Eventually she found a guy wealthy enough to get pregnant to him, she left him before their child was born and made him pay to look after both of them, as the law compelled him to do.

Last I saw her she was a mother, still single and unsatisfied with life, and still living for the weekends. Her habits were very well established.

Anita provides a clear example of sexual desire mismatch – she wanted to have a lasting satisfying relationship but was only ever engaging in Social Sex to try to achieve it. As a result she made it next to impossible to fulfill her dream of a satisfying family life. In our modern world it can be easy to find ourselves caught up in a sexual desire mismatch – just like Anita did.

◎

You want sex to lead to a long-term relationship; he wants it so he can boast to his mates. You want sex to build the closeness between you; he wants it for exercise and stress relief. You are having Social Sex but you crave a close relationship that never seems to happen. You want sex when he doesn't. These are just a few classic examples of sexual desire mismatch.

Sexual desire mismatch happens when we actually have sex. It is not when we can't find anyone to have it with. That is a sex deficiency, which we won't be discussing.

Sexual desire mismatch is having sex in a way that doesn't meet the desires we want it to satisfy. In other words we are having sex but it isn't making us feel the way we want or need it to. As a result it can leave us feeling anything from disappointed, to frustrated, or heartbroken. The three types of sexual desire mismatch are mismatch of:
- dreams and intentions
- dreams and actions
- strength of desire.

We can suffer from one, or all three. What do they mean?

Mismatch of dreams and intentions

Mismatch of dreams and intentions means the dreams and intentions of the two people having sex are very different.

A classic example of a mismatch of dreams and intentions is a person like Anita – dreaming and intending to meet a man she can build a life and family with – Mr Right. While the guy is dreaming of how his mates will be impressed that he scored with someone as classy as Anita. Another classical example would be you dreaming one night of hot Social Sex – while he's dreaming of a longer-term relationship and how great you would be as a couple with a family.

In a mismatch of dreams and intentions you are dreaming of satisfying one of the sexual desire types, such as the desires of Family-Positive Sex, and they are dreaming of satisfying the desires of one of the other types, such as Self Sex, or Social Sex.

Essentially one of you is having Family-Positive Sex and the other is having either Self Sex or Social Sex. You both want sex but with different long-term intentions. Mostly this isn't going to end well.

Imagine you are having Family-Positive Sex and he is having short-term Social Sex. From the beginning his intention is to have sex then be on his way. You on the other hand have the long-term in mind – a stable relationship and a life together. Every time you have sex together he validates your dream of your possible future together – it seems to be coming true.

Every time the sex validates your dream the more you become emotionally connected and caught up in your dream; more immersed in the hopes of the dream coming true.

Then when he inevitably breaks up with you, not surprisingly, you are totally heartbroken. The more your dream was validated by having sex with him the more heartbroken you will be. Suddenly every emotion of every desire and hope of your dream has been dropped from a tall cliff and smashed into little pieces. It can work the same way for him. If he has dreams of you both being together for a long time – dreams you don't share – the more sex you have with him the more you validate his dream and the more heartbroken he will be.

Often two people go into sex with different dreams and intentions.

Clearly the mix of short-term and long-term dreams will lead to someone getting hurt. The longer the breakup takes the more the person with long-term dreams will get hurt. Sex won't be satisfying once we realize it will no longer validate our dreams. We will explain more about why mismatch of dreams doesn't work, especially with regards to Social Sex, in the next chapter and then offer strategies to lessen the chances of anyone getting hurt as a result.

Mismatch of dreams and intentions is common. I have seen many women and men heartbroken and emotionally scarred as a result, many reluctant to try their 'luck' in relationships again; all because of this avoidable mismatch.

Mismatch of dreams and actions

Mismatch of dreams and actions means what you are doing – the type of sex, and how you go about it – isn't going to satisfy your dreams and intentions of why you are having sex in the first place. As a result, it will leave either you or your sex partner disappointed, or heartbroken, and ultimately unsatisfied by the sex.

Suppose you want to have Family-Positive Sex with a guy you are really attracted to, but you barely know him. Your dreams and desires for him are so strong you want to just take him home this minute! Will that impulsive action automatically provide you with a long-term fulfilling relationship?

Probably not.

When we have sex with a person without developing a friendship first we are behaving as if the sex is Social Sex – or even Self Sex – rather than Family-Positive Sex. In Social Sex and Self Sex we don't need to know the person to have sex with them. We are attracted to them and they are attracted to us, we don't need to have similar goals, dreams, or ambitions, you just have sex. We don't need to know if we are truly compatible and can be close friends. This is in contrast to Family-Positive Sex where we need to develop a close friendship and bond and be compatible. Developing a close bond of friendship and seeing if we are truly compatible takes time. It won't just happen in a few minutes, hours, or weeks. We can't expect a close friendship to happen just because we are having sex, no matter what we feel about them. Until we can be sure we can be close friends we are having Social Sex. Once we have that close bond and want to continue to be with each other then we can be sure it is truly Family-Positive Sex.

Anita was an example of someone suffering from a mismatch of dreams and actions. On many occasions she intended to have Family-Positive Sex, she wasn't just out to have a good time (Social Sex). Unfortunately instead of treating her best chance of a long-term relationship like Family-Positive Sex she treated it like Social Sex – the type of sex she was familiar with – and just hoped it would change into something more. It didn't. She never worked on developing a close friendship.

Treat a relationship like Social Sex from the start and that is what it is. Often that is what it will stay for reasons we will consider soon.

Having Social Sex but treating it a bit like Family-Positive Sex doesn't work very well either. If our intention was never to stick around why build a bond of friendship? All it will lead to is one or both of us getting hurt when we inevitably leave. If it isn't Family-Positive Sex there's no point in acting like it is by trying to be close or even casual friends. The longer the friendship lasts the more someone will get hurt when the Social Sex inevitably ends. We can miss the friendship.

When we don't act in a way that satisfies the desires we want to fulfill, we don't treat it like Family-Positive Sex or Social Sex from the start, we are creating a mismatch of dreams and actions that will almost inevitably hurt or disappoint us.

Mismatch of strength of desire

Mismatch of strength of desire means you want sex when they don't, or vice versa; your desires for sex are not similar enough so that you both want sex at the same time.

> **Mismatch of strength of desire is very common. None of us always want the same things at the same time.**

You aren't necessarily hungry or thirsty when I am, or anyone else for that matter. It is no different with sex; we don't all want sex at the same time. Yet if one of us has a strong desire and the other person doesn't meet it then someone will be left sexually frustrated and very unsatisfied.

Mismatch of strength of desire can happen no matter what type of sex we are having. For example, imagine bringing home a guy you think might be 'the one' and as you go to the bathroom you hear him snoring from your bed. He might be there for Social Sex and you might be after Family-Positive Sex but there won't be much of either if he's so tired or drunk he simply falls asleep. You can't expect to have sex if he doesn't have enough desire to stay awake and actually have sex with you.

Time of day can play a role in sexual desire mismatch. For instance, some of us prefer sex in the morning; some prefer it at night. If you like sex in the morning and your partner wants it at night then you have a clear strength of desire mismatch.

Making ourselves sexually aroused enough to want sex when our partner isn't aroused can also lead to a clear sexual strength of desire mismatch. For example, if you have just been watching a romantic or erotic movie, or reading an erotic novel but your partner has not, then you could want to have sex with them as soon as you see them, or right now! But they may not have had the same build up. They may not be as interested.

There can be many reasons and many different circumstances where we can want sex but our partner may not. The frustration of sexual desire mismatch can be just as annoying no matter the cause. At times it can be far more than just annoying or an inconvenience.

For instance, if our friendship is failing – we don't see each other, don't talk much, and we don't enjoy time together – when our partner rejects us it can mean more than just one person wanting sex when another doesn't. We can take their rejection personally; they are rejecting us, our friendship, and our needs, not to mention disrespecting our desires. It is easy for sexual desire mismatch to become far more than just an annoyance; it can be our prophecy that our relationship is going to fall apart.

Strength of desire mismatch will often test the strength of any sexual relationship.

If the relationship is based on more than just sex, and a close bond of friendship is there, then strength of desire mismatch can just be an annoyance, frustration, or inconvenience. If there's no close bond however, then the desire mismatch can be the last straw, or the beginning of the end.

How do you cope with strength of desire mismatch? Is it more than just frustrating, annoying, disappointing, or an inconvenience to you?

We will consider strategies to help deal with strength of desire mismatch shortly.

Why sexual desire mismatch?

Why come up with the idea of sexual desire mismatch in the first place? Because like it or not many men are only after Social Sex, while many women are after Family-Positive Sex. We often both want sex, but for very different reasons.

It will take too long to explain all the reasons many men can be drawn to having Social Sex rather than the lasting and more satisfying relationships of Family-Positive Sex. The bottom line and problem for women is that men don't need a close bond of friendship to be satisfied by sex. On the other hand, most women I have met and have spoken to do need that closer connection to feel the level of satisfaction with sex that they desire. That doesn't mean women can't have Social Sex too, many do during certain times in their lives. Some women are drawn to have sex primarily to satisfy social desires such as to feel noticed, respected, or to increase their status or power. But for the most part, just to generalize, more women seek Family-Positive Sex than men do. This leaves women open to being severely disappointed, fooled, and dejected in their attempted relations with men. See sex in terms of the desires it satisfies and what intentions and dreams we want met by them and we can lessen the chance of women being used, abused, misled, and heartbroken in their sexual experiences. We can help you see past the men who were never really interested in a long-term relationship with you. We can also help you see that if you engage in Social Sex you won't be able to have the satisfying stable relationship you are after, and can also lower your Essence of Woman in the process.

As we have already mentioned the desires you satisfy with sex are essentially up to you. If however you want to be more satisfied with sex then first you have to understand what you are using it for, and if what you're doing will work for you. If there's a mismatch between you and a partner you can avoid it early or overcome it altogether.

How do we do that? We begin by being honest with ourselves.

Chapter 26:
Overcome sexual desire mismatch

'You can't find a good woman these days, they all just want to have sex,' is a comment I often get from many different guys. Bill used to say this a lot, he would have sex with over a hundred women a year. I won't tell you the disrespectful names he called them. Yet he was often lonely.

Bill was always out to impress. He too was into partying; he lived for the weekends. Speak to him about women and he'd tell you he had standards. The women had to be gorgeous, or he had to be drunk enough to think they were gorgeous, before he'd even think of having sex with them. He wasn't great looking but trendy, confident, had a well-paid job, and was playful enough to have a sufficient number of women interested; he could have sex with a few different women per week. I remember him mentioning a young woman he picked up in a supermarket. He complained about certain sexual features she had. It was like he found her hot to look at but then wasn't as impressed. He was annoyed he couldn't find a good woman.

What was a 'good woman' for Bill?

A woman who didn't do recreational drugs – like he did – who would say no and not have sex at the drop of a hat with any guy she happened to like, and who could be supportive of him. He didn't think he was asking for much. He never considered he was being hypocritical. In his mid-forties Bill was once married, but that didn't last long. I once saw him try to have a longer-term relationship with a woman. Interestingly, she wasn't as attractive as the women he usually chose. I learnt later that although they lived together for many months he claimed he never had sex with her. He said he just couldn't do it, even if she was sleeping in the same bed and the lights were turned off; the thought gave him the shivers. He never did say why he started the relationship in the first place. It seemed like she offered him psychological support – he found someone who could listen. Once she finally left he was back to his weekend routines.

'What's wrong with women?' he'd ask.

His single male friends would often ask the same question.

Blaming others – like Bill and his friends were doing – doesn't work. If we want positive change we need to take an honest look at us first.

In a society having so much Social Sex it is easy to tell ourselves what we want to hear. Oh, he has had Social Sex with many women, but he is having Family-Positive Sex with me – he will be different with me, I love him. He must be having Family-Positive Sex with me; my feelings for him are so strong – this is the real thing! Social Sex is so common and our desire for a long-term relationship can be so strong that we can tell ourselves what we want to hear and see what we want to see. If we are to have any hope of overcoming or preventing sexual desire mismatch first we have to start by being honest and see the reality. Only then can we see the mismatch if there is one, and work towards something to prevent or correct it.

So let's begin by getting honest and looking for the truth of the desires we are seeking to satisfy with sex. Then work out if there is a mismatch and see what we might do about it.

Honestly, what type of sex is that?

As a general rule, if you are NOT having sex with the intention of having a long-term satisfying relationship **and close friendship** with him it is Social Sex, until proven otherwise. The sex he is having is also Social Sex until he becomes a close friend and is truly interested in a long-term relationship with you. It is not Family-Positive Sex just because you have strong feelings of sexual attraction to each other, or because it is what you need it to be.

Let's be clear. Every sexual encounter you have at a party, after a night out with a person you barely know, is Social Sex. If you are using sex to just feel that you are still attractive, it's Social Sex. If you're using sex to have fun or improve your career prospects, it's Social Sex.

If you *aren't* building or maintaining a long-term close relationship and close friendship with your partner it is Social Sex.

Similarly if he barely knows you he is having Social Sex. If he wants to have sex with you after just one or two dates he is having Social Sex. If he barely even talks to you it is Social Sex. Even if you really like him, even if he is nice to you, and even if he buys you expensive gifts, if he isn't taking the time to develop a close friendship it is Social Sex. It could be Self Sex, but most sex that isn't Family-Positive Sex is going to be Social Sex. If you have any doubts about what sex he is having with you then look to see if he can prove otherwise.

How can he prove it isn't just Social Sex?

By showing he wants to know and care for you in the long-term, and that he respects you and wants to see if you can be close friends. In other words by him being prepared to take the time to get to really know you before you have sex. If he can't do that then we can pretty much guarantee he's after Social Sex.

Don't be caught up in a romantic dream. Just because you want it – or need it – to be Family-Positive Sex doesn't mean he's having that with you.

Points to clarify

Let's take a moment to clarify.

You can have Social Sex even in a long-term relationship.

You can have Social Sex and be married.

For example, it isn't uncommon that a man seeking to achieve or maintain a level of status – meet his social needs – will find a good-looking wife to have by his side to have sex with. To marry and have sex with a good-looking partner is a mark of status and can meet many social needs. Yet that doesn't mean you can be close friends. Wealth, status, or power have nothing to do with if we can be close friends or not; they aren't the qualities we look for in friendship. Yet if we can't be close friends it will not be Family-Positive Sex; it'll be Social Sex. Social Sex can continue for a long time, at least until one or other of the couple can no longer meet their partner's social needs. For a woman her looks can fade. For a man his wealth, power, and status may be lost. When the foundation of the relationship crumbles the relationship is doomed to end. Just because you want to be in a long-term relationship with him, and even if you are married, that doesn't mean you're having Family-Positive Sex together.

Sadly, sometimes we won't know what type of sex we've been having until they leave us. Not until he finds a younger woman, or she finds a wealthier man, or vice versa, do we see that our friendship mustn't have been very close, and all they were having was Social Sex.

Social Sex can change into Family-Positive Sex with time, but it won't just miraculously happen.

The longer you are with a partner the more you can appreciate them and even like them, and perhaps a close friendship can grow. But Social Sex is unlikely to turn into Family-Positive Sex for two powerful reasons: sex is ultimately just a form of validation, it stabilizes the views we already have for the other person. Plus Social Sex can be highly addictive; a habit that can be very difficult to change.

Suppose we start off having Social Sex – being lovers, a liaison, but with no intention of a stable relationship – we see the other person as one who primarily meets many of our social needs, as our lover. Every time we have sex we validate this image of them and that image becomes more ingrained. We may develop a friendship with them but the back of our mind holds an image of them as our lover, and it's the image our brain most remembers. Every time we have sex this image arises and will be validated again. The more sex we have the more that image will become seared in our memory. It can take great time and effort developing a close friendship for that image to change, and even then it still might persist – we will still just see them as our lover. As you can imagine this social image can get in the way of us developing a close friendship and a closer and more lasting bond.

As we mentioned earlier sex validates our dreams. If we are dreaming they are 'the one' for example then this view is reinforced every time we have sex with them. Sex doesn't change our dreams, it simply reinforces them. So if we don't view our partner as a close friend before we have sex we simply validate that view every time we have sex with them. Sex can make our image of a person we are having sex with very persistent.

Social Sex can also be addictive. It can give us an emotional high, like a shot of a powerful drug. When we are feeling down, a hit of Social Sex can help us feel better. The reason is that Community Self desires – the desires we try to satisfy with Social Sex – are some of the strongest desires of all. We can feel some of our strongest emotional highs when we have Social Sex because they satisfy such strong desires. Often in life we can feel unhappy or unsatisfied and Social Sex can help us escape our emotional pains. If we are using it to help us feel better we won't be interested in close friendships, they risk causing us more emotional pain. It is so much easier just to have Social Sex and not get deeply involved. Use Social Sex enough times and it becomes a habit – like it was for Bill and Anita above. Keep the habit long enough and it can be hard to break. We can be so addicted to Social Sex and how it makes us feel we might not even know what a positive alternative may feel like any more. Addictions to Social Sex make it very hard to ever change any sex we have into Family-Positive Sex, or even start our relationships having Family-Positive Sex; Social Sex may be all we know.

So look at the sex you are having and be honest with yourself. Is it Social Sex or isn't it? Is it contributing to a stable relationship and close friendship or isn't it? Are you simply using the other person to feel better about yourself and don't really care about them? Then it isn't Family-Positive Sex. It doesn't matter how much you may like them. It doesn't matter if they say they like you, if you can't see them as a close friend it isn't going to be Family-Positive Sex. And don't expect Social Sex to miraculously morph into Family-Positive Sex; it doesn't work that way.

Four simple sex rules

1. If it starts as Social Sex expect it to stay that way.
2. If it is Family-Positive Sex and you don't maintain the close friendship then it will almost inevitably fall into Social Sex and the relationship will destabilize.
3. If it starts as Family-Positive Sex and you maintain the close friendship it can stay as Family-Positive Sex and help increase and maintain your close bond.
4. Don't expect Social Sex, your casual sexual encounters, to be anything more than just casual sexual encounters. They do not miraculously just change into long-term satisfying relationships.

If you are still uncertain what sex you are having ask your Inner Self, as described in Step 3. You will know in your heart why you really want sex. Your instinct will tell you what he wants it for too.

We now have a better idea of what type of sex we are having and can more clearly see what mismatch exists, if any. So what do we do about it?

Chapter 27:
Mismatch solutions

Have you identified a mismatch of dreams and intentions between you and your partner? Do you constantly mismatch dreams and actions? Or do you have differing strengths of desire? Here are some simple tips to avoid or prevent these problems, before heartbreak sets in.

Overcome and prevent dreams and intentions mismatches

- **Don't assume.** Never assume you know what the other person wants from you. Don't have Family-Positive Sex and assume he wants the same; you will get hurt.
- **Be clear and upfront.** If you want sex for purely social reasons make it clear before you have it. Inform him that is all it can ever be, don't fuel his hopes of something longer-term.
- **Don't expect Social Sex to build a lasting relationship.** If you want it to be Family-Positive Sex start it as Family-Positive Sex. Build the close friendship first.
- **It takes two to be close friends.** Make sure he is having Family-Positive Sex too. If you are unsure about his or your level of friendship ask your Inner Self; what does it tell you when you are calm and communicating with it? (See Step 3.) How about going out on a limb and asking him?
- **Know each other.** It isn't close friendship and true Family-Positive Sex for both of you until you really know each other. Expect it to take a minimum of months, perhaps years.

- **Go by his history.** If he's had many short or casual relationships he's in the habit of Social Sex. Don't expect him to just change or you will get disappointed, hurt, or both. One of the best predictors of future behavior is past behavior.
- **Time does not define the type of sex.** Just because you are married, or in a long-term relationship, doesn't automatically make it Family-Positive Sex. If you aren't working towards or maintaining a close friendship it is Social Sex. If you want it to be Family-Positive Sex, work on the friendship.
- **Give friendship time to develop.** It can take time to know if you can be close friends or if he's just trying to impress you to have Social Sex. If he is really attracted to you he will stay around and let the friendship build.

Social Sex can be an addiction, and a person can crave how it makes them feel. When he is stressed, or not feeling good about himself, don't be too surprised to see him return to his Social Sex addiction.

It's easy for us to get hurt in relationships. These days we come from such different backgrounds and have such varying ideas about our roles and expectations of each other. We increase our chance of being hurt by going in blind and not recognizing why each of us is using sex. Be aware that many men who want Social Sex are well trained and practiced at telling you what you want to hear. Search for what desires drive them, make them prove they truly desire to build a close bond of friendship with you before you emotionally bond even deeper with shared sexual intimacy and you lessen the number of heart-felt tears.

Overcome and prevent dreams and actions mismatches

- **Treat it like Social Sex from the start,** if that's what you want.
- **Treat it like Family-Positive Sex from the start,** if that's what you want.

- **Don't confuse the actions.** Don't treat it like Social Sex if you want Family-Positive Sex. Work on compatibility and developing a close friendship early.
- **Keep Social Sex simple.** Don't try to be close or deep casual friends if you don't want it to last. That is disrespectful of the other person's feelings – it will hurt them more when you leave them.
- **Let Family-Positive Sex grow.** If it is Family-Positive Sex give it time to grow, don't be impatient that it isn't yet what you want. Take your time. See if you are compatible and if certain deal breakers make it impossible to stay together in the long-term. Can you tolerate each other's families? You aren't just marrying him; you're marrying into his family.
- **Keep up maintenance.** Family-Positive Sex will fade into Social Sex or no sex at all if you don't put in the effort to stay close friends. (See Step 2.)
- **Take precautions.** If it is short-term Social Sex use protection so you don't get pregnant or get a sexually transmitted disease. Sex still makes babies, and people still get sick. Leaving a child without the support of a proper family is selfish; disrespectful of a child's needs for both parents and a community to support them. Children fair better if they grow up among parents meeting each other's friendship needs.

Overcome and prevent strength of desire mismatch

- **Make it a shared issue.** Never make it seem a lack of desire is their problem, or that there's something wrong with them that they want sex more or less than you. That can destroy the relationship. Make it a shared challenge you can work on together.
- **Negotiate.** Talk about it, work out the best compromise for you both; it is not just for one person to have to change.
- **Make sex fun.** Play more outside of sex to enhance your friendship then bring the play and fun to the sex too. We are more likely to want it if we enjoy it.

- **Give the gift.** They may really need it right now. We may really need it when they don't want it. If we both agree to not refuse and make it a gift, a gesture of giving towards our bond of friendship, then we leave our partner happy and meet their needs.
- **Create the interest.** If we know our partner may not want sex we entice them, we don't just expect it at the drop of a hat. Create anticipation for something you can both enjoy and you increase the pleasure of the moment. Some of the greatest pleasure we get is when our mind creates the fantasies ahead of time.
- **Never force the issue.** Forcing sex on your partner is never ok. Neither is making them feel guilty or punishing them if they don't give it to you. Accept their decision and go back to the previous suggestions.
- **If one of you has lost attraction for the other you need to talk about it.** What do you or your partner need to do to become more attractive? Go back to Step 5 and work on that, together. Do you need to be more of an authentic woman? Do you need him to be more of a 'Real Man'?

Sex in a relationship is not a right that must be met on demand. It is a gift to be shared, a privilege that is offered; part of a friendship that is grown.

What if one of you no longer wants any sex?

That is ok if you can both agree to it and still meet each other's relationship and friendship needs. I have met several couples who no longer have sex. In some of these relationships one partner wants sex but they have accepted the other does not, and because they value the relationship they live without it. These are usually couples with children, or those who have been together for decades. They have a sexual desire mismatch but they have learnt to accept and live with it quite well.

If one of you needs the sex and can't accept not having it, then you may have to consider if you want to still be in the relationship. For many of us not having sex with a partner is a deal-breaker. It is not something we are prepared to accept. Each of us has to decide for ourselves just how important sex is and what part it plays in our relationship.

If there is a medical problem, such as pain with sex, depression that lowers your libido, seek medical attention early before it creates an unnecessary strain on your sexual relations.

Never trivialize a sexual issue or difference, sex is important to many of us and deserves to be treated with respect.

As we have seen we can all have sex to satisfy many basic human desires. The key to feeling satisfied with sex is to make sure we are clear about the desires we want satisfied, and making sure we act in a way that will achieve it. We want to avoid sexual desire mismatch when we can, and preferably prevent it happening. That way you will be more empowered to choose the type of sex you want from them and they will be less able to fool you and break your heart. As a woman you can choose what sex will most satisfy you. You can also choose the type of sex that will most increase your Essence of Woman; the type of sex that empowers, not belittles. What type of sex most increases your Essence of Woman? You have probably already guessed. The answer is obvious.

Chapter 28:
Sex to raise the Essence of Woman

The type of sex that increases the Essence of Woman more than any other is fairly obvious: Family-Positive Sex.

Why is that? Family-Positive Sex meets more of your needs.

When you have sex with a man who is your close friend and who makes you feel safe and secure you are meeting many needs all with one man. Your physical desires, friendship needs, and your needs to be with an authentic man can all be fulfilled in one package. You are being true to the woman nature intended. That is not the case if you have Social Sex.

Social Sex can decrease your Essence of Woman.

How?

There are several ways.

Firstly, Social Sex will divert you away from the stable relationship that can make you more complete. If you are focusing on Social Sex, as we mentioned before, that can become your habit. Soon you may have no idea how to have a stable and satisfying relationship with a man, if you ever did. You can be trapped never feeling fully satisfied – like Anita described earlier.

Secondly, the more Social Sex you have with men the more you increase the number of men in our community who have Social Sex. Have Social Sex with a man wanting Social Sex and you validate it for him, and reward his behavior. This will ensure more men out there will not respect you as a woman. More men who use women as a way to feel better about themselves; a use and throw away item. Men don't respect women who have Social Sex. Yes, it's a double standard. But if women don't deny them Social Sex then men will continue to not respect them. This in itself will lower the Essence of Woman in the women they have sex with and in society in general.

Social Sex can also lower the Essence of Woman when women use it to satisfy male orientated needs, like wealth, power, and status. The more you have sex to meet such needs the more you lower your Essence of Woman and promote the qualities of a man within. If you are true to yourself you'll primarily be interested in caring, nurturing, and bonding deeply with a partner who can be there to fulfill your needs. Competing with men, having Social Sex like a man, or using sex to achieve the desires of a man to be the best provider and protector will not be high on your agenda.

It should be recognized there will be times in a woman's life when she may be driven to increase her wealth, power, and status, especially when she is young and establishing a career. If society only values you if you have wealth and status then many young women will be driven to achieve these aims. At times when power is more important than family, and wealth more important than friends, and where Social Sex is the preferred sex – Family-Positive Sex is not on the agenda. I have met many women who regret this choice later. It seemed like the right decision at the time but on reflection – when their life is less hectic and they have time to connect with their heart – they feel a sense of emptiness and longing for the womanly needs they never had an opportunity to satisfy. They grieve over the potential of the authentic woman they left behind, and never fully realized.

We have to remember the male-dominated desires of our society are strong. The competition for wealth, status, and power is all-pervasive at times. These desires and competitive drives will draw men to have more Social Sex. Why? So they can show off their status and power in the arms of a good-looking or powerful woman. As we mentioned in an earlier chapter men who are driven by wealth and status aren't interested in being close friends; usually they're using others to achieve their goals. The type of sex they have will reflect this; they use it to accumulate allies and tokens of their success. Having Social Sex with such a man validates his wealth, power, and status orientated ambitions; thus ensuring women continue to be disrespected and treated as objects rather than real people. In a male dominated society Social Sex becomes a way to continue to oppress and abuse women.

Many think Social Sex is just fine. We all seem to do it so what is the harm? Unfortunately the more we have Social Sex the more we devalue Family-Positive Sex and ourselves.

It seems an old fashioned notion, having sex primarily to build close and stable relationships. To some extent it is, but it is also a practical one. In a time when friendships aren't given the importance they deserve by making Family-Positive Sex the ideal, we give ourselves another way of increasing the value of friendship in our lives, and increasing the stability of our families and our communities in the process. We are giving power to friendship rather than to wealth and status, and lessening the oppression and abuse of women in the process. We are also giving ourselves another way of increasing our own self-worth. When sex is cheap, we are cheap. Perhaps this isn't as much an old fashioned notion as one that is practical, sensible and wise.

If we want the Essence of Woman to be raised in our society then you as a woman must show you are valuable at all times. You won't do that if you act as though you are not worthy of respect and true friendship.

You are a woman with many options. The choices you make when it comes to sex are important, for your long-term fulfillment and satisfaction. You choose how much you let men deceive you. It is easy for sex to confuse us, it can be hard to know when to have sex and with whom. You can better understand sex and make wiser choices by simply considering sex in terms of the basic desire types. Be honest with yourself about why you want sex. Seek proof about what your partner wants too. Doing this will put you in a much better position to have the mutually satisfying relationship you desire. Sex can either raise you up as a woman or bring you down. The choices you make regarding sex are important; make them wise.

Are you being sex-wise?

What about romantic love?

With all this talk of desires and sex where does romantic love fit into the picture? A love for someone so strong it hurts and yet can send our heart soaring within a single breath? It is still there, but we might like to be more careful how we use the word 'love'. The term 'being in love' can mean many things. In terms of how it helps guide us towards building stable and fulfilling relationships it has become almost useless.

The feeling of being romantically in love can mean anything from simply being attracted to them, to wanting to have sex, to dreaming of the fairy-tale romance, the family, and the happily ever after. However now we know claiming to be romantically 'in love' doesn't always end up in a long-term stable relationship.

Can we understand what this feeling of love is all about?

You have already started to see what it means for yourself.

As we have seen our brain always looks to the future, it is always dreaming and creating hope – seeing how we can satisfy our basic human needs. When we become attracted to someone we are drawn to a dream of the other person. Every desire our brain sees in its dream of us being together combines to give us a wonderful feeling. The more desires it sees that partner will satisfy, the stronger and more powerful and wonderful the feeling. We call the feeling of attraction to them – the result of our dream about them – as loving them, or 'being in love' with them. We love them – or are in love with them – because they promise to meet many of our relationship needs. If you don't believe me take the time and see for yourself, ask your Inner Self what you feel, what does your love promise to satisfy? Would you feel the same love if the other person didn't potentially meet your needs?

Try it. Sit down and put the scenarios to your Inner Self as we learnt to do earlier. Imagine the person you love didn't meet a need; say they didn't respect you. Imagine it in detail; when you are home, or out with friends, or when you have a disagreement. Imagine it as if it is actually happening. What would it feel like? How would you feel if he never treated you with respect? Or if you felt he couldn't be trusted? Imagine he hypothetically broke your trust. How would your love change? Would you still have the same feelings of love? What if he abandoned you when you needed him most, if he didn't care for your feelings, how would your love change? See for yourself how your love can shift according the desires it does or doesn't satisfy for you.

When we break up we're not grieving the loss of the person; we are mourning the loss of the dream we had of being together. It hurts so much because we feel the pain of promising desires being lost.

It's easy to give love almost superhuman qualities. To believe that it can conquer all and change the world. Yes we want love to be all-powerful, we need to be so attracted to each other we will stay together, however just wishing it to be so doesn't make it so. Look beyond what you need or wish love to be and see its reality. Search for its truth inside you and see if you can notice the desires that define it. Often strong emotions such as love seem to have one all-powerful feel; usually beyond logic. But as you have seen when you question this feeling with your Inner Self even love and its true nature will reveal itself and its parts to you.

Perhaps if we truly wish to continue to use the term 'love' and 'being in love' – romantic love – we should be more careful about it? Considering being in love can mean we are having short-term Social Sex, or even Self Sex, perhaps we should call all attraction without close friendship or the intent of long-term relations as 'lust'. In other words we are in lust when we start any relationship and not in love until the closeness of our friendship has been tested and we still want to be with each other and care for each other. At least by defining love in these terms we are less likely to fool ourselves into believing just because we are deeply attracted that it will magically end up as happily ever after. At least this way we will be more careful, take our time before we have children and decide to truly commit.

Are you in love with your partner, or is it merely lust? Perhaps you simply feel the lust of Social Sex or Self Sex? Which would you prefer, true love or lust?

When we feel the joy of a wonderful romantic love it whips up so many all-consuming feelings. Perhaps we might take a look beyond the feelings and search for the desires driving us to have sex with each other.

By looking in this way we need not take anything away from the great joy we have for one another. Yet this perspective can help us find that one person we need and truly desire for a close, stable, and mutually fulfilling relationship.

⓪

It was never nature's intention that woman was subdued, unheard, without influence in her family or community. Women were traditionally highly influential and played a critical role in family and community affairs. This involvement helped balance the Essence of Woman with the Essence of Man and further helped women be truly valued and respected in a manner they rightly deserved, for the benefit of our families, our children, and our society. If we want the Essence of Woman to rise again, not just now but for generations to come, then we need to reawaken this part of the ancient wise woman within.

So how do you exert your womanly influence?

A very simple yet powerful action you can take every day is to be more actively involved in decision-making.

Step 6: Get actively involved

A bunch of a certain number of shell (wampum) strings each two spans in length shall be given to each of the female families in which the Lordship titles are vested. The right of bestowing the title shall be hereditary in the family of the females legally possessing strings shall be the token that the females of the families have the proprietary right to the Lordship title for all time to come.
If at any time it shall be manifest that a Confederate Lord has not in mind the welfare of the people or disobeys the rules of this Great Law … the War Chiefs shall then divest the erring Lord of his title by order of the women in whom the titleship is vested. When the Lord is deposed the women shall notify the Confederate Lords through their War Chief. The women will then select another of their sons as a candidate and the Lords shall select him. When a Lord is to be deposed his War Chief shall address him as follows: 'So you, _____, disregard and set at naught the warnings of your women relatives. So you fling the warnings over your shoulder to cast them behind you.'
'Behold the brightness of the Sun and in the brightness of the Sun's light I depose you of your title and remove the sacred emblem of your Lordship title. I remove from your brow the deer's antlers, which was the emblem of your position and token of your nobility. I now depose you and return the antlers to the women whose heritage they are.'
The War Chief shall now address the women of the deposed Lord and say: 'Mothers, as I have now deposed your Lord, I now return to you the emblem and the title of Lordship, therefore repossess them.'
Constitution of the Iroquois Nations[11]

The Iroquois women – before the arrival of white man – held great power and influence in the decisions affecting their lives. They even had the power to remove men from office if they didn't heed the women's wishes! Women today can be just as powerful and influential as their ancient counterparts.

One of the most powerful ways you can spread your womanly influence is to be actively involved in decisions. The more decisions you take part in the more these decisions spread your point of view and spirit among people and across the world.

An effective way to ensure the decisions you make have the most positive impact on our children, our families, and our community is to be well educated. Two types of education can most benefit a woman in this respect: socially recognized education, and personal education.

Chapter 29:
Types of education

Socially recognized education includes formal learning at home or at a school, college, or university. Most of us are familiar with this type of formal education, as most of us in the West have had formal schooling. What many of us are less familiar with is personal education.

Personal education involves learning from your experience and perspective, without reading a book, or learning from someone else. We often neglect personal education because our society doesn't value it, but it can be the most important education of all. It is from personal education that we learn how to be tolerant, compassionate, empathic, and friendly human beings living true to ourselves. Via personal education we become wise. If we want women to spread their natural qualities among us through the decisions they make then surely we want those decisions to be wise, compassionate, and understanding from caring, tolerant and knowledgeable women.

The aim is to increase the power and influence of women in our lives as themselves, not as women behaving as men. Education helps give women this power and influence.

Can women have power and influence and remain true to themselves?
In a society dominated by men that can be hard, generally speaking men will not listen or respect you unless you have a similar ruthless and competitive nature. They are not out to value a woman's caring and compassionate side. However, being authentic to yourself and having great power and influence are not mutually exclusive; you don't have

to sacrifice one for the other. A good example of how women can have power and influence and still remain true can be found in the tribes of the Iroquois Nation before the European settlement of the Americas.

As the quotation at the beginning of this part reveals, in the council of tribes of the Iroquois Nation the men sat in council as the Lords and representatives of their people. But the women elected them. If the men didn't listen and act in a way the women thought was in the best interests of their people, the men would be deposed and replaced by men who could. In terms of being true to our natural desires as men and women that meant the men could act as the protectors and make decisions regarding helping keep the peace, allowing them to be true to their natural provider and protector roles. The influence of the Essence of Woman was strong in their society; all the women were actively involved in the running of the tribe, their families, and the state. Their caring and nurturing ways were spread into every aspect of their lives and they had powerful influence.

We may never make women the only citizens to vote, and to only vote for men who listen to women's interests. We may never make women the sole shareholders of a company and let them determine what men become the directors and CEOs, making them accountable to the women who vote them in. Perhaps we should. But we can learn from the wise ways of people like the Iroquois Nation. Their approach helped them to live in relative peace for hundreds of years while still giving women in society a powerful influence and encouraging them to remain true to their authentic selves. Tribes and confederacies like those of the Iroquois Nation are not a one-off; tribes around the world have valued the powerful role of women.

By helping women once again play a critical role in all decision-making we have a real chance of increasing the power and influence of the Essence of Woman in societies again.

In the following chapters we will consider some of the benefits of formal education to helping a woman meet her authentic needs. Formal education can be of great benefit to women in many ways; take it too far however, and it can work against them. We will offer suggestions as to how to balance formal education with life in the next chapter. We will also explore what personal education represents, how it can reduce social anxiety, increase tolerance, empathy, and compassion for others, and how it can help you personally change your life and make you wise so you can apply these qualities in your decision making. We will then look at how you can increase your decision making in the four critical aspects of your life, in decisions about: yourself, your family, your community, and in governing the state.

With so many people in power it can be easy to believe we can make no difference in the greater scheme of things. This is simply not true. Every decision in every part of your life changes your life and the lives of those around you, such as the life of your children, your family, and your community. Now more than ever we need you as a woman to spread your influence by actively participating in more and more decisions in every aspect of your life. We can begin by ensuring all women are well educated.

Chapter 30:
Socially recognized education

Quality formal education – using recognized curricula through institutions such as colleges, schools, and universities – is invaluable to a woman in the modern world. It is essential for her be able to meet many of her needs, including motherly, social, and the relationship components. Women can attain amazing levels of formal education. Unfortunately, there are times when this can restrict her ability to satisfy her authentic self. The key is to find the right balance so you can be better informed and influential in your decision-making, but remain true to the authentic woman within.

How does quality formal education help women in our modern world? Can too much formal education really be bad for you?

Quality formal education teaches us enough to thrive as individuals in our modern societies.

We often take our formal education for granted, but it helps us every day in ways we may not realize. For instance, a quality education can help us get a good job that pays enough money to survive and perhaps have a family. It allows us to be able to shop, read labels, know what we are buying and how much we should pay for it. It helps us catch a bus or train, pay for a taxi, read road signs and understand what they mean. Quality education also helps us to think critically.

Want to know if ingredients listed on a packet of cereal are good for you? Want to know if politicians are trying to fool or misguide you? Want to know if what is advertised in the media is true? With a quality education you can research topics, see if what others are saying is valid or true. You can determine how to better care for your health and the health of your family – to help you be a responsible mother. With a quality education you are better prepared to participate in the discussions that affect our lives. Give us a high quality education and we can better survive and thrive in a modern competitive world. It also helps meet many important social needs.

As we mentioned education holds status. When you have more formal education people are more likely to listen and take you seriously. Those with higher social status usually have quality formal education. Those without out it can be looked down upon and treated as inferior. Formal education will help garner you social respect. Being valued and respected are important to women's social needs.

A quality formal education helps lessen the likelihood of being abused and dominated by your partner.

If you have a formal education and can live an independent life. Some men will be less likely to abuse you because they know you can leave them any time you choose. If you have insufficient education to live independently then that leaves you vulnerable to his outbursts and abuses when he gets stressed. Why would he worry about upsetting you if he knows you are dependent on him? As we have seen all women need to be valued and respected in a relationship, but this is less likely to happen if he's better educated and can be more independent than you.

It is a crazy irony. Many men across the world still believe women should not be educated. They believe that education is the right and privilege only of men. Besides, the men have to work so they need the education, the women should stay at home and care for the children and the man's needs, what need do they have for education compared to a man? This is still a view held by many men in some countries such as India, Pakistan, and Afghanistan. This view was highlighted by the shooting of Malala Yousafzai, a Pakistani schoolgirl who in 2012 was travelling on a bus in Pakistan when men opposed to the education of women shot her in the head. (Thankfully she not only recovered but became a voice for the right of women to be educated everywhere, and is now a Nobel Peace Prize recipient as a result of her considerable efforts.) Yet if women aren't allowed to get an education the relationship won't be balanced. This will leave him more unsatisfied even though he may feel more powerful and secure due to his dominance. The most satisfying relationships are with those among equals because only then – as we noted earlier – are our close friendship needs met. Keep a woman less well educated than a man in a relationship and the level of satisfaction in the relationship will be less. A woman can be more herself when she is as educated as he is.

Can a woman have too much formal education?

If you spend so much on an education, many of your needs will be neglected. For example, if you value education so highly you don't spend any time having relationships then your relationship skills might be lacking and you may be much less likely to find a compatible partner. If you study till you are thirty for instance, to the exclusion of a social or family life, then you will be older than the younger women competing for the same men around you. Similarly if you leave having relationships too late you may no longer be able to have children. I commonly see this in general practice and the fertility specialists are driving this home to us regularly – don't leave having a family too late! If you have left it till you are over thirty-five, even with the wonders of modern medicine, with sophisticated in vitro techniques, it may be too late. Make gaining an education too much of a priority and you may not be able to fully satisfy your authentic woman needs to be a mother.

We have to remember we live in a society that is dominated by the need for status and wealth. If you let this male driven desire seduce you to be like a man, and work primarily towards achieving status and wealth by making education more important than being a woman, then many of your authentic needs won't be met. This is the risk. Formal education can be liberating for women, it increases their status and value in a society and in relationships, it even gives them a much needed sense of independence, yet if it is made the priority – to the neglect of many other needs – it may lower the Essence of Woman.

Does this mean women shouldn't strive for the highest education levels they can achieve?

Not at all. It simply means we have to balance the education with other needs, needs that can only be met within a certain time in your life. If these needs aren't prioritized, they may never be satisfied. Is this ok with you?

There are many opportunities to further an education without compromising your desires as a woman.

For example, education of children needs to have a higher priority preferably not at the expense of quality time with friends and close women role models such as mothers, aunts, and grandmothers. We still need girls to learn how to be compassionate women and good members of society. Balance life with schooling and children can learn a lot.

In puberty women can receive an education and begin to explore relationships – there can be a balance here too. College and university education for instance gives a woman a great opportunity to find an intelligent man with whom she can be compatible. Never will a woman find so much choice and opportunity for a partner in such a small area in her lifetime. Yes, it sounds like a bit of a meat market, but it is also a unique opportunity. If study is all she focuses on her future happiness and satisfaction as a woman can be put at risk. Clearly if a woman decides not to have a family, that is her choice.

Once a woman's children have left – assuming they have been raised so they do leave – her study levels can once again increase.

Don't get me wrong; this isn't about women abandoning study just because they become – or have decided to become – mothers. It is about those women who chose to become mothers finding a functional balance.

I recently met a mother of two children under ten studying to be a nurse. It was the first thing she had done just for her in years and she really enjoyed it – she was getting very high marks. But she was doing so many hours of study – cramming as much of the course into the shortest time possible – she was neglecting herself and her partner. Her weight ballooned by over twenty percent in less than six months – she was comfort eating to feel better, and stopped exercising – and her husband was complaining they never had time for each other anymore. Yes, the study was immensely satisfying, but the rest of her life was feeling rather lonely and miserable (hence the comfort eating), the children were seeing less of their mother, and their relationship was at real risk of falling apart.

This isn't about whether women who want to be – or are – mothers should study. It is about acknowledging that if we make study the greatest priority it can restrict a woman's ability to reach the full potential of her authentic self.

Being a mother doesn't mean being locked away in a dungeon all day, or stuck doing household chores.

Women in tribes used to meet regularly with other women to keep informed.

When women were no longer burdened by the immediate needs of their children then they were freer to spend more time in other pursuits. The grandparents of the Pueblo Indians of early America, for example, took on a larger role in their society; they would not get locked away in an aged care facility or sent on some holiday, they remained full participants in their community. When women are freer of the immediate needs of their children not only can they increase their study, they can spend more time sharing their knowledge and wisdom with other women, their grandchildren, and their society.

Of course if women help each other more, join to support each other raise their children together, then each of them also gets more free time and time for other pursuits. When we had closer families and communities the assistance of other women was far more readily available.

In the end it comes down to priority. If we make being a woman a high priority, but still make education important, then we can have both.

As was mentioned before, the key is finding the right balance. We won't find that balance if we value education more highly than being true to yourself.

Ultimately a quality formal education helps you to be well informed.

The more informed you are the more other people are likely to listen to you. With a higher level of education, and the status that goes with it, the decisions you make are more likely to be taken seriously. Do you listen to people who don't look like they know what they are talking about? Not many do.

The following recommendations aim to help ensure you're at least as educated as men, yet not at the expense of being true to yourself. How you wish to apply them – or don't – is up to you.

Recommendations for formal education

- **Educate all women.** All women should be formally educated to the level of their choosing. They should be able to live as independent women and offer a valuable contribution to society. Ensure you and all girls and women in your community get a formal education.
- **Remain true to yourself.** Don't let education become so important it stops you meeting your needs. Don't let it get in the way of your relationships, having a fulfilling family, and being the mother your children need you to be, or the nurturer caring for society.
- **Keep informed.** Keeping up to date with the new discoveries affecting your life is important so you don't feel left behind, but also so you can keep up with your children. Formal education doesn't stop when schooling stops.
- **Find an equally educated partner.** Try to make sure your partner has a similar level of education as you. This will mean you have a better chance of a close friendship between you.
- **Share your formal education.** Share what you have learnt with your children and others around you so they too can be well educated. Pass on your discoveries to the next generation so that the women who follow can be as well educated as you.

Formal education for women helps women meet many of their needs. It also helps women to make informed decisions that are more likely to be taken seriously. But formal education isn't the only education a woman needs; she also requires a high level of personal education. If you want to make decisions that not only spread the Essence of Woman but also share tolerance, compassion, friendship, and wisdom so we live in a more peaceful and less threatening world, then you will need to increase your personal education.

Chapter 31:
Personal education

Liana cried in frustration as she spoke of her mother. 'She doesn't change! She still does the same stupid stuff that made my life hell. I love her, I just can't stand to spend time with her!'

I had known Liana for many years, a courageous young woman with children of her own with a terribly traumatic childhood that had left many deep emotional scars. Every moment with her mother behaving as she had always remembered left her visibly distressed. Her mother, Cecilia, had suffered terribly too. Her way to deal with the many emotional pains in life was simple, to study, read, and listen to others more than herself.

Cecilia had read every self-help book she could find. Now she was studying psychology, and listening to a Tarot reader and professed clairvoyant on the side. She tried all their advice and then came in one day crying and asking me 'Why can't I change?' Then she quickly picked herself up and told herself she was being silly, and apologized to me for being so weak. Cecilia believed all she had to do was listen to the wisdom of others, eat well, exercise, and do what others said and she would feel great. She had learnt to use the vast knowledge available to her to hide from the depths of her feelings, searching in vain for a less painful solution she was prepared to accept. Long ago she had learnt to stop listening and learning to the one person who could help her most – herself. It was less painful to learn from someone else. The only problem was it just wasn't working.

What is personal education?

Personal education is learning about you; why you think and feel as you do, using your life experience and your point of view to learn about the world, other people, and yourself. It is not about learning what others teach us or from reading or any type of formal education. With personal education you are the teacher, and you are your student. We have the potential to learn amazing amounts about the world and ourselves without reading a book, a scientific paper, or asking someone else to explain it to us. We all educate ourselves every day. Take what we all naturally do even further and not only can we learn more about the world and ourselves from personal education, we can also help reduce social anxiety, increase tolerance, empathy, and compassion, and help make it easier to make friends. Increasing personal education can also help make us wise. Listening to the wise ancient woman within will put you into a much better position to make wiser decisions that can benefit us all.

How to increase personal education

There are two classical ways to increase personal education: learning from experience, and learning by putting ourselves in someone else's shoes – imagining we are in their position and circumstance.

> **Your own experience is a great way to learn more about the world, yourself, and other people.**

At a basic level you can learn what works and doesn't work by trial and error, by making mistakes or learning from being hurt. You can learn from a burn for instance, not to put your hand into the fire. You can learn not to get angry if the consequences mean those you care about will leave you. If you choose to you can learn so much more.

By simply reflecting on your behavior and the consequences you can learn much about who you are. You can learn what you think and feel and why, as we have been doing by asking questions of our Inner Self. Without reading a book or listening to anyone else you can learn what hurts you, what you are afraid of, and how these either work for or against you in making a fulfilling life. You can learn the workings of a human emotional heart and what makes it tick and drives it. You can discover the truth of your own humanity. In the process you can learn a great deal about other people too.

As we have seen all human beings have the same basic desires and drives; the ones that make us human. This means the more we understand our human desires and how they make us think, act, and feel, the more we can understand everyone else around us too. If we are different, then most of that variation between us will be because we have grown up under different life conditions and circumstances. Understand enough about our own humanity and we can see that we too would react as our fellow human beings if we had grown into their life circumstance and conditions.

Increasing personal education is simply doing more of what we already do.

We already learn from experience. Many of us already try to imagine putting ourselves in other people's positions so we can better understand what they think and do. To increase our personal education we simply do more of it.

For example, we can spend time reflecting and learning more from the limited experiences we have had. We can learn more about how we tick, and in so doing learn a lot about each other in the process. Why do we keep having trouble with relationships? Why do we get angry, frustrated, or afraid? See for yourself. Explore, find out what our relationship needs are, look inside your heart and from your own experience and see for yourself.

What if we get it wrong? What if we just fool ourselves and only see what we want to see?

Then connect with your Inner Self in the ways we described earlier (see pages 94–111) so you will be less likely to fool yourself. Keep searching for the truth; keep developing your ideas. As long as you keep searching your ideas, your understanding will continue to grow and your experiences and predictions will test them and become more accurate and complete. Without reading a book you can develop a very detailed, realistic, practical, and personal understanding of who you are. Initially your ideas will not be as accurate as you like, but the more you develop, test, and put the ideas together the more you understand about yourself in a way that feels honest and true, is practical to your life, and touches your heart. By using this approach I eventually came up with the Balance of Self (BOS) Model. Only much later did I find out it stands up well against many current scientific and psychological approaches and theories.

To help you develop an even greater personal understanding of others and yourself simply spend more time also putting yourself into other people's positions.

Often we can see a part of us in other people. We can be angry or in conflict with them because we see something in ourselves we're in conflict about. The more we look into the hearts and lives of others the more we find ourselves reflected back. Wouldn't you be crying like your friend if a guy you were really close to dropped you out of the blue? Imagine how you would feel in their position. The more accurately you imagine yourself in their shoes, the more you understand yourself, the more you can see what it would be like to be just about anyone in the world.

How does increasing personal education make us less anxious and more tolerant, empathic, and compassionate? How does it make it easier for us to be friends? By making us more alike and more predictable.

You will recall earlier when we looked at how to master fear that we are afraid of the unfamiliar; we feel fear when we encounter the unpredictable. When people are unpredictable – we don't know how they will react or behave – they can make us extremely anxious. A good example of this is a child living with an abusive alcoholic parent. When the parent gets drunk they can get extremely violent about the smallest of things. Not being able to predict when they will lash out can leave you living in terror, because you don't know when the violence is going to start again. When anyone around us seems unpredictable, when they seem so different we can't be sure how they might react, then they make us anxious. The more we can understand them and make them predictable the less anxious we will be around them. It is similar when it comes to tolerance, empathy, and compassion.

Suppose you were depressed because a close friend just passed away. As a result you have taken time off work, locked yourself away from everyone, and avoided your responsibilities. If all I saw was you shirking your responsibilities I could get very angry and not tolerate your behavior. If I had never lost anyone close I could still not understand or tolerate what you were doing. But if I also suffered the loss of someone close and knew how that felt, and I too acted in a similar way when it happened to me, then I would be much more compassionate, empathic, and tolerant. I would have learnt about personal loss and what it is to feel depressed. The more I understand about myself and the more I can project myself into your circumstances the more tolerant, empathic, and compassionate I will be. I will also find it easier to be friends. On the other hand, if I thought you were being silly – mainly because I didn't have enough experience or self-understanding – then I would be far less tolerant.

You will recall that 'sameness' was one of the Ten Basic Desires of Community Self in the BOS Model. The more similar you are to me the more you meet an important friendship need and the more likely that we can be friends. Not surprisingly then the more we can see ourselves in other people, in what they think, feel, and do, the more we see them as similar to us, making them less of an enemy and more of a potential friend.

Do you ever see people fighting in other countries on TV? Often these people seem very foreign to us, they dress strangely, have different customs, and look like they want to harm us. Because we see them as different we struggle to treat them as our friends. See that they too care for their children, worry about their partners and relationships, want only the best for their close friends and family, and suddenly we can relate to them; they're people just like ourselves. By increasing our personal education enough we can all look very similar; like potential friends.

It is worth pointing out by making everyone a potential friend we also reduce the level of threat in our societies and between countries.

The less threat the more the Essence of Woman can be raised and the easier it will become for you to be true to yourself.

One of the most important benefits of increasing your personal education is it makes you wise.

What qualities make us wise?

Knowing how to live a balanced life as a lastingly satisfied human being. Knowing how to be human.

A wise person has learnt from personal experience and understanding what they need to be a lastingly satisfied human being. They know how to meet their basic human needs and by so doing know what the rest of us need to do, how we need to act, think, and behave. Think of a wise person and who comes to mind? Would that person really do anything foolish that would threaten their own safety, the safety and happiness of their family and friends, such as make unnecessary enemies, or do anything that would threaten their lives? Of course not, that would lead to unnecessary pain and misery, and wouldn't be very wise. Wise people have learnt not to let emotions cloud their judgement; they have learnt that too much indulgence now can have terrible long-term consequences. Experience and self-understanding have made them wise.

Personal education is a direct way to become wise.

What if our society has lost its wisdom, and no longer knows what works? That means there's only one source we can count on: ourselves. Everything you learn about yourself and others helps you understand your humanity and how to have your needs met. The more you learn how to do this the wiser you become. Learning from others, such as by what they teach us, can help us understand more about ourselves too, but not in as an intensive and direct way as when we educate ourselves. Much of what others teach us is based on their experiences, or their studies or reading. We are learning second-hand. The majority of what they experienced we will never know and so we will never truly see their point of view and gain all we can from their experience. The one person's point of view we can really know well is our own.

It is up to you to become wise; no one can be wise for you.

Below are some recommendations about how to increase personal education:
- **Make personal education time.** Take the time to reflect on what you can learn from your day-to-day and life experiences. Connect with your Inner Self to help you and see how much you can learn.
- **Change your point of view.** Whenever you see someone acting or behaving in a way that disturbs you or you don't understand don't just quickly judge them, try to understand their point of view instead. The more points of view we embrace the closer we come to the truth about them, ourselves, and the world.
- **Keep learning.** The moment you think you have someone all worked out is the moment you can guarantee you haven't. So many pieces make up the puzzle of who we are, we can never know them all.
- **Keep your unique perspective.** If someone else has a different view look for what they read or experienced that led them to see it differently, don't just substitute their view for your own. Always remember, your point of view is as valid as anyone else's.

One of the best things about increasing our personal education is that it always rings true. This is because it's based on our experience, not on someone else's theory, idea, or experience. It rings true to our life. Nothing else we ever learn can feel like that, no other idea, theory, or description of someone else's life. We may read of someone else's experiences or ideas and feel great because they validate our own, but taking them on as our ideas and views is not the same as developing our own.

I have met many people like Cecilia described at the beginning of the chapter who read widely and quote wise sayings from people to whom they can relate. The only problem is they don't seem to get any wiser, they continue to suffer because they never really change. Many insist that the only way to learn is by reading widely and seeking out the advice of those who know. However, the way to meaningful change and wisdom isn't by reading but by working things out for themselves.

You may think, 'This author is a hypocrite, I bought his book didn't I?' Yes you did. But the key to getting the most from a book like this isn't to use intelligent or wise quotes to impress your friends. The best way this book – or any other book – can help is if it stimulates you enough that you learn for yourself.

You have a chance to make a positive difference by developing and sharing greater wisdom, empathy, compassion, and friendship. To make the most of that opportunity you need to become actively involved.

Chapter 32:
Active involvement

At home, in the family, in matters relating to our community and state we often let others make decisions for us. The more you get involved the more you influence change. Even making small decisions can spread positive influence and change through your life, your family, and throughout society.

Active involvement means taking a personal interest and participating in the decision making process in matters all around us.

Do you let others make decisions for you? How often do you just let things happen and not really participate? What shall we have for dinner? I don't know, what would you like? Where shall we go tonight? Oh you decide. When are we meeting up as a group? Can't someone else organize it? The more decisions others make for you the less influence you have and the less the Spirit of Woman inside you impacts on the world. If you want the Essence of Woman to once again influence our families and communities then women like you need to participate, and be actively involved; you need to be making more decisions. Four areas of your life where your decisions can make a positive impact include decisions related to self, family, local community, and state.

Self

Active involvement begins with matters related to yourself. If it involves you directly get active, participate in the decisions; let your opinion and voice be heard.

We sometimes like to think our decisions don't make an impact, that even if we live alone they can't be that important. It isn't true. They are very important. Every decision we make affects more than we can immediately see.

For example every type of food we buy had to come from somewhere. By us deciding to buy it we are supporting how it was produced, how the land was used that it was grown on and how the farmers cared for it, and how the animals were treated. Every decision about work, how you relate to others, how you decide to treat them affects how they treat others. Even the type of job is an important decision, especially if the business you work for doesn't respect its workers or contributes to world degradation and pollution. By you simply working for such a company you support it and its methods and impact on the world. Every decision has an influence.

Of course if you live with others then every decision you make impacts on them too. How tidy you decide to be can affect the level of mess others have to tolerate or live in. If you don't work and do your share that leaves more work and chores for others. How long you leave lights, the TV, the washer, and the dryer on, or how long you leave the water running, all adds to the bills the household has to pay. When you shower, when you eat, everything we do in a close group effects the lives of those directly around us. Live in a group, a household, or a family however, and it can be easy to let others make decisions for us.

This is to say nothing of how long people have to work to pay for such bills, and the price the environment has to pay in pollution, global warming, loss of natural resources etc for your consumption.

It can be easy to let others decide things for us, especially in a group or family. We simply let them be the leader and take responsibility. Often we can do it just to keep the peace so we don't have an argument. Soon we aren't very active in decisions directly affecting our life. Little by little, or all in one go, we can let others decide when we eat and what we eat, when we watch TV and what we watch. We change our life to fit in with theirs, as if what we do isn't important. We may even let others decide for us what we will wear!

Whether we live alone or with a group or family every decision we make is an important opportunity to make a difference. For you as a woman it is a precious opportunity to let your Essence of Woman impact on your life and on the world. Unless you become actively involved in decisions directly affecting your life the influence of the Essence of Woman will fall.

How do you get more actively involved in decisions regarding yourself so you can spread your womanly influence?

You start by being aware of the choices and decisions around you. Begin by seeing just how many decisions you give away.

Exercise

For one day carry a notebook and list the decisions you let someone else make for you. It could have been what you ate, what time you left the house, what time you had dinner, who cleaned up, or the house roster – if you have one. It could be what movie you saw with your partner, what you did on the weekend, or what holiday you planned on taking. If someone else made the decision for you, you didn't feel you had a say in the matter directly affecting you, then write it down. Write them all down.

At the end of the day, look at your list. Now imagine no one else was going to decide what you did, this time it was only your choice, your decision to make. What would you have decided?

Try this for a week. Every day note what decision you let others make for you and then later that day work out what you would do if you had to decide. Think about it carefully, listen to your heart, what would you decide?

Now start deciding. Participate. Get involved in the decisions that directly affect you.

Does this mean you should take control and prevent others making their choices and decisions?

No.

Being actively involved in decisions affecting our life doesn't mean we disrespect other people's choices, it means respecting their decisions and choices as well as our own. It means seeing our decisions and choices as being of equal value and importance so our influence can be shared as part of a balance and not dominate. We don't like it when someone takes away our ability to choose and neither will other people, not if they respect themselves. People who respect themselves make sure they have a say in what happens to them. They are not satisfied when someone tries to dominate them.

Are there people who like to be dominated, who prefer others to make the hard decisions they don't want to make?

Of course there are. But these people also have a low Personal Self, they have not been taught the value of their own opinions, they have often been abused or coerced into believing their decisions don't matter.

When we make decisions affecting our lives we can ensure our needs get met. Nature needs us to have our basic human needs met or we don't survive as a species.

Every day make the effort to practice being actively involved in decisions directly affecting your life. Become mindful of the decisions and choices you have given away and take them back. Get involved in discussing and negotiating decisions that affect your life. You are not lesser than anyone else. Make decisions that directly affect you that prove it. Spread your Essence of Woman, your compassion, and friendship and let it influence those around you and the world.

Family

The decisions you make in the home are important and can affect the affairs of state. It may seem ridiculous but household decisions can be the basis upon which a nation develops. Even the Ancient Romans recognized the link between the running of a household and the running of a state. Understanding this link gives you the great opportunity to create a balance at home that can be an example and spread its influence across a country.

My first-year university philosophy teacher taught us that many Ancient Romans considered the running of their household or Villas analogous to running cities and states. If you could efficiently manage

Active involvement

your slaves, your expenses, your supplies, and your family then you had the skills to manage a city – the Polis – or a large state. Both need good people and sound financial management. Both need to ensure they run smoothly so you can have a comfortable and not too troubling place in which to live. They quite reasonably recognized the skills and affairs that have been learnt at home and with our family could be translated to affairs affecting the greater community.

If you can restore a balance between the desires of women and men at home you offer an example and hope for our community and the state.

If it can take place at home it can happen in the greater community, and across the country. The good news is you only have one man to create this balance with at home, whereas if you're trying to restore a balance in the whole community a few more men are involved – thousands, sometimes millions.

How do you restore a balance between the desires of men and the desires of women at home?

By actively being involved in decision-making at home, but also ensuring no one person dominates the decisions.

When a man becomes dictator of a family and dominates the decisions the man's desires dominate. When a woman dominates the home and decisions the woman's desires dominate. When each allow each other to be respected as having equal say in the decisions within a family then the influence of a woman and man's desires are balanced.

Being passive and letting oneself be dominated by a man in the family lessens the Essence of Woman in you and in every member of the family.

You are the source of the Essence of Woman in the family, if that gets lowered the only person who can offer the Spirit of Woman to your children and your partner is gone. They are absent. They are not there for the family.

Young boys and girls need to see and experience the Essence of Woman in their lives. The girls need to know it so it raises their Essence of Woman and helps them to be true to being a woman and live a fulfilling life. The boys need to experience it so they learn its value and to respect it from an early age, so they will respect the important role of women throughout our society. You are their most powerful example. If you don't show balance of the Essence of Woman and the Essence of Man then they can struggle to learn it later. If what it is to be a woman isn't respected in your household why will your son – later as a man – truly respect and value women outside the household, especially in his relationships?

The less you are actively involved in decisions in the home the harder your sons and daughters will find it to have respectful and balanced fulfilling relationships as adults.

What does being more actively involved in decisions at home actually mean?

It can mean taking control of your finances and more control of where the household money is spent. It can mean both of you deciding how to raise the children, what house rules you set, where they go to school, how much time they should spend on their computers. It can mean both of you being actively involved in the decisions affecting everyone's lives in the household. Like a tribe everyone should be allowed to have their say, and it should be validated and not dismissed out of hand. Their opinion should be explored and fully expressed. Once you have everyone's say then you can all make an informed decision.

Does this mean children should have a say too?

Children need to feel heard and validated just as much as the rest of us. They are not a parent or adults however, they lack life experience; they do not know the consequences of their actions. They should be allowed to have their say but until they are adults – or reach puberty – both of you as parents will decide what they do. If you don't work together on this your children will play one of you against the other, searching for the weaker link. They will also start to argue and have tantrums if you try to negotiate with them. Don't negotiate, set the rules once they have had their say, make the decision and stick by it. If the children know you mean what you say and will follow through on any consequences the house will be in a much greater state of peace. Give in to them even once, make the rules seem they can be changed by them crying or getting upset, and they will test the rules ten or twenty more times just to see if the rules have changed. After all they changed last time – when we gave in. Don't be consistent with the rules, even on a bad day, and the whole household will suffer from their tantrums and be much less of a happy place.

As a woman and parent the less decisive you are the more your children will test you.

The less powerful you look in their eyes compared to their father and others around you the more they will also test you. If others are allowed to abuse you or disrespect you the children will learn to do the same, they can even come to hate you. After all children are just small human beings, if one of our pack – our family – doesn't respect themselves why should we? We will get angry that they don't stand up for themselves, as we know they should. We will resent their weakness and can easily hate them for it.

Be actively involved in decisions regarding the family. Don't be weak and submissive. Don't let the man dominate.

Treat the home like a small tribe where women and men have equal say and are treated with equal respect and value.

This will raise the Essence of Woman in your home and restore a balance. You will be the example to our community of how we should all create and restore a balance between the desires of men and the desires of women. You will spread this influence among your children and to us all.

Local community

Every decision made by your local council or neighborhood group will affect the services for, and living conditions of your family. If you don't want these decisions to be driven by individuals motivated by wealth and status, and want them to be more family-orientated, then you have to be actively involved in local community decision-making.

It's easy to blame local governments or councils for what's wrong in our suburb. When they choose to build a twenty storey building next door or down the road instead of a park for local families it's easy to just claim they're all corrupt and leave it at that. If we are really angry about a decision we might write a letter. But unless many people write that letter before the decision is made then nothing can be expected to happen. 'It's the council's fault!'

No, it's our fault.

If you want the influence of woman to transform your local community you – personally – have to get actively involved in the decisions of the council. Yes, you are busy. Yes, many of you probably have children, work, a thousand obligations.

But if you don't actively participate in local matters then they'll remain under the dominating influence of men.

Better still, if you are a grandmother – a woman who has been in touch with her Essence of Woman and knows what it is to have a family – get actively involved. Mothers may not have the time but you probably do.

As we have noted, in tribes women's views were heard. Councils are nothing more than big tribal meetings. Make yourself heard.

The local councils and local governments need the balancing influences of the Essence of Woman to counter the Essence of Man. Without this balance what is in the best interest of our children and our families can be lost. Only women in touch with the Essence of Woman within can give us the balance we need in councils and local governments.

Don't just get involved in councils; take your influence even further!

Matters of state

A country makes decisions on our behalf. The decisions they make will be determined by the influence we, as individuals, have on the leaders we allow to represent us. As we have seen if we leave it to men to dominate these affairs in the interest of protecting us a state of chronic threat can exist in many countries, lessening the respect for women all over the world, and leaving our children feeling unsafe and living in fear. The way countries behave towards each other reflects the desires, will, and beliefs of the people living in that country.

> **Countries are in many ways just people, interacting like we do; trying to have their basic needs met.**

The same desires that drive us as individuals drive the people that run a country. What this means is every country also seeks to have the Ten Basic Desires of Community Self met; they seek to feel safe and secure.

Does your country behave like a friend to other countries, or does it see them as hostile competition? Does it act like there are enough resources for everyone to share, or as if there isn't enough to go around, and they must fight and dominate others for their share? Does it treat other countries like we are the same? Or does it treat them as different and alienate them? Does it respect the will of the people of other countries or try to exploit and use them to benefit its own interests, no matter the cost to the people? Does your country treat others as respected equals or try to rule and control? How does your country truly represent you?

Yet you are the country; an integrated part of the people of your great land. Your government acts for you. When the masses of the people speak the governments are forced to listen. If the people don't make their views heard then the representatives of your land will follow their own will, or the will of the companies whose interests they represent.

> **If the leaders of the government and companies are men then men's desires will dominate. Their desire to increase wealth, power, and status will weigh heavily on their agenda.**

As a woman your active involvement in decisions made by your country's government is critical.

Do you want your children to grow up and live in fear and feel unsafe? Do you want them to worry about enemies out to get them? Or do you want your family to feel safe and secure and live in a country that knows how to be friends rather than enemies with other countries?

Our governments have a stark choice: treat everyone else as the enemy, demonize them, fight them, and treat them like an obstacle to their supremacy, or work with other countries with less of a 'you are either with us or against us' attitude. Instead promote friendly competition that spreads benefits among more than just a select minority or few. Treating countries as hostile competition fosters wars and acts of aggression, just as treating people around us as a potential threat – rather than friends – means they are more likely to become defensive, aggressive, and more likely to fight. We may wonder why people on the other side of the world are so hostile towards us, want to kill us and attack our way of life, but what part has the approach of our government played in making us a threat to others? How much has the dominating agenda of men for ever more wealth and power ultimately made us unsafe?

Do you want your children to feel threatened by people from other countries because your country – your government – acts like an enemy to everyone else? Do you want a country that represents your family's best interests? Then you have to get actively involved!

How do you get actively involved in matters of a country's government?

Active involvement in governments

- Keep abreast of what your country is doing to represent you overseas.
- Maintain close contact with your government representative. Ask them about the country's policies and ask them to explain so you understand them and can have an informed say. (Do your own research to ensure you have a balanced view.)
- Make your opinions heard. Write to your government representative regularly.

- Form local groups of friends with similar views. Contact your government member as a group, letting them know of your views.
- Use social media to form bigger social groups of women with similar views and then each of you write to your government representative and leader – create a bigger voice.
- If you don't have heavy responsibilities consider running for office. Especially if you have the education behind you.
- Most importantly of all – VOTE! A woman's voice cannot be heard if she doesn't vote for candidates that represent her values. If there aren't any candidates that can best represent you either run for office yourself or find a woman or man who can best represent your views.

The more you are true to your Essence of Woman the more your country needs to hear your voice. Be heard, let those who represent you know your views. Form groups that offer a bigger voice that cannot be ignored. And above all vote!

Every time just one woman chooses not to vote she lessens the voice of the Spirit of Woman and the Essence of Woman among us all.

Every vote is your opportunity to raise the Essence of Woman among societies everywhere. Your vote affects the agenda of your government, who gets in and if they champion the desires at the heart of women. Change the agenda of your government away from threatening male dominant desires and your government becomes less of a threat to other governments. When this happens the desires of women can then rise in those governments. As we have seen, lower the level of chronic threat and the desires of men no longer need to dominate. Your vote as a woman not only influences change in your government and your country, it changes the level of influence of women in governments everywhere. Women can change agendas of governments and how governments treat each other and the world. Your vote, as a woman, changes the world.

The world needs women like you to represent her people. If you are unable to stand for office support women and men who can champion your cause, who put family above profits, friendships above status, and compassion above an insatiable need for power. Encourage the natural caring and nurturing nature of women who represent you, don't let them feel they have to be like men to have a voice. Make your voice count and let your personal powerful influence change your government and the world.

Decisions matter. Choices affect lives. As a woman you have a wonderful opportunity by becoming well educated both formally and personally to affect positive change in your life. You have an opportunity to raise the Essence of Woman in your family, local community, in your state and worldwide. Women do not have to live under the scourge of chronic threat. They do not have to feel like second-class citizens, subservient to any man, suffering abuse and disrespect at his hand.

It is up to you to be actively involved in decisions so the Essence of Woman stands tall and receives the recognition and respect it deserves.

If you want to make a real difference in your life, decide to.

Another powerful way to help raise the Essence of Woman and spread the power of the Spirit of Woman among people of the world is to be more spiritual. In a mostly logical and rational modern world we have come to dismiss or ignore the cravings of our heart for spirituality. If you truly wish to be and feel true to being your complete self, then consider enhancing your spirituality.

Step 7: Enhance your spirituality

Our spirituality is a oneness and an interconnectedness with all that lives and breathes, even with all that does not live or breathe.
Mundrooroo[12]

Spirituality is important for you as a woman, and for us all. One of the greatest benefits of enhancing your spirituality is that it can help you raise the Essence of Woman within so your true self can be fully and more completely realized. It can do this by reconnecting you emotionally to the world, and giving your life a greater sense of purpose and meaning. Spirituality can offer us what science and logic never can; a personal and relevant insight and experience that helps make us whole.

What do we mean by 'spirituality'?

The term 'spirituality' can mean many things. There is currently no one accepted definition of what it is or represents. The word's origin can be traced back to the Latin *'spiritus'* that describes 'soul, courage, vigor, breath'. Today being spiritual can conjure up images of religion, God, mysticism, paganism and the belief in spirits of the natural world. It can also give us the image of a spirit or soul, a part of us that survives beyond death. In the context of increasing the Essence of Woman enhancing the spiritual refers to creating stories and experiences that go beyond oneself and yet remain true to our heart. We'll explain this shortly.

Many rational people don't take spirituality seriously, and why should they?

Spirituality often isn't logical, it isn't founded on reproducible experiments or agreed upon facts, and it doesn't search for truth in a critical way. In short, spirituality isn't scientific. This makes it seem a waste of time.

Nothing could be further from the truth. It's far from a waste of time. As you are about to see often most of science is more of a waste of time than enhancing the spiritual. More importantly, science unchecked can be an enormously destructive force. For example, its discoveries have contributed to climate change, pollution, and the decimation of untold plant and animal species. Enhancing the spiritual, if done in a practical way, can help keep science in check and help give it personal context, guide its future, and give it greater personal meaning. Only develop the rational and logic ideas of science, without giving them a spiritual context, and we create an imbalance between nature and us that can threaten us all.

How can most of science be more of a waste of time than enhancing the spiritual? How can the spiritual keep science in check so we don't develop a destructive imbalance?

The answer lies in better understanding stories.

Chapter 33: Stories

We live by the stories of our brain. Some stories can help us live fulfilling and satisfied lives in balance with nature and in contact with our true selves. Other stories can do the opposite.

We have already learnt our brain lives its dreams and fantasies. It lives to make its visions of the world come true so the world seems predictable, so we feel safe. As we have previously noted, in effect all our dreams, fantasies, memories, and self-image are really just types of stories our brain creates that we live by. The stories we create determine our actions and behaviors; how we think, act, and feel. In the end both science and enhancing the spiritual are just about creating stories.

Behind all the complicated ideas and theories science is really just a collection of stories to help us make sense of the world and ourselves. Enhancing the spiritual can also help in this regard, but with a different emphasis and feel – we will discuss the differences more in a moment. Because stories determine what we think and do ideally we want to be creating functional stories, stories that see us strive to have our needs met so we feel fulfilled in our lives, but also see us live in a way that is sustainable and in balance with nature. Often the stories of science are not very functional, and can be a waste of our time. The same can't be said for stories that enhance the spiritual.

Why are most of the stories of science not very functional, and often a waste of time?

Most science-based stories are not personally relevant. Worse than that, they also detach us emotionally from the world and ourselves and make the world, its creatures, and even ourselves something we can have great difficulty caring about.

For example, how personally relevant are most of the theories we come up with in physics? Learning about the particles that make up matter, and what mathematical model best explains the collisions that occur in atom smashing particle accelerators, doesn't help you be a woman and live a fulfilling life. Sure it can be fascinating and inspire great curiosity and personal interest but most of the knowledge science uncovers can be completely irrelevant to you as a woman and how to live a wonderful and fulfilling life. Over four million scientific papers are submitted to scientific journals every year, and aside from the fact many are substandard and rejected the vast majority will not help you directly to be truly satisfied as a woman – most scientific stories aren't that personally helpful. This is in contrast to seeing the world in terms of spirits, a method of enhancing the spiritual.

When we were all tribal our spiritual stories helped us make sense of the world, learn our roles in society and taught us the rules. We knew from tales of spirits of the land, the plants, and animals, how to hunt and find food and when and where. We learnt which food or animals were not to be harmed and what land should be avoided due to dangers; we learnt what was sacred and taboo. We even learnt from tales of the spirits where to find water, such as how the koala bear lost its tail.

In the story of how Koolah the koala lost his tale – a story from north-west New South Wales, retold with permission by June E Baker in the book *Gadi Mirrabooka, Australian Aboriginal Tales from the Dreaming* – we hear a story of great drought. In the tale we learn of the struggle of a mother carrying her child and being tempted to leave them and search for water, tempted by old man kangaroo – Bundah. Soon Koolah and a new companion Euro – a male wallaby – find the sands of a big dry riverbed. Koolah pretends that she's too tired to dig for water and leaves the job to Euro. Feeling sorry for Koolah, Euro digs for them both. Once the water appears Koolah jumps up looking fit and well and eagerly drinks from the hole, making Euro so angry that he cuts off her tail. To this day we notice the wallabies and kangaroos hopping over the land with their long tails whilst the koala sits lazy – without a tail – high up in a tree.

From the spirits of Koolah and Euro we can learn many lessons. One important lesson is when water is scarce is to dig in the dry sands of a large creek or riverbed to find it. Another is where to find a koala, and something of their nature should we want to catch them – they are often slow and lazy and found high in trees. The more we learn of the spirits the more we know how to survive on the land.

Our brain used its creation of spirits as nature's translator. Nature spoke to us in the will and actions of the spirits. Spirits were very relevant in our lives; the stories we had of them helped us survive. They also helped us connect emotionally to the world and ourselves.

By creating spirits – real or not – we give the land and its creatures feeling, like we have feeling for our parents, children, brothers, sisters, and friends.

Creating spirits in all things offers us a way to give plants, animals, and the landscape itself, personality. Who cares about the plants if they are just bits of green stuff we study under a microscope? Who cares for a monkey that is but a collection of chemicals and hormones? Who appreciates the mountains and forests if they are just chunks of minerals and ecosystems? But if the flower has the spirit of life that can cure a troubled heart, the monkey has a spirit of curiosity and kinship, and the land and forests have the spirit of a mother nurturing its children, then we feel more of a connection with them. We feel they all have greater personal meaning for us and we will treat them differently, care for them as we would care for our own, and treat them with something closer to the respect they deserve.

For over forty-five thousand years – perhaps much longer – the Aboriginal people of Australia lived in balance with their environment. They had a rich spiritual culture involving tales of the spirits of animals, the land and the seasons. They could have exploited their world, treated it as a resource or something to use, and they could have destroyed it to the point where they could barely survive. Instead they respected it, developed a personal emotional connection with it through seeing spirits in all things, and lived often happy and fulfilling lives. When Captain Cook first came across the Aboriginal people of Australia he described them in his log as some of the happiest people he had ever met.

It is harder to care for what has no personal emotional meaning or connection to us. It is harder to restore a balance with nature and within ourselves if we view everything with the emotional detachment of science.

By connecting with everything on a spiritual level however we once again make it more personal and help us restore the balance we need.

Spiritual stories also help us deal with death.

We are all mortal, we all die, but many of us have trouble dealing with the idea our life will end. However by creating a spirit inside us that defies death we give ourselves ongoing hope. We transcend the idea of death and can give our life a greater meaning. If our spirit is to join the stars, or our ancestors or family after our death for instance, we can take comfort in the night as we look up and see our loved ones shining back at us. We can take solace that we will someday once more hug and be close to those we have loved. Then we can get on with life and not think everything is meaningless. What meaning can there be if we just die? Spiritual stories can give our life meaning and help us cope.

But the spiritual stories aren't true. At least the scientific ones are; we can test those. That should make us lean more to the stories of science, right?

Actually neither is true.

Even scientific theories and ideas are just stories. They are not true, and no scientist who understands science will admit they are true; they are just the best theory – story – they have at the time. In fact because we can't know everything no theory we ever come up with will ever be entirely accurate, it will never ultimately be true.

Why is this important?

If the stories of science aren't ultimately true, and the stories of the spiritual aren't true either, does the truth of a story really matter that much to us in our lives?

Isn't it more important if our stories actually work for us as people, if they are functional stories?

As western science makes ever more discoveries we remain largely out of contact with our Inner Selves and nature, we emotionally detach ourselves from them. We no longer consider ourselves part of nature but separate to it. We have become so emotionally detached using stories of science that we don't care what happens to the world, as long as we can buy our new phone, TV, car, or computer. And we are prepared to destroy the natural world to get them. Our stories of science are creating more of an imbalance between nature and us, and making it harder to find a balance within ourselves. In just a few hundred years of scientific discovery and advancement we have brought our earth to the brink of destruction. We have polluted our airways and waterways in the hunt for material to fuel our modern lives. The extinction rate of the estimated one hundred million species of plants and animals on the planet is considered one thousand to ten thousand times higher than the natural extinction rate thanks to man. We are currently estimated to be losing ten thousand species every year.[13] Without the discoveries of science we would not have created so much damage to the natural world. Yet we consider the stories of science to be more valid and valuable than the stories of ancient tribes and ancestors who could meet each other's human needs and were able to live in balance with the land for over tens of thousands of years.

We currently consider some of our most dysfunctional stories to be the most important of all.

Don't get me wrong, the methods and approaches of science can be very helpful, but they are far from our salvation. I grew up with science, as a doctor I came to know it well and use the products of it every working day – it helps save lives and lessen human suffering. Science can help us adapt to an ever-changing world and offer us lots of benefits, it can even help undo some of the damage it is largely responsible for, but in the process of using it we risk losing ourselves.

Science will not increase your Essence of Woman. Science will not help you be true to yourself. But right here and now by enhancing your own spirituality in a way that raises your Essence of Woman you can become more complete than science can ever help you to be.

Enhancing spirituality can be a powerful tool for personal change. It can help you fulfill your deepest desires.

How do we enhance your spirituality in a way that raises your Essence of Woman? We can:

- connect with the spirit of all things
- create stories of spirits true to your heart.

But wait. Aren't we going back to a more ignorant and superstitious way by re-embracing the spiritual? No.

This is a forward step; a progressive approach very much worth considering.

Science is narrow; it has trouble seeing the bigger picture, and its own relevance. This makes it potentially hugely destructive. The spiritual helps us engage with our humanity, connect with the bigger picture and can help restore balance by keeping the destructive potential of science in check.

Would we really have made atomic weapons that can destroy all life on the planet if we had remained emotionally connected to all things? Would we continue to make new diseases just because we can and yet have the potential to wipe out whole species? Would we use science and technology to destroy so many trees, create so much pollution, change our world so it can no longer sustain us with enough food, water, and diversity if we had remained emotionally connected to it? Yes, we can discover it, we can build it, we can change the world, but what do we feel about it? Does it feel like the right thing to do?

We noted earlier there are parts of the brain that deal with the present or short-term, and parts that deal with the long-term. The short-term parts focus on the rational, they don't look far into the future. The long-term parts don't focus on the rational, they look beyond what is narrow, far beyond what we consciously see; they relate to feelings and intuition. When we focus more on what we feel we can see what is beyond us, yet still has great meaning. Science is very logical, but it is restricted by its own logic. Enhancing the spiritual helps us connect beyond the rational, but is still critically relevant to the world, ourselves, and our long-term survival and fulfillment by reconnecting us to all things with feeling.

Without the spiritual we are running full speed ahead, without knowing if we are headed towards a cliff. Enhancing the spiritual helps us see the bigger picture so we can better choose where we are going, so we don't wipe ourselves off the planet in the process.

However, enhancing the spiritual comes with a potentially devastating risk. Enhancing the more intuitive side of us can create just as much imbalance and destruction as unchecked science. If we aren't aware of this risk then enhancing the spiritual can do more harm than good.

How can enhancing the spiritual potentially be so destructive?

The risk is in doing what we have done before; giving the spirits we create too much power.

Chapter 34:
The great danger of the spiritual

We were always going to create spirits to help us make sense of the world and the many forces we didn't understand. We were destined to give them too much power. Becoming farmers didn't just lead to the inevitable fall of the Essence of Woman, it prompted some of the most destructive stories of all. Stories that would not only see us destroy each other but also reduce our sense of choice, sense of responsibility, and for the first time enable us to disconnect personally from nature. The fall of the Essence of Woman is not just a tale of chronic threat and farmers. It is also a story of our inevitable changing relationship to spirits and the supernatural.

Live off the land, move from place to place, and it pays to know the spirits of the animals and land we travel. The more intimately we know the spirits of the animals we hunt for instance the more we can predict how they will behave and the easier it is to teach each other to stalk, catch, or kill them so we can feed our families. The more we know the spirits of the land the more we know the places that might be dangerous and the ones where we can find clean water. A farmer doesn't need to know any of these spirits since he no longer needs them to survive. What a farmer needs is to know that his crops and animals will grow, and the harvest will be plenty. He needs powerful spirits that govern the winds, the seasons, and the rains. If the rains don't come then the crops will fail and there won't be enough to feed the animals. If the winds are strong they can destroy the farms. If the seas are harsh they can kill us as we seek to harvest its bounty for our family.

As farmers we don't need spirits that are our equals, we need powerful spirits that we can bargain with, coerce, and manipulate.

Farmers don't need spirits; they need all-powerful gods.

A powerful god can change the weather, the seasons and the sun, the fruitfulness of the harvest, prevent pestilence ruining a crop, and give farmers the plenty they need to survive and thrive. Farmers need gods of fair trade so they can sell their excess, they need gods of fertility so they can have children and be able to continue to grow what they need, and they need gods of song to celebrate their bounty. There are many examples of gods being created by farming cultures that had powers such as these.

For example the powerful early Indo-European god, Dyeus, could control lightning, the rain and the wind. The Roman god, Vertumnus, had influence over the seasons, plant growth, fruit trees and gardens. The Greek god, Hermes, the Roman god, Mercury, and the similar ancient Arabic god, Al-Kutbay, were powerful gods of commerce or trade. There were numerous fertility goddesses such as the Greek goddess, Aphaea, the African goddesses, Ashanti, and Igbo, the Aztec goddesses Chimalma, Coatlicue, and Xochipilli, the Celtic goddesses Brigid, Onuava, and Epona, the Hawaiian goddess Haumea, and the Roman goddess of female fertility and the earth, Libera, to name but a very few. And the Greek god, Dionysus, was a god of wine, vegetation, pleasure and festivity. All of these gods were powerful and could help farmers enjoy success.

It isn't enough these gods just have great power they also need to be gods with human features.

If a god doesn't have human features we can't predict them, we can struggle to understand and make sense of them. More importantly, if our gods aren't like us we can't bargain, beg, coerce, and manipulate them to help us. We need gods to be like us so we feel they relate to us. We can pray to a god with human features as we might ask a parent or a leader with great power for help. If they can relate to us they will be more likely to care for us as we care for each other. Besides if a god thought of us as we think of ants why would they want to listen to us? Do you try to listen to the needs of an ant? The more human features we give our gods the more secure we can feel. All of the gods we just mentioned had human qualities and features. This would allow us to better relate to and bargain with them through prayer, worship, and offering sacrifice. The more we believe in gods when we are farmers the more we have hope. Once we became farmers we were always going to create gods.

The big problem with creating powerful gods is we also create people who claim to represent them.

As we have seen once we become farmers we are more driven by the desires for wealth, power, and status. Create a powerful god and what better way to increase our power and status than to ally ourselves with them? Besides, who can question us if we speak the will of a god? Who would dare question the power of a divinity we mere mortals couldn't hope to understand?

Create many gods and the drive for power and status will inevitably lead to a conflict for power among the followers of the gods. A classic example of this happened over three thousand years ago.

Amenhotep IV was a pharaoh of Ancient Egypt who died around 1334 BC. Egypt at the time was a place divided. Some of the most powerful and influential people were the priests and priestesses of the various gods and temples, all competing for power and influence, a power that could threaten a pharaoh's rule. Amenhotep's solution to restore order and consolidate his power was to make himself the sole prophet of one God, Aten – often depicted as a sun disc on hieroglyphs or pictograms. He made Aten the most powerful and only god, and Amenhotep was the only one who could speak for Aten. He outlawed all other gods and priests. In the process he changed his name to Akenhaten meaning 'horizon of Aten'. As the sole prophet of one all-powerful god he could then unify Egypt under one absolute ruler: himself. His efforts didn't last long however. After his death the other priestesses and priests regained their power by reinstating their gods. They tried to wipe away all history that Akenhaten ever existed. Just enough pictograms survived to tell us of his tale.

Create gods and we can expect men will fight for power and influence in the name of their gods.

They will try to destroy each other just to prove their god is most powerful. In essence trying to prove they are more powerful, since they are fighting as men on their god's behalf. Create gods and we create destruction as we fight each other, not for land or resources, but purely for power. Yet because we have created gods we can justify a battle of good versus evil, a war against an Axis of Evil, or against evil barbarians who threaten our way of life – if they do not follow the will of our god they must be evil. Whole countries can be destroyed just to satisfy human based desires, not the desires of the gods but the very human desires at the heart of a man that can never ultimately be satisfied – the search for ultimate security through wealth and power. Create gods and we also create destruction by reducing choice, personal responsibility, and emotionally disconnecting us from nature.

Create prophets and priests and we create people we can go to when we need advice and need to decide what to do. When should we plant the crops? Let's ask the priest or priestess of the god who controls the harvest. Want a baby? Let's ask the priest or priestess of the fertility god what we should do. Want to make war, or be a successful merchant, or our children to be born healthy, just ask the relevant priest or priestess what we have to do, what tribute we need to make, what actions we need to take. How do we know the right course of action to take? We ask the so-called representatives of the gods to make the decisions and choices for us.

We hand over our power of choice to those who are supposed to represent the gods.

The Auger – a powerful group of priests of Ancient Rome – would interpret the will of the gods by studying the flight of birds. Their interpretations determined matters of war, commerce, and religion. According to Cicero (106–43 BC) – a Roman consul, philosopher, lawyer, and politician – he considered the Auger the most powerful authority in the republic. The Augers could overturn laws, and were consulted to determine who would ascend to be a magistrate, even a king. The Auger's acceptance of any proposed position in office would lead to 'inauguration', a term we are still familiar with today, a ceremony held to instill a new official to their post. It is a tradition that has been handed down and we can still see remnants in the ceremony that installs the president of the United States on the day of his 'inauguration' every four years. The Augers – the representatives and interpreters of the will of their gods – made many powerful and critical choices for their people that defined the course of a once great empire. But to hand over the power of choice to others can come at a price.

As we have previously noted when we reduce our sense of choice we lessen our sense of self. This leads to a reduced self-respect; thus making us more likely to destroy the world, each other, and ourselves.

Create gods and we also lessen our responsibility.

Create gods and we are not the reason our relationships fail. It isn't our fault the crop failed. We committed the crime due to the evil god that made us do it. We could destroy great tracts of land and still not take any responsibility. There wasn't anything we could have done; it was in the lap of the gods. Or worse still, we could claim we are only following the will of our god; it was my god that inspired me, much as the Augers could be inspired by their gods to send Rome to war, or a leader today can be inspired to send his or her soldiers into battle.

Create gods and we don't have to look to us to change, or to understand what happened so it doesn't happen again, we can simply blame the gods, or the prophets, priestesses, and priests that are supposed to represent them. They didn't pray enough. They didn't make powerful enough offerings, or properly interpret the signs. They didn't stop the storm from destroying our farm's crops. It wasn't our responsibility.

The more we believe in the power of the gods and the power of their representatives on earth the less we need to look to ourselves to change and take personal responsibility.

The less responsibility we take the less we learn and the more mistakes and destruction we are going to make. Without personal responsibility we can be very destructive.

We can also be very destructive when we are emotionally disconnected from the world and ourselves, as we noted earlier when discussing the emotional detachment of science. Creating gods helps us create a similar level of destructive emotional disconnection to that of science.

Create gods that create or control all things and we invoke an image of people with great powers – like the Gods of Mount Olympus in Greece. Gods such as Zeus, Apollo, Ares, Hermes, and Aphrodite are not part of everything, they stand above it; they control and manipulate it from on high. Once you create an image of beings controlling the natural world you create an image of us as human beings being able to control it too; if the gods can control it and they have human features like us then so can we. By creating gods we create the idea that we too can be gods some day and control and manipulate nature, each other, and ourselves, as we imagine they do. This idea that we can be like gods or a god detaches us from the world. No longer are we a part of all things we are separate to it, we are better than it, we don't answer to the natural world we control it, and it answers to us.

Contrast this to when we were tribal and believed in spirits. At that time we were part of the spirit of all things. Everything affected us and we could sense it. We could feel the effects of all things. Hear the stories of the ancient nomadic tribes such as the Aboriginal people of Australia, the North American Indians, even the current tribes of the Amazon such as the Yanomani, and we can see this. The Yanomani for example believe that every creature, tree, rock and mountain has a spirit. They remain in close contact with the land; they respect it and live in balance with it – though the land that sustains and nourishes them is currently under threat from mining.[14] It is clear they learnt to be part of the land and not be separate to it. I have heard it said by many Indigenous people of different lands that they define themselves in terms of the land, that they are the land, and the land is them. They don't believe in gods, they believe in spirits.

It is worth pointing out that without a belief in spirits and then gods we would not have developed science.

Only once we detached ourselves emotionally enough from the world could we see it 'objectively' as science insists we do. This ability to emotionally detach from the world and ourselves can be traced back to us developing the idea of gods rather than spirits. Only with the advent of gods did we begin to treat everything as being truly separate to us. Until then we were emotionally linked and intimately connected to everything.

Detach us emotionally and it is easier to destroy or kill those with which we have no emotional connection, including plants and animals. It is easier to destroy the world itself. Create a belief in gods, give our spirits too much power, and we risk destroying our societies, and the world. Much of the destruction we create, including our wars, can be considered a direct result of us giving spirits too much power and making them gods. Some of the most destructive stories we have ever created are the stories of gods we were inevitably going to create once we became farmers.

There is a risk in us going back to seeing the world as spirits. It can lead to us giving away our choices, losing a sense of self in the process and living less fulfilling lives as we lose touch with our own personal needs. It can lead to us taking less responsibility for our actions and not learning about ourselves as we could so we become wise. It can lead to us emotionally detaching ourselves from all things, even each other, so we are more hostile and destructive to the world and the people around us. It can also lead to us losing connection with our inner selves – the Essence of Woman and the Essence of Man inside us – and creating an imbalance with nature. But this will only happen if we choose to give our spirits too much power, by making them more supernatural than they need to be. And only if we give people permission to speak for a spirit or god on our behalf.

Before we created gods and powerful supernatural spirits we didn't need anyone to interpret the will of nature for us.

We could listen to it and interpret it for ourselves, much as you have begun to do by listening more to your Inner Self. Nature has written inside us who we need to be. We can be distracted from its truth inside us by giving power to beings that never actually had it and listening to others who claim to speak on their behalf.

Enhancing the spiritual is not a backward step. It can be a forward step if we don't give the spirits we create too much power. Through vigilance and keeping our spiritual connection to all things simple we can make enhancing the spiritual a positive and practical forward step that can once again give our lives a sense of emotional connection with the world and each other, and give it the meaning and purpose we all need.

Even better, increasing your spirituality helps to directly enhance and raise your Essence of Woman. It doesn't just do it by directing you to listen more to your Inner Self, it also helps you personally connect with the spirit of all things and allows your caring and nurturing nature to more completely express itself.

See the spirits in all things and the woman within can more fully blossom.

Chapter 35:
Connect with the spirit

It is a crisp spring morning and the crackle of dried leaves and small branches under foot add texture to the birdsong echoing softly in your ears. The trees along the path are tall and majestic. The bushes between them, scruffy and short. Beams of light flicker as the swaying branches brush the sky with leaves scattering new morning light. And the view is breathtaking. Before you, to your right, just past the closest of thick timber, is a valley rolling in carpeted shades of mottled green.

Suddenly you see it differently.

With a clinical eye you see a cliff on the hillside and notice its folded layers of earth and stone. You see the rocks at your feet and notice their volcanic origins. You examine leaves of plants and begin to name them according to genus and species. A flower is no longer a thing to enjoy; it is *Calochilus paludosus*. The butterfly no longer a white beauty but *Delias harpalyce*. And the once pretty dark small bird with a black and orange fanned tail is no longer a chirping friend but *Rufous rufifrons*. Where beauty once touched your heart there are now only names and classifications.

A girlfriend you let walk ahead comes strolling back; her eyes to the clear glowing bright blue sky and tree tops. 'Magnificent, isn't it?' she says as she stands beside you. 'Can't you feel it?'

'Feel what?'

'The life, the essence, the spirits all around us, touching us, flowing through us, and changing us.'

You stop a moment and check how you feel. You notice something. It's there, behind the names and the unemotional detail.

'You know, I think I can feel it.'

'Hard to describe, isn't it? Like coming home.'

Like our friends above we all choose how we see what we see. We also choose whether we connect to emotions and our heart, or keep our observations distant and less personal. You have the choice of seeing a forest of wood for housing and timber, or a land filled with the spirits of wise old trees. You can choose to see animals that might bite or sting, or the spirits of creatures that are like the children of the land. You will not want to care for and nurture a forest of wood. You may not even care for animals that might annoy, scare, or harm you. But you would be more inclined to care for and nurture the spirit of a being in the form of a majestic, patient, yet vulnerable tree, or the childlike spirits of a maternal land you hold close to your heart that nurtures us all. By creating a connection with the world through its spirits you evoke the natural feelings of the Essence of Woman within; they emerge and blossom.

How do we create a way of seeing the world in terms of spirits so we reconnect with everything emotionally? We think and analyze less, and feel more.

To increase our spiritual connection to all things we want to use the parts of our brain that see beyond detail; outside the logical and rational. Seeing the world in terms of feelings is a great way to do that. Details have clear limits. For example the letters on this page stop, they don't just fade into each other or we would have trouble reading them; they have clearly defined edges or limits. Feelings in contrast are more nebulous; more like a cloud with fuzzy edges. Fly up into a cloud and we can't see exactly where it begins or ends. Feelings have no clear beginning or end, often they blend or flow from one into another such as the feelings of enjoying the company of good friends blending and flowing seamlessly with the feelings of having your much-loved partner by your side. Spirits are also nebulous; they have no clear beginning or end.

For example, if I spoke of a spirit of the real woman inside you what image would come to mind? Would you think of a solid woman within; a spirit that you could touch or hold? Or would you think more of a ghost, a more mist-like apparition? We often give spirits poorly defined qualities, they are more mist-like rather than solid as say a stone or piece of rock.

Feelings and spirits go well together, they both have mist-like qualities, and this is what we want.

Spirits are something we feel, we don't measure. We sense and conjure them, but we can't clearly define them. This allows them to change, be personal, blend with the world and each other and blend with us. Conjuring or creating spirits helps us connect and blend with all things in a personal way. You are more likely to feel for trees, animals, and the land as spirits than you ever will as objects of study that are precisely defined.

Create the spirit in all things and you can more easily care and nurture it.

Give the land and its many parts qualities you feel and relate to, give everything the feeling of being the child of a greater motherly spirit, and you raise the Essence of Woman inside you as your inner woman seeks to naturally care for and nurture them.

Creating spirits in all things helps raise your Essence of Woman by giving you so much more to care for and nurture.

Your potential for caring can feel almost infinite, if you let it, as you feel the spirit in all there is that has no end. The key to experiencing and feeling this is to simply begin to see the world in terms of spirits.

Below are some suggestions of how you might do this.

See the world as spirits

- **Walk in a park or a nature reserve and imagine all the trees, plants, and animals as inhabited with spirits.** Feel their presence. Feel what it might be like to be them.
- **Imagine the earth as a great spirit.** It grows and nurtures so much that all becomes part of it. What might that feel like if you were that motherly spirit?

- **Look in your heart, what essence of womanly spirit do you find?** What qualities would you give it? We have created the image of the Essence of Woman, what form might that take as a spirit? Would it be a young naïve woman for example, or the wise ancient mother spirit we alluded to in earlier chapters?
- **Imagine the spirits of your ancestors.** Can you see their spirit in your children? Can you feel their spirit in yourself?
- **What does the spirit of the sky feel like?** How does the spirit of the sea make you feel?
- **And within the greater spirit in all things what smaller spirits make the whole?** What children, what stars, planets, worlds, life, and people are a part of its greater self?
- **Notice the spirit in your pets, see their human-like qualities if you don't already.** Get to know their unique and different spirit and see how nature made them. For instance, what happens if you treat your dog as a human child? Is that what nature made them to be? Do you notice how they act if you baby them; like a leader of the pack – leader of you? Getting in touch with your pet's spirit can help avoid behavioral problems.

There is much that we don't consciously see. We can begin to touch it and grasp its connection with us and feel its value with connecting to its spirit. We can't do that if we just name it, dissect it, or try to classify it. Can we still examine it if we want to? Sure, it isn't going anywhere.

As a general rule I tend not to look for the spirits in technology, such as cars, computers, phones and the like. This tends to give them an unnatural value.

The more we value what isn't made directly by nature the more we value what can destroy nature.

We make our technology by destroying parts of nature not by working with nature; for example we destroy forests and mine the minerals that make our computers and TVs. The more we emotionally attach to what was created by destroying nature the more we are likely to destroy nature rather than create a sustainable balance with it.

Does this mean we should be against technology?
No.

It just means it can be more useful if we simply keep the technology a tool like an axe or hammer is a tool rather than give it human or spiritual character. The more we spiritually relate to technology the more we can get absorbed in it and give it an unnatural power.

The more power we give it the more important technology becomes in our lives compared to the natural world and the more we are likely to destroy the parts of nature that keep us alive just to get more of it.

We can have technology and develop a balance with nature. That can be next to impossible if we imbue technology with a powerful spiritual feeling.

Feel the world every day. Search for the essence in all things, find its spirit and let it touch you. Let it welcome you and let yourself know it in your heart as it really is, as your Inner Self sees it.

Keep it practical

It is worth pointing out that we can take the caring and nurturing of nature too far. You can be so connected spiritually to all things and want to care for them so much you may never want to harm a thing, not even to eat it! How can we even think of killing something we care so much about? That is impractical – we don't eat we don't live.

I remember seeing a documentary where a small African native tribesman ran down a large antelope – running on two legs allows us to run for longer than animals on four legs. At the end, as the antelope stopped, fell over, and started dying of heat exhaustion, the small weary tribesman gave thanks to the animal, spoke calmly to it and tried to ease its distress. Then he calmly cut it so it would bleed and die more quickly. He did not attack it; he did not cut it up while it was still alive. You could say he respected its spirit. He thanked a fellow creature for helping him provide for his family.

We can still care for life on the world; treat it with respect and still be human. If we don't take the ideas of caring for all things too far, we can find a balance and take our place among it closer to what nature intended.

Another powerful way of enhancing your spiritual connection to all things is by creating stories. Stories that can also help you know yourself, consolidate your emotional connection with everything, and help raise the Essence of Woman even further. We look at this in the next chapter.

Chapter 36:
Create stories of spirits true to your heart

Creating and sharing stories of the spiritual is a great way of consolidating and spreading stories that can positively change our lives. We have seen how powerful and influential stories are; they determine everything from what we think to what we do and feel. By creating and sharing stories of the spiritual – as our ancestors once did – we can help foster the functional and wise aspects of our lives, how to live in a balanced way that helps us have our needs met. Better still we can also enhance and help raise the Essence of Woman. Every spiritual story that helps emphasize the power, value, and importance of woman in a society helps the Essence of Woman be raised once more, and restore much needed balance. Every story you create or share matters.

Does this mean you have to be some wonderful storyteller to make a real difference?

Not at all.

Remember your brain is a natural storyteller. All you need to do is use this natural ability and give it focus.

We have already started doing this.

A moment ago by giving plants and animals a spiritual essence we made them easier to want to care for and nurture. When we did this we created a spiritual story. The story helped raise your Essence of Woman. The story of Mother Earth as a great spirit of creation and caring is another such story.

Considering the earth as a motherly spirit evokes feelings of caring and nurturing, this time of all that exists on the planet. Any story that enhances the power and value of the womanly spirit and influence raises the spirit and Essence of Woman, especially among women who hear it.

Another example is the Keres Indians of New Mexico's tale of Thought Woman, as woman creator giving life to all things. This evokes images of giving birth and bringing new life into the world, a desire within the Essence of Woman to have children and a family. The more people believe this story the more it can raise the Essence of Woman in those who tell and share the tale; it imparts strength, power, and validation to many powerful womanly desires.

Though we look at her as a mother, the Keres Indians considered Thought Woman to be a father also. She had features of both. As well as raise the Essence of Woman her image also creates equality and balance with the Essence of Man.

Every story Australian Aboriginal women told as part of secret woman's business raised the Essence of Woman among all who heard and told it.

Stories can help raise the parts of us that lie dormant in our hearts.

The ancient tribes knew the power of their stories, if not consciously then at least subconsciously. They knew their stories held greater power and personal connection especially if they involved spirits with characteristics they could all relate to.

So create and share stories of the spirits of the world and the feelings they evoke just as our ancestors did. See the world from different spirits' eyes and allow that to be your storyteller. For example, imagine the world through the eyes of the spirit of an eagle, or through the patience of the essence of a tree. Perhaps see it through the cheekiness of a magpie, or the vigilance of the ever-watchful meerkat. Feel the spirit of the land as it talks to you. Learn its stories and know its heart. And in all this, search your own heart and find the spirit of the woman you know you are and you know you want to be.

I once remember explaining the concept of Land in the Balance of Self Model to a female patient feeling depressed. I explained how most of our human communication is still non-verbal; body language. For most of human existence we never really spoke, certainly not with a complex language. That meant we simply noticed what others did and then interpreted what that would mean, such as the behaviors of someone who was angry, or sad, or happy. People's actions had – and still have – meaning to us. The seasons of the land can also have meaning. For example, the Aboriginal Australians of Kakadu in northern Australia learnt when the berries are ripe on the tree it is time to collect eggs from the wild geese. As we spoke she told me her grandfather was Aboriginal. As a child he told her if she listened the land would talk to her. She didn't know what he meant. Now she understood. The land has many stories to teach us, tales we can share with each other, if we are prepared to consider them, and listen.

Following are some suggestions to help you create stories involving spirits.

Create stories with spirits

- **Recognize and feel the Spirit of Woman in all things.** In everything that gives life – protects it, nurtures it, cares for it – recognize her in it. It could be a flower, vine, tree, an insect, animal, river, mountain or fertile plain; notice the womanly spirit that unites them, as if it is the same spirit shared among sisters. But don't just notice it, feel its presence as if it flows and resides in everything. Search for this womanly spirit and see where you find it.
- **Search only for the Spirit of Man in men.** If you see common features of a motherly, maternal, or womanly spirit in a man you will only diminish the Essence of Man in him and other men. The more you see of the Essence of Woman within him the less he will be able to satisfy you by being a man. Find a womanly spirit in the heart of men and not a manly spirit and you make him one of the girls and will then wonder why he cannot satisfy you.
- **Recognize and feel the power of the Spirit of Woman.** The more you do this the more you empower yourself and make your Essence of Woman stronger.

- **Notice the influence of the maternal and motherly spirit.** Notice how it molds our children and transforms a society. Feel the great power of the woman spirit inside you.

Many of the North American Indigenous people recognized this power and shared stories expressing it. As an example Maria Chona of the Papago in *The Spirit of Indian Women* (p 92) said: 'Women have power. Men have to dream to get power from the spirits and they think of everything they can hoping that the spirits will notice them and give them some power. But we have power. Children. Can any warrior make a child, no matter how brave and wonderful he is?'

This short story reminds us, men can build the largest companies, govern the largest country, and yet have no power at all. The great power, if women choose to accept it, is in the natural spirit of the woman and being mother of the child who will change a nation. Every child changes the world.

Embrace the spiritual stories that empower you as a woman and your Essence of Woman is raised.

Stories through actions

Words can't accurately explain much of what you feel of spirits and nature, of feelings from your heart. So not all stories our brain creates can be spoken. This doesn't mean they cannot be shared.

We share a story by expressing it in our actions. You share the Spirit of Woman by acting true to being a woman to your children, your partner, your friends, your family and your community. Imagine the great Spirit of Woman being passed with good will to all those you know. How much better will they be for it? How much can we all benefit from this sharing?

We can also share stories evoking and embracing the Spirit of Woman through art, music, movies, games, and in the more familiar novel or written word. To create such works requires tapping into the heart of the Spirit of Woman. Much as art and culture can be used to increase our Personal Self it can also raise your Essence of Woman if you draw from it as you create it and gain inspiration. The more you share the Spirit of Woman the more it transforms you and the people with whom you share her.

Share tales and actions of the Spirit of Woman with your daughters, your girlfriends, granddaughters, nieces, and aunts. Enhance its power by making it secret. Create the sharing of your own woman's business much as many Aboriginal Australians once did, and some still do today.

Do not share all your tales of women with or around men however. When you come together and share tales of women being women, of the spirits of nature and the balance of life, the Spirit of Woman is finally allowed to freely express itself. This cannot happen when men are present; their spirit will naturally dilute the power of the womanly presence. Regular meetings of women and sharing women's business is a powerful story creating and sharing experience.

Let the Spirit of Woman rise as you share a part of yourself that only a woman can truly know.

In a world full of stories and all manner of beliefs it can be easy to lose our way. By seeing spirits in all things of the natural world and inside our heart we can once again be guided by them as they guided our ancestors and their ancestors before them. When a path is blocked or looks dangerous sometimes we have to take a few steps back before we can change to another path and once again move forward with safety. Enhancing the Essence of Woman by seeing and feeling the spirits in all things is not a long-term backwards step, it is a bold forward step that can help us find the fulfillment and balance we have been losing. We do not need to actually believe in real spirits to gain benefit. We can simply embrace our imagined spirits' feel, their understanding, their point of view, and intent. For when our mind can search and be among spirits it can transcend this physical world. Then we can begin to see and experience everything closer to what it really is, including ourselves. We can begin to see all things closer to how our Inner Self sees it.

The spirits can guide you if you let them.

Many ancients were wiser than we'd like to believe. Perhaps we should finally respect their wisdom as it was reflected in the stories they created that filled their hearts and helped them live as fulfilled and satisfied human beings. Perhaps we should reconcile the stories of the past with the stories of the present and decide what stories will serve us best as human beings in the years to come. Perhaps scientific stories, and the stories of all-powerful gods, are not the types of stories we should be trying to find salvation in.

Warning

Never let spirits control your actions. You control what you do; they do not control you in any way. Once you believe otherwise you will no longer listen to and be guided by your Inner Self, you will be steered by ever-greater delusion and fantasy that will lead you astray. That is how our brain works. If you give it permission to lose control to the fantasies it will, without hesitation.

And never let anyone speak for the spirits on their behalf.

Only ever learn to listen to what you notice of them personally. Don't let someone else control you and take away your sense of self. Your personal communication with nature should be paramount.

A good way to help keep the spiritual world in check is to be mindful, meditate regularly, and communicate with your Inner Self. Your Inner Self will always know the truth and how much is your fantasy or creation. It can always offer a reality check if you are quiet of mind enough to let it.

The seven steps have been offered as a guide. Their aim has been to help you become and feel more true to yourself as a woman, and better understand what this means in the context of living in the modern world. What you may not have noticed is how each of the seven steps also helps create a more peaceful, safe, and secure life for us, while also raising the Essence of Woman. As we began to see earlier, if we don't work to reduce chronic threat the Essence of Woman will naturally fall and women will continue to be treated poorly. You can help reduce chronic threats simply by following each of the seven steps. By you becoming more authentic you begin to eliminate the reasons you have not been appreciated, valued, and respected as a woman.

How does each of the seven steps help reduce chronic threat?

Consider the following.

Create a more secure world

We have always held to the hope, the belief, the conviction that there is a better life, a better world, beyond the horizon.
Franklin D Roosevelt[15]

It's hard to be valued and respected as a woman in a family, society, or nation under the influence of ongoing threat. Chronic threat is poison to a woman's soul and spirit; it robs her of the joy and satisfaction in her heart of being the woman she knows she can be. The good news is each of the seven steps you have just applied goes a long way to reducing the state of chronic threat among us, perhaps in ways you haven't considered. Let's look at this more closely.

Chapter 37:
How the seven steps reduce chronic threat

Step 1: Respect

The more we practice respect for men and women the more we respect each other as human beings. This reduces tensions and helps us finally end the extremely destructive battle of the sexes.

> Many of us still do this; we blame all men, or all women for the problems we have with each other.

We say that the world 'can do without men; it has been biologically proven!' We resent and get frustrated that the opposite sex isn't meeting our needs. We can resent them even more if they abuse, disrespect, or oppress us. We make the opposite sex the enemy. This battle between genders simply adds even more tension between us and begins to create a state of chronic threat in our families, communities, and relationships. Unfortunately, every time a woman makes a man the enemy she increases the state of threat between us, she makes men less of a friend and less likely to help her feel safe and secure. The longer this threat lasts – as minor as it might sometimes seem – the more the desires of men will dominate and the more likely women will be less valued and appreciated in our society, opening them up to even more abuse by men.

> Nobody wins a battle or war between the sexes but women especially fair badly, as it further lowers the Essence of Woman among them.

Focusing on what is common between the sexes does the opposite, it helps raise the Essence of Woman and reduce the level of threat. You will recall we become friends by focusing on the sameness between us, not the differences. Respecting each other's differences whilst placing our focus on the vast similarities between us – we are more alike than we are different, we are both human beings after all – goes a long way to reducing threat and preventing a state of chronic threat ever existing in our relationships, families, and societies. Who cares if men are from Mars and women are from Venus; we share the common human experience of living on the same life-giving Earth.

Every part of our life where there is a state of threat – where we do not feel safe and secure – increases the level of threat in our society. Even the threats we pose to each other as men and women simply because we are biologically different. Respect and value the differences in each other yet keep focus on what we have in common and we go a long way to reducing a state of chronic threat ever developing or maintaining itself in our communities.

Step 2: Friendship

It goes without saying the more we can be friends the more we reduce the level of chronic threat in our society. The more we meet each others' needs of friendship the less we fight, compete, and become aggressive towards one another in our relationships, families, and within our communities. Meeting the same ten needs of friendship also goes a long way to reducing the level of threat between countries.

The same skills we learn to make friendships are what we need to develop in friendships with other countries. As we noted earlier every country is like every person in that it seeks to be respected, valued, appreciated, heard, it seeks to be noticed, cared for, supported, and protected in times of need. When we can be friends with each other we can lower the state of threat in a society or country. When we can be friends with other nations we lower the state of threat everywhere.

Practice the skills you learn to improve your friendships with other women and your partner and share them with everyone and you lessen the state of chronic threat around you and around the world.

Step 3: Listen to you

With the practice of mindfulness and communicating with your Inner Self you become calmer, more tolerant, more understanding, and more peaceful inside. This calm, peace, and tolerance make you less of a threat to others. This spirit of calm and peace can be contagious and spread among your colleagues and friends and lessen tensions wherever you go, thus lowering the level of chronic threat around you and in society at large as your influence ripples its positive effects through your community. Listening to your Spirit of Woman by connecting with your Inner Self can also help in a more direct way.

The more you see what it is to be an authentic woman, the less you will have to compete with men on their aggressive terms.

The more your caring and nurturing nature rises as you discover it through communicating with your Inner Self the more you will want to share and care for those around you, not fight or compete with them. The more sharing and caring you become the less threatening you become and the more others can follow your example. The more you listen to the truth of your inner nature as a woman the more you can pass on these nonthreatening ideas and approaches with everyone, including the men in your life so they too can spread these more compassionate approaches among other men.

The more you listen to the inner-you the more we all feel the benefits of you naturally reducing states of threat.

Step 4: Be attractive

Increasing your attractiveness though raising your Personal Self can reduce chronic threat in several ways. One obvious way comes by you increasing your self-worth and self-respect.

When we respect and value ourselves we are less tolerant of other people's disrespect.

This means we will be less likely to tolerate abuse and physical violence against us. The more people are allowed to get away with abuse and physical violence the more people will suffer it and the more the level of threat then rises in a family and community. Worse than that, if we don't stop the abuse then our children will either suffer it or be the ones abusing others when they grow up. The stronger our self-worth and self-respect the lower the level of threat we will tolerate around us, and the lower the level of threat in every aspect of our life.

The more you become and remain attractive as the real you, with a raised Personal Self, the less the chance of a state or chronic threat existing in your family, community, and country. The more others see the benefits of you having a strong Personal Self with an inner strength that is better able to prevent abuse and deal with it when it arises the more they are likely to follow your example.

Step 5: Be sex-wise

What sex we have can affect the levels of chronic threat in our society. For example Social Sex can be used to increase and validate status and power. When we are all seeking status and power we're not friends we're competitors and possible threats to each other's security. Using sex to gain power or status just emphasizes and reinforces this state of competition over friendship, contributing to us feeling even more insecure since we have so few people we can truly trust or count on. Social Sex can easily add to a state of threat among us.

Family-Positive Sex on the other hand, that is founded more on close friendship than on building power and status, can lower the level of chronic threat. It emphasizes and helps teach us how to be close friends.

It then offers a role model to our children. By emphasizing the value of friendship and relationships over wealth and status Family-Positive Sex helps us improve the community thus lowering the level of threat.

> **Being sex-wise will determine if we raise or lower the level of chronic threat in our society.**

Step 6: Be actively involved

As we have seen by increasing your personal education you raise your wisdom and insight. This helps you to empathize with others and be more tolerant and compassionate towards them. Formal education means more people are likely to take you seriously – education is a form of status. Combine formal education and wisdom and people are more likely to take notice of your womanly wisdom and experience and consider and adopt your empathic, compassionate, and tolerant ways.

> **Compassion, tolerance, and understanding go a long way towards reducing conflicts with others and reducing the chance of a state of threat developing between us.**

We are more likely to make enemies from those we don't understand or relate to. Be actively involved in decision making as a well-educated woman and you help spread qualities that naturally reduce a state of threat and chronic threat wherever you go. The more levels of society you actively participate in, the less threat in your society and around the world.

Step 7: Enhance your spirituality

As we just noticed the more we see the world in terms of spirits the more personally connected we become to all things. This makes us less likely to destroy it and become more motivated to work in harmony and balance with it.

Work with nature and we reduce the threat of famine and drought by ensuring waterways and land are preserved so they can sustain us. Fight or disrespect the land and we can all soon start fighting for what few natural resources are left. Seeing the world in terms of spirits can help us reduce long-term or short-term threats of starvation. It can also help calm us.

With the natural world full of spirits we can also more easily connect with natural peace.

We can let the slow flowing river, the blue sea, and the tall steadfast tree connect with us emotionally and let it calm our own spirit. Try it; let yourself feel their calm, then spread the calm among your community. Nature doesn't fight us, the more we see it as a collection of friends with a calm and peaceful nature the more we can share this nature among others and reduce threat in our families, cities, and communities.

Every step you take to becoming more your authentic self helps create a sense of safety, security, and peace among us all. The effects of chronic threat need not continue to poison the lives of women and societies. Women do not lessen chronic threat however by being like a man, such as taking on more of his provider and protector role and playing his games of seeking wealth, power, and status. We can help create a peaceful society that respects and values women, and the vital contribution we need from them, by women like you simply learning to listen to you and being the woman you feel you are deep in your heart. The seven steps have been written to help you achieve this.

Women like you give us our greatest and most realistic hope.

Chapter 38:
Realistic hope

For eons women and men like you and I lived in close contact with the land that nurtured and sustained them. By simply living in its presence the land helped teach us to be authentic; nature helped define our roles for us. As we wandered the land it touched our hearts and taught us how to live in balance with it. By simply existing in close contact with the land its calming and often-soothing influence helped create a peaceful balance within. It wasn't always smooth sailing, many hardships had to be endured, and life within and between tribes wasn't always great, but we survived well this way for more than a million years. Then we changed; the land helped do this.

Nature provided special places with plants and animals that allowed us to settle so we no longer had to roam vast wildernesses to survive. It allowed us to settle and farm, and soon we farmed animals and plants, developed towns and villages, and eventually cities and vast civilizations. Soon we lost direct contact with the land that taught us who we are. In a matter of a few thousand years we lost contact with the truth in our hearts, with what we felt deep inside.

Today we struggle to know what it is to be our authentic selves. Chronic threat now dominates the world creating an imbalance between the Essence of Woman and the Essence of Man. In the process women are being abused, undervalued, and disrespected simply for being women. They're being driven by basic human needs to be like men.

We live in a time when the male dominant drives for wealth, power, and status rule our lives. Friends have been replaced by allies, mothering replaced by childcare, supportive communities replaced by the dollar. Relationships are failing and not satisfying us like we know they should, families are being torn apart, communities are struggling to meet their citizens' needs. Every day we see in the media evidence of violence, wars, starvation, torture, and abuse. We are surrounded by fear and insecurity. It can all seem overwhelming and hard to take. It can leave us feeling powerless, and rob us of any hope.

There is a hope, and as many of you may have become aware it won't be found in a leader, a genius, or science or faith. Our greatest realistic hope is you.

Written inside you is the key to our salvation, to a life of satisfaction and deep fulfillment nature has offered since humanity's very inception.

Inside you is the influential and powerful woman we all need, for our relationships, our families, and our communities. Inside you is the ancient spirit and Essence of Woman that can counter the poisonous effects of the domination of the Essence of Man. Once and for all she can help restore the peace and balance we crave.

Nature made us with potential weaknesses. We respond poorly to long-term threats. We can detach ourselves from the natural world and begin to believe we are above it or separate to it. You can help bring us back to our true and natural realistic self.

The future needs women to stand up and be true to themselves. Not to become what others might think they should be, but as women feel, based on what's written in the honest depths of their hearts.

I see a promising future, with women as valued and respected members of the community. I see relationships changing as we once again value close friendships over alliances, wealth, and status. I see us changing how we treat the world and each other as we emotionally connect with our Inner Selves and the world in ways many of us used to in ancient times. I see us reconciling the stories of the past with the tales of the present, science and faith no longer disregarding the wisdom of our ancient tribal ancestors. The past and present is integrated to see us take bold new steps forward creating more functional and useful stories that can help us most. We are products of our environment and the weaknesses nature instilled in us to help us survive. We are also conscious beings able to change our behaviors and the course of our future. I see great promise in the world; tremendous power that can make it happen. It isn't found in books, movies, papers, research, or texts. It is, and always has been, inside you.

The time of Thought Woman is upon us, and long overdue.

Appendix 1

A balance for parents

Time	Activity	Aim or reason	Human essence
1–2 hrs/wk	Quiet time	Be in moment. Listen to self	Personal Self
1–2hrs/wk	Enjoyment time	Connect with self. Fun	Personal Self
1 evening-night/wk	One-on-one couples time. No kids. To talk. eg Restaurant together	Relationship Build and maintain friendship	Family Self
1 weekend every second month	Couples time alone together for a weekend	Relationship Maintenance, fulfill man/woman needs	Family Self
2–3 x 1 hr sessions/wk	One-on-one parent–child time. No disturbance by others for 1 hr minimum	Have fun. Play at child's level doing what they like	Family Self Personal Self
2–3hrs/wk	Time only with friends	Male–male and female–female bonding. Talk. Have fun	Community Self
1 lunch or dinner/month	Extended family time. Time for extended family to socialize	Build family ties and supports. Share problems and good times	Family Self
< 40hrs/wk	Work/Job	Income	Community Self

Appendix 2

Further reading

Bar, M (2011). *Predictions in the Brain: Using our past to generate a future.* Oxford: Oxford University Press.

Diamond, JM (2012). *The World Until Yesterday: What can we learn from traditional societies?* New York: Penguin.

Fitzgerald, J & Fitzgerald, OR (2005). *The Spirit of Indian Women.* Bloomington: World Wisdom, Inc.

Gunn Allen, P (1992). *The Sacred Hoop: Recovering the feminine in American Indian traditions.* Boston: Beacon Press.

McKay, Helen F (2001). *Gadi Mirrabooka: Australian Aboriginal tales from the dreaming.* Englewood: Greenwood Publishing Group, Inc.

Ramsay Smith, W (2003). *Myths and Legends of the Australian Aborigines.* Mineola, NY: Dover Publications, Inc.

Sedhoff, W (2011). *A Balance of Self: A new approach to self understanding, lasting happiness, and self-truth.* Fremantle: Vivid Publishing.

Standing Bear, L (1933). *Land of the Spotted Eagle.* Lincoln: University of Nebraska Press.

Notes

[1] Boston: Beacon Press, 1992, pp 13–15.

[2] Black, MC. Intimate partner violence and adverse health consequences: implications for clinicians, *American Journal of Lifestyle Medicine*, 2011, 5(5): 428–39.

[3] Australian Bureau of Statistics, Paper 4128.0, 1996.

[4] WHO Fact Sheet No 239, Updated October 2013.

[5] Such as the stories described in *The Sacred Hoop*, and *The Spirit of Indian Women*, Bloomington: World Wisdom Inc, 2005.

[6] Centerwall, BS. Exposure to television as a cause of violence. In: Comstock G ed. *Public Communication of Behavior*, Orlando: Academic Press Inc, 1989, 2:1–58.

[7] Liminal Songlines, Sacred Women's Business www.liminalsonglines.com/2010/08/womens-business-womens-ceremony-2.html (accessed December 2014).

[8] The Insulted and Humiliated, *Vremya*, 1861.

[9] *The Spirit of Indian Women*, p 19.

[10] *Land of the Spotted Eagle*, Lincoln: University of Nebraska Press, 1933, p 162.

[11] Constitution Society, Constitution of the Iroquois Nations www.constitution.org/cons/iroquois.htm (accessed December 2014). Credit given to the National Public Telecomputing Network and the Constitution Society.

[12] *Us Mob*, Mudrooroo, 1995, p 33 quoted in www.creativespirits.info/aboriginalculture/spirituality/what-is-aboriginal-spirituality (accessed December 2014).

[13] World Wildlife Fund http://wwf.panda.org (accessed December 2014).

[14] Survival International www.survivalinternational.org/tribes/yanomami/wayoflife (accessed December 2014).

[15] Franklin D Roosevelt, 'Address on Hemisphere Defense, Dayton, Ohio', 12 October 1940. Online by Gerhard Peters and John T Woolley, *The American Presidency Project* www.presidency.ucsb.edu/ws/?pid=15870 (accessed January 2015).

About the Author

Dr Winfried Sedhoff is a physician with a special interest in mental health. Born in Germany he grew up in the small southern New South Wales country city of Albury, Australia. He graduated medicine from the University of New South Wales in 1987.

In his early twenties and barely two years after graduating, having endured many years of intermittent depression – especially at high school and university – Winfried suffered a life threatening personal crisis. Forsaking all he believed, including a promising specialized medical career, he spent twelve months in self-imposed isolation in a small rental unit in Sydney and began an internal quest to find himself, and a sense of unquestionable truth. His success has allowed him to create a life that has been both personally satisfying and feels his own. He no longer suffers depression. Over twenty years later his personal realisations form the foundation of models and ideas that continue to successfully help patients overcome depression, anxiety, and develop a true and honest sense of authentic self.

Winfried lives in Brisbane, Australia.

Index

Aboriginal Australians
  Awelye 23
  gender based ceremonies 23
  role of land in culture 5–6, 262
  spirituality 241, 251
  women's stories 261, 264
abuse of women
  Australian statistics 8
  consequences of submission 40
  domestic violence as provocation for murder 7
  responding to abuse 42–5
  US statistics 7
  World Health Organization statistics 8
active involvement 225–36, 272
addictions 30, 89, 192, 195
Afghanistan 14, 211
Amazon Yanomani 251
Amenhotep IV 248
attractiveness 141–3, 146, 271
Augers 249–50
authentic men
  bad boys 163
  Family Self 5
  friendships 68, 83–4
  giving support to 74
  needs 142–3
  respect for 46–9
authentic women
  attractiveness 141–3
  education 210, 212
  Family Self 5
  friendships 52, 65, 69, 85, 92, 138
  Inner Self 93, 136, 270
  needs 48, 69, 143, 212
  qualities 26–8, 30, 37, 45
  respect 31, 47, 49
  sexuality 174, 197
  uncovering 21, 24

Baker, June E 240
Balance of Self, A (Sedhoff) 161
Balance of Self (BOS) Model

Community Self 26, 80
  definition 1–2
  derivation 220
  human desires 94, 112–13, 120, 176
  Land 152, 261
  Personal Self 144, 151
  social needs 12
battle between the sexes 268
bonobo chimpanzees 175
brain functions 95–6, 129
breathing
  controlled 101–2
  feeling the breath 106
bullying 40, 90, 126–7

caring and nurturing 34–5
Center for Disease Control and Prevention [USA] 7
choices
  increasing 156–8
  questions to help 129–35
Chono, Maria 263
chronic threat
  influence of 10–15, 275
  steps to reduce 268–73
Community Self
  needs 143, 167, 175–6
  place in Balance of Self Model 2
  ten basic desires 4, 26, 31, 53–4, 72, 80, 90, 221, 233
creativity 171

decision-making
  within community 232
  within the family 228–31
  having influence 225–8
  involvement in politics 233–6
  threat reduction and 272
Diamond, Jared 55
disrespect from women 38–45
Dostoevsky, Fyodor 25

education
  personal 207, 209, 217–24
  socially recognised 207, 209–16, 272
emotional pain, questioning to relieve 112–17
empathy 220–1
Epicurus 51
Essence of Man
  desires 11, 14, 29
  effects of dominance by 13
  male friendships 67
  raising through friendship 52–7
  reactions to threat 11
  time spent with women 67
Essence of Woman, *see also* Spirit of Woman
  benefits of family-positive sex 199–204
  creating spiritual stories 260–6
  danger of spirituality 246–53, 265
  depleted by social sex 199–201
  desires 14, 28, 31
  effects of chronic threat 10–15
  effects of farming 16–22, 274
  enhancement through active involvement 225–36
  enhancement through education 207–24
  friendships with men 66–84
  friendships with women 58–65
  imbalance with Essence of Man 11–12, 274
  inevitable downfall 7–9
  motherhood 37
  questions to understand 136–40
  raising through friendship 52–7, 91–2
  raising through respect 25–45
  romantic love 202–4
  spirituality 237–8, 240–5, 253–9
  strong Personal Self 146
  time spent with men 67, 81
Ethiopia 8

Family Self
  desires 5
  needs 143, 175–7
  place in Balance of Self Model 2
farming, effects on relationships 16–22, 274
fears, questioning to resolve 118–28
feelings 255–6
flashbacks 123
friendships
  attractiveness and 142–3
  befriend yourself 165–8
  close 56–7, 69–77
  with community 90–2
  enhancing 60–4
  with family 86–9
  as means to reduce threat 269–70
  with men 66–84, 138
  with other men 77–84
  with partners 51, 69–77
  Ten Basic Desires of Friendship 80, 91, 142, 176, 178
  ten desires of the Community Self 4
  types of 52–7
  with women 58–65

Gadi Mirrabooka, Australian Aboriginal Tales from the Dreaming (Baker) 240
gender roles 12–13
gods 247–52

hope, creating realistic 132–4
Human Essences 2

India 211
Inner Self
  accessing memories 107–10
  communicating with 96–111
  definition 94–6
  emotional pain, questioning to relieve 112–17
  fears, questioning to resolve 118–28
  feeling the breath 106
  listening to 270
  mind set for communication 101–3
  place for communication 99–101
  questioning 110–11

questions to help future choices 129–35
timing of communication 96–8
toy boats on a stream 105
understanding Essence of Woman 136–40
Zen meditation 103–4

Japan 8

Land
  increasing contact with 152–5
  place in Balance of Self Model 2, 5–6
limbic system 94–5
Luther Standing Bear 173

meditation 102–3, 170
mindfulness 102–3, 110, 170
mortality 242
motherhood 35–8, 137–8, 214
Mundrooroo 237

nature, connecting with 152–5, 171, 243, 256–7, 272–3
North American Indian tribes
  Blackfeet 141
  Cherokee 8, 87, 93
  Iroquois Nation 8, 87, 205–6, 208
  Keres 261
  Oglala Lakota 173
  Papago 263
  role of women 8, 35, 87, 205–6, 208, 263
  spirituality 251

obesity 163

Pakistan 211
Papua New Guinea 55–6
parenthood 277
Personal Self
  befriend yourself 165–8
  in children 169–72
  components 3
  enhancing 144–9
  expressing culture 154

increasing choices 156–8
increasing contact with Land 152–5
increasing self-worth and self-respect 159–64
needs 143–4, 175–6
place in Balance of Self Model 2–3, 149
self time 150–1
Post Traumatic Stress Disorder 124
power
  leading to insecurity 20
  male dominant desire 20
  social sex 200
  used to protect wealth 18–19
praise and encouragement 33–8
purpose, creating future 134–5

respect
  being proud of other women 45
  caring and nurturing 34–5
  disrespect from women 38–45
  within families 88
  increasing self-worth and self-respect 159–64
  loss of pride 29–30
  as means to reduce threat 268–9
  motherhood 35–8
  praise and encouragement 33–8
  respect for other women 33–45
  self-respect 25–32
  speaking well of women 38, 44
role models 86, 89, 139, 165, 213, 230, 272
Roman Empire 21
romantic love 202–4
Roosvelt, Franklin D 267
Russian Revolution, 1917 19

science 239–44, 251
secrets, sharing 75–6
self time 150–1
sex
  basic human needs 175–9
  being sex-wise 173–4
  family-positive sex 177–9, 193, 195–6, 199–204, 271–2

masturbation 176
mismatch solutions 188-98
self sex 176, 179
sex wisdom as means to reduce threat 271-2
sexual desire mismatch 180-7
social sex 176-7, 179, 189-93, 195-6, 199-201, 271
social sex addiction 192, 195
Sheehan, Barbara 7
Spirit of Indian Women, The (Chona) 263
Spirit of Man 262
Spirit of Woman, *see also* Essence of Woman
  ancient internal spirit 41
  connecting with 135
  decision making 225, 235
  defending 41, 43
  importance to family 229
  Inner Self 270
  sex wisdom 172
  spirituality 236, 262-4
  united strength 43
spirituality
  connecting with spirit 254-9
  creating spirit stories 260-6
  dangers of 246-53, 265
  enhancing 237-8, 240-5, 272-3
  Indigenous people and 251
status
  leading to insecurity 20
  male dominant desire 20
  social sex 200
  used to protect wealth 18-19
stories
  creating spiritual stories 260-6
  importance of 239-45

Tatsey, Joseph 141
television 14
Thought Woman 261, 276
toy boats on a stream 105
trust 74-5, 77

voting, importance of 235

wealth 17-21, 200
Wendling, Gisela 23
World Health Organization 8
World Until Yesterday; What can we learn from traditional societies?, The (Diamond) 55
World War 1 21
World War 2 21

Yousafzai, Malala 211

Zen meditation 103-4

www.ingramcontent.com/pod-product-compliance
Lightning Source LLC
Chambersburg PA
CBHW050528300426
44113CB00012B/2004